SEE
WHAT I SEE

MORE BOOKS BY GREG GERKE

There's Something Wrong With Sven
BlazeVOX Books, 2009

My Brooklyn Writer Friend
Queen's Ferry Press, 2015

Especially the Bad Things
Splice, 2019

SEE WHAT I SEE

Essays

Greg Gerke

Introduction by Steven Moore

ZEROGRAM
PRESS

Los Angeles, 2021

ZEROGRAM PRESS
1147 El Medio Ave.
Pacific Palisades, CA 90272
EMAIL: info@zerogrampress.com
WEBSITE: www.zerogrampress.com

Distributed by Small Press United / Independent Publishers Group
(800) 888-4741 / www.ipgbook.com

First Zerogram Press Edition 2021
Copyright © 2021 by Greg Gerke
Foreword © 2021 by Steven Moore
Originally published in 2019 by Splice (UK)
Many of these works appeared before in the following journals, all in a much different form: 3AM Magazine, Mubi, Full Stop, Los Angeles Review of Books, The Kenyon Review, The Millions, The Rumpus, The Nervous Breakdown, The Fanzine, Music & Literature, Lapsus Lima, The Smart Set, Senses of Cinema
Book design: Pablo Capra

LIBRARY OF CONGRESS CATALOGING-IN-PUBLICATION DATA

Names: Gerke, Greg, author.
Title: See what I see : essays / Greg Gerke.
Description: First edition. | Los Angeles : Zerogram Press, 2021. | Includes index.
Identifiers: LCCN 2020043734 | ISBN 9781953409010 (paperback)
Subjects: LCSH: Literature--Appreciation. | Motion pictures--Appreciation. | Art appreciation. | LCGFT: Essays.
Classification: LCC PS3607.E746 S44 2021 | DDC 814/.6--dc23
LC record available at https://lccn.loc.gov/2020043734

Printed in the United States of America

For Tess and Lily
and
in memory of
Bill Gass, The Master
and
my Father

Contents

REAL LIFE

THE SILVER SCREEN

Foreword

by Steven Moore

GREG GERKE'S *See What I See* is a splendid example of the return of the personal in modern literary criticism. Up until World War II, a reader could often sense a flesh-and-blood person behind literary critiques, but upon the arrival of bloodless New Criticism, such writing became more impersonal, and under the influence of the continental criticism of the 1960s it took on a quasi-scientific tone. As the hermeneutics of suspicion took hold of them, critics distanced themselves from the works they interrogated, and it became hard to tell if they even liked literature. Writing in 1892 of the heroine of Swift's novella *Polite Conversation*, the great George Saintsbury confessed, "I fell in love with her when I was about seventeen, I think; and from that day to this I have never wavered for one minute in my affection for her." Can you imagine a professional critic writing that today about a fictional character? (And make no mistake: Saintsbury is a greater critic than any academic writing today.) Unabashed enthusiasm for a book or a character became the sign of an amateur: a member of a neighborhood book club, or a reviewer on Amazon.

On two occasions Gerke quotes T. S. Eliot's famous line, "The progress of an artist is a continual self-sacrifice, a continual extinction of personality." But I don't think that's always true of *artists*; if you knew nothing about Eliot's life, you could pretty accurately guess from his poetry what kind of personality he had, a totally different one from that which emerges from the poems of his free-spirited contemporary E. E. Cummings. Critics, on the other hand, have indeed pursued "the extinction of personality," even down to the strict avoidance of the first-person "I." In Gerke's case, on the other hand, the personal approach is apparent even in his title: *See What I See*, not what an impersonal "one" sees.

In recent years, however, some critics have woven their personal involvement with a novel into their critiques; I'm thinking of Michael Gorra's *Portrait of a Novel: Henry James and the Making of an American Masterpiece* (2012), Maureen Corrigan's *So We Read On: How* The Great Gatsby *Came to Be and Why It Endures* (2014), and Rebecca Mead's *The Road to* Middlemarch: *My Life with George Eliot* (2014), each of which gave me a greater appreciation for those novels than any academic treatises on them. No difficulty here trying to decide if the critics liked the novels they wrote about, nor did their enthusiasm muzzle any misgivings they may have had about any shortcomings.

See What I See is a welcome addition to this trend. This collection puts into practice William H. Gass's belief that "Works of art are meant to be lived with and loved." In prose as beautiful and imagistic as Gass's, Gerke recounts how he has lived with and loved certain authors and filmmakers. Especially in his discussion of books he often mentions the circumstances in which he read a particular author, the binding of the book and font, even the time of day: "Is late afternoon the best time for poetry? With a sinking sun and the stories of our lives in repose after the often fitful midday, aren't the siesta hours most befitting an artform so benighted by dreams, the sleep of dreams, and dreamlike imagery?" He likes the smell of certain books, is aroused by what he calls (in "Holy Hill") the "eros of language," and dotes on the sensuality of reading. After quoting the opening paragraph of John Hawkes's *Blood Oranges*, he writes "The passage presses its sweet side to the reader," as if the prose had metamorphosed into an armful of warm girl. He gets horny at times, trying to decide if he should "[h]op into bed with [Elizabeth] Bishop or Borges?" and wonders if he should add Henry James's *Italian Hours* to his "discriminating list of books to shag." In the same randy essay ("How to Live, What to Read") we catch him "stroking the spines of a few new books I've just bought . . . clothed or naked."

William H. Gass, it quickly appears, is the tutelary genius presiding over the literary half of this collection. (The book is divided into essays on literature and on film, with an intermezzo on "Real Life.") He's one of the dedicatees of the book, and while not named in the first essay is alluded to twice. ("Art has taken precedence. I've fallen deeply into it and can barely return to life" is adapted from *Willie Masters' Lonesome Wife*, and "Life in a chair . . ." is from *The Tunnel*.) There are two essays on Gass, and he is often cited in the other essays in the first half of the book. What Gerke loves most about Gass is his attention to sentences; Gass wrote several essays about sentences, and titled one of his collections *Life Sentences*, for he felt the main goal of a literary work was to offer as many beautifully crafted sentences as possible. Gerke echoes this belief as he writes of "the music of sentences," of "that gargantuan or miniature unit called the sentence." He praises Henry James's "architectonic sentences," his "singular syntactical sensations," and claims "The beauty of James' sentences victimizes us." Following in the footsteps of these masters, Gerke offers a steady stream of beautiful sentences of his own, rich in imagery. Of his fellow subway riders, he writes: "They nodded off, punched at or swiped the screens of their phones as if scraping frosting from a cooling cake. An older women, with the hard angles of an Eastern European face and short hair colored by a box of chestnut dye, sat hunched with a heavy book." Not an upscale bottle or tube of dye but a "box," and note the alliteration of "hard . . . hair . . . hunched . . . heavy"—perhaps an homage to the *h*- alliterations he had noted earlier in Wallace Stevens's "A Rabbit As King of the Ghosts."

In addition to Stevens—the subject of two appreciative essays and lovingly cited elsewhere—another tutelary genius of this book is Gass's friend William Gaddis, who is mentioned throughout, beginning on the first page. He is the subject of three essays: one on *Carpenter's Gothic*, another on *A Frolic of His Own*, and a review of Joseph Tabbi's 2015 biography. Even in these critical assessments, the personal touch presides: I've read virtually everything written about Gaddis, but never an essay that begins, "There are stolen moments when raising a young child, the let-up during nap-time being a prime example. In one of these recent pauses, I read to my wife the beginning of the fifth chapter or section (they are unnumbered) of William Gaddis's 1995 novel *Carpenter's Gothic*. . . ." In the one on *A Frolic of His Own*, Gerke explains that he read Gaddis's legal novel concurrently with his wife, a criminal defense attorney, and adds anecdotes of his own involvement in the legal profession. Gerke reminds us that novels are read in the real world—he often reads on the subway—by real people with real jobs, which is rarely conveyed, or is considered irrelevant, in academic criticism.

The other recipients of Gerke's loving attention include Rainer Maria Rilke, Louise Glück, Gertrude Stein, Geoffrey Hill, Patrick White, Don DeLillo, and V. S. Naipaul. The final essay in the first half is entitled "Why Write?," which is not merely an academic question. In addition to essays, Gerke writes fiction too—he has two short-story collections to his name, *There's Something Wrong with Sven* (2009) and *Especially the Bad Things* (2019), with a lengthy novel in the works—which accounts for his sensitivity to the fiction of others. As I've written elsewhere, I've always felt that novelists often make better critics than academics for the obvious reason that they know what it's like to actually write a novel:

they've struggled with conceiving and developing an idea, finding a form, breathing life into characters, plotting the narrative, revising and aestheticizing their work, and finally seeing it through the press, sometimes even defending it from doubtful editors. They've walked the walk, and consequently are far more qualified to talk the talk than professors or book-reviewers who have never tried their hand at fiction, and thus have only a theoretical notion of what goes into writing it. Gerke concurs in one the last essays in this book: "Critics carry the stain of envy into the thoughts they print, especially those emboldened enough to critique without having ever made the art that can exasperate them."

The personal takes center stage in the four autobiographical essays in the "Real Life" intermezzo, all engaging, masterfully written, and marbled with references to books and films. Then he shares the stage with several auteur directors for the final section, "The Silver Screen." Gerke confesses in the book's opening essay that filmmaking was his "first passion" as teenager, and in a later essay on director Paul Thomas Anderson he tells us that he attended film school for two years before leaving with "numerous Bergman-enamored screenplays that would never see production." He turned to writing instead, switch-hitting thereafter between fiction and nonfiction. I am not a cinephile and haven't seen many of the movies he analyzes, or even heard of some of the directors—is Maren Ade a real name or a playful pseudonym?—but this half of the book strikes me as just as intelligent and well-written as the first half, and if anything is even more personal.

As with the literary essays, the focus is on the roles his favorite films have played in his life, privileging subjective over objective analysis. As Gass said, "Works of art are meant to be lived with," and in the section's opening essay on Michelangelo Antonioni—whose *Blow-Up* is one of my all-time favorite movies—Gerke gives us a perfect example of that sentiment: "I have to admit there is something about Antonioni that is deeply embedded in my soul, and though the psychical manifestation of his art is a little riven by time, its granite face can still proudly display a freckling of mica by my own sun. It is a force that surely resists many people, and though I believe I've grown out of taking up a cause to rebuke those I would label impoverished, I only extol to eradicate my own glowering, to teach myself the lesson of how as I get older, much of his work only gets better." The Italian director would agree with this approach, for Gerke quotes him as saying, "That is why the best way to watch a film is to have it become a personal experience. At the moment in which we watch a film, we unconsciously evoke what is inside of us, our life, our joys and our pains, our thoughts—our 'mental vision of the

past and the present,' as Susan Sontag would say." Similarly, in his essay on Stanley Kubrick's longest film, Gerke asks, "What makes *Barry
Lyndon* my own story? Have I lived to subsume it or have I subsumed
it to live?" Sometimes a work of art will tell him "You must change your
life"—he quotes the famous last line of Rilke's "Archaic Torso of Apollo"
near the end—and other times he skewers films that can't be lived with,
crass Hollywood productions like *The Social Network* and *Drive* that
"drain me of my life spirit."

Although he can intellectually analyze a film with the best of them,
Gerke has a physical reaction to his favorites: in his essay on Ingmar
Bergman—who, along with Eric Rohmer, plays the same role of tutelary
genius for film as Gass does for literature—he writes, "I can always tell
how good a film is if my armpits smell afterward. The body doesn't lie."
All of his film essays convey nuts-and-bolts information about his chosen
directors, but any film critic could do that; Gerke mixes the informative
with the confessional, and to an extent that not many film critics would
dare.

In some of these essays, the personal becomes almost uncomfortably revealing. In the long essay on Rohmer, for example, he aligns the
actresses in some of the French director's Moral Tales series with old
girlfriends. While not neglecting technical matters, such as the shade
of gray in the 35mm film stock Rohmer sometimes used, Gerke is more
interested in what his films tell him about himself. "How can I see my
past better in this film?" he asks, "for to come to *Claire's Knee* is to be in
the company of a woman I lived with the longest until my marriage, and
to dwell on that time reminds me of my greatest failings." He restates
this at various times in this section, as in the opening of his essay on
South Korean director Hong Sang-soo: "Isn't the miracle of art how we
see the panoply of our own lives via a magical panopticon? Every time
we look, we see something that's really all about us." In the wrong hands,
this approach can lead to the impatient rejection of certain works of art
because one "can't relate" to them. That's why he goes on to caution, "It
might not be easy to see one's life in film—not in the narrative itself, but
in the regard of the camera, the editing, how people say things and what
their silences are like."

In the book's closing essay, in which Gerke alternates between critiqu-
ing director Mike Leigh's *Mr. Turner* and musing on the role of criticism
today, he evokes "poet-critic Guy Davenport, whose essays are jewels,
and who claimed to be 'not writing for scholars or critics, but for people
who like to read, to look at pictures, and to know things.'" That is Gerke's
audience too—though "scholars and critics" could learn a few things

from his personal approach. Whether writing about film or literature, honeymooning in Paris or consuming Combos, Greg Gerke bedazzles us with his keen intelligence, wide knowledge, and stylistic flair. *See What I See* is a beguiling collection of belletristic essays meant for those of us for whom art is a passion, not a profession or a pastime but a way of life.

Society wishes to be amused. I do not wish to be amused. I wish that life should not be cheap, but sacred. I wish the days to be as centuries, loaded, fragrant.

— Ralph Waldo Emerson, "Considerations by the Way"

THE WRITING LIFE

Living Words

I LIVE IN A CITY. The City. I go from one room of books to another. This isn't good for the flowers or the trees. Don't laugh—they want to be looked at. In these rooms full of books I endure a terrible longing to return to those natural preserves. Before I grew up and into a paper and print man, the earth was so near. Because I could not read and thankfully cared little for TV, nature (along with toys) made up most of my reality. Grass, the soft grass of city parks. The dirt of gardens, the dirt of dirt—the way water made it soggy, more appetizing. In our small backyard there were three trees until they became too big and one had to be cut down. Its uneven stump remained. I stared at that stump for hours, trying to remake the presence of the tree—imagination enlivened by ruin. Other extravaganzas of organics influenced. The tyrannical primary hues of spring as opposed to the gray slate skies of a Midwestern winter. The blaze of autumn. Nature taught me motion—turn and counter-turn—she taught me color.

Words conjure. Crack a novel or poem at random and most will have a tiny shout about the outdoors. Even in *JR*, William Gaddis' novel of 87% dialogue, nature bursts into the rooms where the speakers speak: "Sunlight, pocketed in a cloud spilled suddenly broken across the floor through the leaves of the trees outside." One can't keep it out and nature can't keep away—it is the leveler of literature: *Just want to make sure you know I'm still here*, it says, and we say, *Just want to make sure you are still there*. With this understanding we live, banking on the picture of the earth to always be in its place. Is this a happy arrangement?

I turn to Wallace Stevens and the last canto of the *Auroras of Autumn* for help:

An unhappy people in a happy world—
Read, rabbi, the phases of this difference.
An unhappy people in an unhappy world—

Here are too many mirrors for misery.
A happy people in an unhappy world—
It cannot be.

What are we that a poet can take three of the most frequently used words in the English language and mix and match them in such easily understandable and memorable lines of verse? We have to be made of magic, and why I read is to feel who we are, to apprise myself of the distinguished enterprise of being.

This is me—the child trying to be father to the man—who has read *Ulysses* but has not made a son, who has been under Lowry's *Volcano* but never beneath a car to understand its underbelly or twist on an oil filter to save money while hoarding the bragging rights, so my love could speak of her *man*. I continue reading—I am adding and addled by the ideas there, those bristling feelings enjambed in sentences and lines of verse—but is this just filler for what is truly desired?

I often go into bookstores in New York City. Mercer Street Books, The Housing Works, The Strand, Unnameable Books, and Barnes & Noble—though that last one is more of a social mecca. On a cool night I enter the West 82nd Street branch of this behemoth, not to browse but to observe. Many people sit or stand in these stores and read. And although some frustrated friends have bellowed, in despair, "People don't read!", this ugly edict is obviously false. I espy a demure woman in her forties with a brown leather purse and a face that seems stoic, despite the tight cowgirl jeans accentuating her already extravagant ass, as she reaches into the Christianity section and pulls a thin volume from the bottom shelf: *Prodigal God*. In the next instant a mother hands her daughter a copy of *I Am Number Four* before the young girl promptly reads the cover blurb, returns it, and continues with her oversized paperback, *Sarah's Key*.

People are reading. Men finger newspapers and one flicks through a Visual C++ handbook. There goes a young couple with a puppy-care guide, and how about that Upper-West-Sider with *The Dance of Anger*, no dance on that female face stricken by the hard lines of living beneath sixty-year hair dyed henna. There's a man, frowning, gray-shirted, with a pile of mysteries, phone in lap. Oh, they are reading. Why, though, are these people reading at Barnes & Noble? We are a million people reading a million different books, yet our little lives are rounded by the same simpers.

If I wanted to talk to others about books and book culture, shouldn't I be talking to these men and women? The inelegant paradox of life as I see it is that reading is a solitary activity and yet it yields an understanding of our world and the many people who populate it. Or is E. M. Cioran correct when he says, "We must read not to understand others but to understand ourselves"? Reading can be shared—by going to readings, by participating in book clubs, by embarking on a course of study in school. And over the years I've selfishly given friends and family books I like in hopes they would read them and we could talk shop. Some did, most didn't—out of the ignored books given as gifts, one could build thousands of libraries.

My ways and means favor the reading out loud of texts as the most direct route to shared experience. I've read three of Cormac McCarthy's novels to three different lovers, yet my output has not been confined to the continent's most fêted scribbler apart from Franzen. I also cast out *The Emigrants, Disgrace, Desperate Characters*, Stanley Elkin's novella 'The Condominium,' a bevy of short stories, mostly by Chekov and Alice Munro, and poems aplenty, many to myself. I had read all these books before deeming them worthy of taking hours and hours from others' lives. I was then, as now, learning how to write, and I desired to hear the music of the sentences, especially *Blood Meridian*. That this particular armful of tomes bathed in the dark side of life is true. The entire group carried the stink of tragedy in their steely words and stark stories, moving me to think worse of the world and better of myself—I was a little fucked up, but I didn't have the problems of the characters they contained. I wasn't ready to end my life—how could I ever have as good a reason as Sebald's three crestfallen refugees?

I don't know if any of the women were so interested—one disclosed, in retrospect, her hatred of *The Road* (and me)—but we were spending time together, I was reading to them, they had my voice in their ears. What is so powerful about the antique image of a paramour speaking his verses to the high-bosomed lady he loves is that the practice still exists and bolsters seduction—a word not as dirty as the paltry romance novelists who've never read Rilke think. With book love a main component of my affection and even compassion for another, how much of myself still sat in the real world? Enormously interested in their reactions, I wanted them to emote right along with me—cry, like me, when Professor Lurie kills the dog in the final pages of *Disgrace*, or when the woman offers welcoming words to the fatherless boy at the end of *The Road*. It didn't happen the way I envisioned it. A sad clown throughout all those years, I had more expectations than were healthy to harbor a happy relationship.

Nowadays, I might call my dearest into the alcove of her room and share one of Stevens' late poems: say, 'The Novel' or 'Farewell without a Guitar.' I'll read it, we'll remark about such a term as "routemarche," she'll take the book in hand and read it again as I finger the sad edge around the quaggy longing to make us two people we actually aren't. Susan Sontag doesn't sleep next to me, ready to spout a sportive and Spartan interpretation of my choice of art. It's cowardly to think I have something more than a bowdlerized conception of myself to offer the world and those closest to me. *I'm giving you something that probably doesn't interest you, but I know you will look at it because you love me,* I insist like the ham I am—the barest way I can describe the contract as it plays itself out in my years. Art has taken precedence. I've fallen deeply into it and can barely return to life.

On a featureless Thursday I come to the petite library near City Hall Park where the homeless sleep and the mentally ill chortle and upbraid those who dare to chortle near them. On exiting the building, two vivacious ladies laugh, causing the Jamaican woman at my table to stare her computer down and voice a mantra: *Who are you a dunce to try and make me laugh?* She says it five times, stops, then ten times more—a stream most pretend not to notice.

Libraries used to be different—I have this on my authority. If you want silence stay in your house, the furies cry. Nay, but I've written in public libraries for twenty years—I can't just stop. The disenfranchised are my familiars. I'm used to these people, this morbidly-broken set. All of my better ideas were born with someone on the cusp of magnificent breakdown only a few feet away. Their mouths have produced numerous titles for me, their odors haunting my nose even after a second shower.

There are still books in libraries, but what happens when those meaty chunks of paper are no longer stocked on the shelves? *Libraries* won't be the correct term. If personal libraries used to stand for or typify an intelligence, or were a place for showing off, especially since hardcover books were status symbols, before people could even read, and not so affordable, what has taken their place today? Gigantic plasma screens? Exercise rooms? Videogame studies? The term *Arts and Leisure* is bloody wrong.

Life in a chair is the life of the mind. Is this a shuttered life? Is this how I thought it would be at age three, Lego in hand, food on my face? I have a stormy idea that what I make and what I do is foolish and futile but I will never know. Is this why I read Stevens—the highest art attained? I seek cause before satisfaction and to hold my head over a bowl, a golden bowl, a chalice, a stone—something beautiful.

But there's only cold comfort at Brooklyn's Central Library by Grand Army Plaza on a Sunday afternoon. It's open for just four hours and I'll get just forty minutes.

Mudwoman. A new book, reviewed in the *New York Times. That's where I recently read about it,* the librarian barks officiously to a small woman. I've known this particular man for ten years. In my patented autobiographical novel I describe him thus: "One effeminate man in his fifties with thick glasses, silver hair and often plaid, pastel, or beige striped shirts spoke loudly to patrons and other co-workers in a finishing school voice that pronounced every syllable like an all-powerful king at court."

Will he sue me for libel if the novel is published? Will the library order a copy? The better question is, will the *Times* review my bitchy ass? *Mudwoman.* There are many books in a big library. Most all the greatest literature ever written—and that should be read. Imagine trying to catch up in 1877, when Walter Pater taught Oscar Wilde and Henry James had written only three of his twenty-one novels and less than a fifth of the Library of America's 4,700 pages of his collected stories. Then imagine what the anxiety is like 140 years later. Flaubert finally finished out, there was Modernism, then Postmodernism, plus a whole host of bunkum I wouldn't read if you paid me. Then all the new translations of works written before 1877.

Mudwoman. What can be accomplished in forty minutes? . . . Yes, that can. Poetry as well. The reading and writing of it. Something as small as Emperor Hadrian's only known verse, 'Little Soul,' goes a long way:

> Little soul little stray
> little drifter
> now where will you stay
> all pale and all alone
> after the way
> you used to make fun of things

I came to the library to find the quiet nest of myself that goes missing when I'm not able to dictate the words I carry ringed up in garbles, botched rhythms, and frozen streams like overgrown tumors. I constantly find what is outside me more interesting, but not more explicable. This is a sign more simple than I think, but utterly unfollowable—a cyanide to my sham-hearted thought of the writer as more than zero.

What have I done? I answer: I have read the words. Maybe someday I will live up to Howard Nemerov's self-epitaph:

> Of the Great World he knew not much.
> But his Muse let little in language escape her.
> Friends sigh and say of him, poor wretch,
> He was a good writer, on paper.

On or About

REGULARLY, IN ARTICLES and essays, in blog posts and tweets, Virginia Woolf's remark, "on or about December 1910 human character changed," gets bandied around for having pinpointed the coming of the modern age. It is claimed, by such a writer as Edward Mendelson, that Woolf was making a serious joke—and that her pronouncement was a hundred years premature. "Human character changed on or about December 2010, when everyone, it seemed, started carrying a smartphone," he wrote in the *New York Review of Books*. That's a serious joke, too. Both Woolf and Mendelson are probably not right; besides, trying to pinpoint something as elastic and elusive as human character is better left to the hacks. Few persons living or dead would attest to these dates when asked about human character, which most people probably think falls under the rubric we call *life*. Someone much more divested than Woolf or Mendelson, Thich Nacht Than, the Vietnamese Buddhist monk, averred what I now take to be the warmer truth. In a dharma talk I attended some years ago, he said, "You can't compare yourselves with anyone, because everyone is different." It holds that all of us will have different markers to our lives. Some Americans feel September 11th is one, while others could give a shit. I would bet all the money in the world that in the final analysis, the personal outweighs the historical or political in almost every instance. The most mundane and seemingly least important things are our benchmarks. Charles Foster Kane's friend Bernstein, an old man at the time, says it best in *Citizen Kane*:

> A fellow will remember a lot of things you wouldn't think he'd remember. You take me. One day, back in 1896, I was crossing over to Jersey on the ferry. And as we pulled out, there was another ferry pulling in.

And on it there was a girl waiting to get off. A white dress she had on. She was carrying a white parasol. I only saw her for one second. She didn't see me at all. But I'll bet a month hasn't gone by since . . . that I haven't thought of that girl.

Can I say I've had the privilege of living a life tending solitary? I didn't choose it as a child or a teenager—it's just what happened. Divorced parents, a sister seven years older, the ostracization of being taller than everyone else my age and fairly chunky—these facts strafed me and made me separate. I learned to play by myself, creating my own universe and my own reality, taking the role of two players in Monopoly and many other games, and then gorging myself on TV, movies, and reading. It can't be a surprise I traded the usual collaborations of my first passion, filmmaking, for the quiet, orderly hours of writing.

Even before my body grew, I developed a yen for wonderful contrasts: my being solitary while the company of others was not too far away, something exemplified by playing in my own world in the back seat of a car while my parents were in the front. I felt a sort of strange equilibrium, maybe entelechy, but also a security in the sense that I knew life went on—more important worries were being taken care of by older people. I could rest easy and be apart, but remain in the encompassing bubble. I kept testing the limits, and as I experienced the summer vacations, especially during high school, I reveled in the long hours when my mother and sister would be away at their first-shift jobs and I ruled a large enough two-story bungalow. What I gained, besides a thriving inner life, was an adamantine sense of control. You could say I didn't play well with others and I lost some of the social skills one starts displaying at twelve, thirteen, and fourteen, acquiring a shyness most took as vanity, and a sneer that couldn't be called haughty because I was incredibly alone—haughty people need others they can direct. I sneered when scared. Around people, fear ruled.

ONE ORDINARY DAY, a moment in my life came back to me for no particular reason. I've rarely thought of it in the thirty years since it happened. The moment wasn't so much when my human character changed, but indeed something did. The moment itself, which wasn't really a moment so much as a span of time, took place in around an hour. It was June or July of 1988, a Friday. In the evening, but not too late, maybe between eight and nine, when the golden hour would hit Milwaukee, Wisconsin, though it was overcast. I sat inside during the warm night doing what I did best, watching a movie on TV. It was *Friday the 13th* something. Part two, part three? Maybe four. Aren't they all the same? But it was on a national station, so it was edited with commercials, and at that age I already pretty much had the template of the scenarios down. An unsuspecting group in their late teens goes camping. There's the couple where the guy always wants to get into the pants of the girl, plus the nerd and the jock and the well-developed female character who will ultimately survive the carnage. Slowly, inevitably, the script engineers things so that people get separated and easily killed without anyone else knowing until Jason reveals it—and as I write this I have to make a serious joke of my own: how can people wonder about the violence in American society when a thirteen-year-old can recapitulate the methodology behind killing so efficiently, so clearly?

I actually wasn't too tied to the film because in the backyard, just a little jaunt through the house (the TV room was at the front end), my sister and her soon-to-be husband stood with one of his friends and our mother testing the durability of an old tent they were considering for a weekend camping trip. Their imminent departure has stayed in my memory because it was such a different type of experience, even if I would not be the one going on the trip. Trips were scarce, and even when my father lived with us, into the prior year, we were all homebodies (except my sister), whether through TV or depression—aren't they equal? Good for my sister and Joe, I thought vicariously. Getting out there, having fun. This real life corralled my plastic one concerned with baseball, baseball statistics, and films about a real life I couldn't understand. I could scarcely imagine the prospect of women and their honeys—I wanted the baseball Brewers to win the pennant. Where was real life? "The fair courts of life," James Joyce called it; that is order, peace, honor, and beauty in whatever form we live our adult time. But I had enough years of watering a quiet wish for what would eventually have to happen in some form for me as well. I couldn't conceivably live at home forever. I'd have to get a job and eventually fall in love, with someone, or I'd be a failure.

Was this the dawn of yearning? Jealousy? Envy? Surely I had all those before, but I couldn't name the words to encompass the feelings. I continued to observe. Not vanquishingly and not without disinterest. I stood in the house's enclosed porch, looking down on them in a yard with two trees, an oak and a cherry, planted by the man who bought the house but no longer resided there. The yard was once my play area, yet I retreated to my father's former den (the TV room), which stood out of the safe zone, where the unexpected is more likely. These people obviously participated in the fair courts of life, while I eschewed people for control, for artifice, and somewhat for my own unattainable glory. I pressed to join them, but was hamstrung.

Listening to their plans, I stooped, vaguely aware they were about to head out for the woods like the people in the movie I was watching. Hey! I was watching a movie and the commercial was probably long done, so I went back through the house to the TV to see Jason staring at one of his imminent victims. They were by a barn, but I viewed this with an eye to reality. The cool kids (my blood) were going into the forest. Wasn't that more interesting than edited death by machete impaling? Mmmm. Beginning to watch a soft-core car commercial, I asked if we (I) had a will to do what we wanted? But really, sitting beside my closest friend, the TV, did I know anything else?

I returned. Joe and his friend were packing up the old tent—it would do. This time I went outside. I had a flicker of how I was being viewed by the others when trying to stand eagerly, but unable to be a party to anything. Myself: tall, very overweight, morose. Who did they see? How could they help him? Because, of course, what I was doing there was asking for aid, even though I didn't know I did so. My mind said, *Come play with me*, or, *Come watch the movie with me*; although I couldn't always align actual words with emotions just yet, I could feel them accumulating in a large face growing more and more punitive toward the world, more repelled while marooned on the wrong avenue of my desires. Soon, people said their goodbyes. The moment just ended.

I don't think there are as many epiphanies in our lives as we report. Things accrue and one day there is a jettisoning, but much has contributed. Our lived years bring us to the cusp of realization, but all that went in comes out in fits and fizzles—and maybe it's only real when we can give those fits and fizzles language, to be understood. I went back to the television. My mother started going through the week's newspapers in the kitchen. I could write in an epiphany, but to say it came to me then would be false. I simply succumbed to entertainment. My yearning? To see everyone killed, like I'd been taught to expect—except the final girl, who would somehow destroy Jason, with a little help from a Hollywood screenwriter. After I got that, I perfunctorily hoped nothing like this would come to pass in western Wisconsin where my sister camped. My small prayer might have been the beginning of something, some parceling of feelings, maybe some inner voice whispering that I would soon have to take responsibility for my life, especially if I was to participate in it to the extent my sister participated in hers, but it wouldn't manifest for some years. In essence, I had my first ideas of what I was missing. Now . . . how would I give up the make-believe world to get there?

On Influence

WHY NOT STAND UP straight for art? Rainer Maria Rilke's older lover, Lou Andreas-Salomé, cared greatly about Rilke's relation to words and made him improve his handwriting, urging the poet to take control of everything in his life before communing more with the muse. Soon Rilke purchased a standing desk to improve his circulation while he wrote—by changing his methods, he changed what the methods produced. This might speak to a few things about influence and who we are willing to listen to (Andreas-Salomé, also a former lover of Nietzsche, was a distinguished psychoanalyst and writer), but undoubtedly, art is at least as physical as it is emotional.

Often, at the heart of concerns about my art (writing) and art in general is the fiction writer and essayist William H. Gass. He may be more completely defined as a philologist and a philosopher of language, one who worked poetic designs into his prose no matter the format. Slowly, I once digested Gass' books, reading twelve of the fourteen. His creations kept me spellbound as I sought to refine my art through close examinations of the masters. His essay on Auguste Rodin in *A Temple of Texts*, which also serves as an introduction to Rilke's monograph on the Frenchman, is a piece as much about Rilke and how he shadowed the grand sculptor, asking him how to live, while indeed he did live with him. Gass writes:

> All of us have emotions urgently seeking release . . . opinions we think would do the world some good; however, the poet must also be a maker . . . and . . . like every other artist, should aim at adding real beings to the world, beings fully realized, not just things like tools and haberdashery that nature has neglected to provide, or memos and

laws that society produces in abundance, but *Ding an sich* . . . things in themselves.

Why do we pick up the pen, dance the keyboard, fashion clay, and mix green with blue only to ruin it with yellow? How hard does one have to work to get it right, and why create ephemera when we have a chance to construct something that sticks? I wanted to make fiction that could last. I wanted to become the maker Gass urged me to be.

I saturated myself with art—seeing, sensing, and feeling films, books, music, and visual art to hold my head up in a climate enriched and enlivened by my forebears and spiritual family. To return and return was a homecoming. Another reason to re-read Wallace Stevens' 'The Snow Man', or to watch, re-view, and then return to Robert Bresson's *Au Hasard Balthazar*, was to spark the sense that I was not alone, that these artists' visions communicated to me, that everything was a little more beautiful and, possibly, more tolerable.

From the age when I was ready, art began to color me. Certain films, poems, and books ready one for the masterpieces that might need to be entered from a door not so readily visible. For instance, Woody Allen's comedies and dramas of rumination—specifically the autumnal *Hannah and Her Sisters*, *Crimes and Misdemeanors*, and *Husbands and Wives*—prepared me for the more forceful feelings of Allen's own master, Ingmar Bergman. People under siege from religion and artists under siege from society typify Bergman's *mise-en-scène*, as often beautiful, pale Scandinavian women and stilted, tight-jawed men are photographed in close-up, retching or destroying themselves in the face of demons inside and out—Bergman's main demon being death. Later, a rash of Rilke reading in youth was augmented by Gass' great *Reading Rilke*, read at thirty-five, ten years after the book itself came out and ten after I sat on a cement enclosure above the Neckar River in Mannheim, Germany, huffing through *The Duino Elegies*, cracking into my German pronunciation of those grandiose lines, but riveted by those cries of angels, as Stephen Mitchell calls them. Reading Rilke Gass-style was re-reading Rilke and was what I needed to do to find my own voice and drop the imitation act—craning my consciousness to see above and under a work of art, see it in different weather, see and understand the clarity in which the object or subject is rendered, see to be able to fashion sentences and trains of sentences that are *Ding an sich*, as each word is the work and the whole becomes more complex, more dense, encouraging multiple readings.

I still need to re-read Rilke, along with most everything I love to read, because the authors themselves re-read their works countless times as they honed their words and brought them to life—fashioning, as Stevens indicates in one of his stark, late poems, 'Not Ideas About the Thing but the Thing Itself.' Art, in my life, and many others, is not some simple flash of inspiration or passing entertainment—it is a life's work. It took seven years for Joyce to write *Ulysses*, while Rilke spent six on *The Notebooks of Malte Laurids Brigge*, and, in the eighteenth century, Bach devoted twenty-six years to his *Mass in B minor*. This kind of time demonstrates a streak of perfectionism in the creator, but surely the hours of toil that wax into days and weeks become more than just clock time and the first forays into these classics only tap the topsoil in the excavations that must take place in order to strike at the singular strains of mind which have formed such vivid, heartily hewn prose and song—as demonstrated by this treasure from Gass' *The Tunnel* (twenty-seven years in the making) wherein the narrator is in mid-recall of a childhood car accident:

> As I rebounded from the floor of the car my ears received, like the rapid rasp of a saw, a series of terrible sounds: of rending metals, shattering glass, pissing vapors, unstaged screams.

Being an apprentice writer is a challenge. What comes easily can't always be trusted. Only masterpieces like Vermeer's *The Milkmaid*, Woolf's *To the Lighthouse*, and Tarkovsky's *Solaris* carry any sort of unconditional sentence—they are fully realized, full-flowered works to compel, disturb, and urge others to create similar objects of such clear, beatific, unbridled consciousness. I couldn't strive for anything less and I knew the masters would demand the same of me, given their incredible travails.

Elizabeth Bishop rewrote her poem 'One Art' at least fifteen times over several months. It ended up as a villanelle, nineteen lines in length. What began as maudlin—

> You may find it hard to believe, but I have actually lost
> I mean lost, and forever, two whole houses,
> one a very big one,

—she finally begat as masterly—

> I lost two cities, lovely ones. And, vaster,
> some realms I owned, two rivers, a continent.
> I miss them, but it wasn't a disaster.

For Bishop, who only published 101 poems in her lifetime, the composition of this poem over many months was in fact very quick—she couldn't believe it, and later described the experience as "like writing a letter." 'One Art' was one of Bishop's last poems, but that it was easy in her terms does not take away from the fact that, on average, she let barely one-and-a-half be published each year of her sixty-eight on earth.

It told me that I would have to spend more time with my writing—and the more I read the masters, the more I found laziness and mistakes in my own efforts. Yet, after I edited and edited again, I would feel proportionately edified that what I held was something closer to an ornate object—a fine clock, not an empty milk carton.

As we ride the rough road of writing fiction, our equipage must be heavy in splendor. If one hasn't read a lot of Shakespeare, why hasn't one read a lot of Shakespeare? If one doesn't "get" Henry James, one must ask why one doesn't "get" Henry James. While licks of love are sweet, little can compare with full immersion. Not excerpts, not one painting in Philadelphia and three in Paris, but the whole book, an entire room of an artist's work over a time. Example after example of form fronting for feeling. A slab of years, not one season's trellis.

Inspiration is a wonderful, delicate thing, but it can be a misleading wind. It may be mandatory to create by inspiration, but only mandatory in the way that physical attraction is between lovers. For lovers to get over themselves and into love requires another, higher caliber of emotional sensation, and if they have summited the chalky pinnacle of "love," they are well advised to be fully equipped with the reach and reaction times needed to nestle one another and think of themselves second to stay there. What artists do, probably unconsciously, is destroy their notions of what is good enough again and again. Good enough can never be good enough. Let a story sit for four seasons, rewrite the poem until it is another poem. Artists think of themselves second in order for the art to be fully conscious, fully conceived. And the connection between art and love is not some tenuous, new-age conceit; rather, it is as real as rain. Love takes time because we don't know what we love until the bloom retires and we are left with a presence not endowed with a glow, but a cast-iron reality. Because a consciousness created *The Portrait of a Lady*, the book itself holds its own being as well. As Gass says in *Fiction and the Figures of Life*,

> The aim of the artist ought to be to bring into the world objects which . . . are especially worthy of love. . . . Works of art are meant to be lived with and loved, and if we try to understand them, we should try to understand them as we try to understand anyone—in order to

know *them* better, not in order to know something else.

We love certain types of art because they challenge us and make us happy or maybe angry; they frustrate and disturb, they move us to stray from the path of our preconceived harmony. Their beauty tugs us to step outside the familiar aura of the smiley-faced quotidian we often engage each other and the world with.

Love and love in the art. John Hawkes, in the opening paragraph of his 1971 novel *The Blood Oranges*, is writer enough to attempt a definition, surely incomplete, of that most elastic and misunderstood emotion:

> Love weaves its own tapestry, spins its own golden thread, with its own sweet breath breathes into being its mysteries—bucolic, lusty, gentle as the eyes of daisies or thick with pain. And out of its own music creates the flesh of our lives. If the birds sing, the nudes are not far off. Even the dialogue of frogs is rapturous.

The passage presses its ravishing side to the reader, while the narrator introduces his powerful, eidetic voice, rinsing his ruminations with the words of love: tapestry, gold, sweet, breath, breathe, bucolic, lusty, gentle, daisies, thick, music, flesh, birds, nudes, rapture. Yet studding this field of genteel hopes is a stunning aside: "thick with pain." In only four sentences, Hawkes creates a voice that is accomplished, authoritative, and—most importantly—seductive.

Splendid conjunctions and influence are often at work between masters. Sharing a similar opening ode to love is Shakespeare's *Twelfth Night*, a precursor to *The Blood Oranges*, which begins with Duke Orsino's famous words: "If music be the food of love, play on; / give me excess of it, that, surfeiting, / The appetite may sicken, and so die." For both Shakespeare and Hawkes, love and music (and, by extension, natural sound) are linked in an effort to examine the mysteries of the former; and by the hand of each writer the phrasing of lines settles onto the reader's radar with its own harmonic qualities. These lines are stately, conspicuously wrought pieces of art—as beautiful as a Caravaggio or a Bernini. They transmit through language the sensation and the emotion of love with the best words in the best order.

Art should be taken as seriously as marriage, from the making of it to the meaning of it. No other practice suspends human beings and all animate life in such beauty. With reverence does one open the munificent pages of *Ulysses*, or pass through the massive doors of Notre-Dame, or come into view of Michelangelo's audacious Florence Pietà, or sit in the dark while the obtuse, sensuous, and maddening prologue of Bergman's *Persona* plays out on the silver screen.

Great art knows how to unmask. It can force one to encounter what we dare not unfurl to others. It can absorb our horror show of melancholy, swampish thoughts, ill-fit opinions, and webbed anxieties with its silent grandeur, its *élan*, its exquisite anchor of being timeless and fully alive. The work of art is never changing but the receiver is. We experience time and its spoils and wretchedness amidst the seesaw of being, whereas the Cello Suites of Bach retain their higher consciousness forever with no note unplayed. Similarly, *Othello* never grows another line—we can always only find "the Moor" speaking the same words from the same bed after killing the wife he falsely thought false:

> Speak of me as I am; nothing extenuate,
> Nor set down aught in malice: then must you speak
> Of one that loved not wisely but too well;
> Of one not easily jealous, but being wrought,
> Perplex'd in the extreme; of one whose hand,
> Like the base Indian, threw a pearl away
> Richer than all his tribe . . .

Inside this soliloquy, the high school student, focused on newfound sexual relations, will find something very different from the twice-married, twice-divorced man of letters down on his luck. When I first read Gass' novella 'In the Heart of the Heart of the Country' in college, I didn't have a clue about love or compromise and what that word's kernel, "promise," meant when it stood up to the hurricane winds of despair, deceit, and disunion. The sentences were gorgeous, the delights many dappled, but the driving force underneath—a man "in retirement from love"—was something suspect. It was a nice idea but it was as much a bunch of bunk to my pea-sized mind as people retiring from life to bird-watch, or embarking to Florida or Arizona to spend their last years being restive under too much sun—satisfied enough to balance grandchildren on their knees. I could be silly and stupid then because I did not know the color of pain, had no inkling of real responsibility or the battered escutcheon of tidings I would later brandish after a dozen years of fits and starts, fiddles with feelings, and falling for tits and talk of Dalí before scouting the terrain of my beloved's soul—sensing how trusty the one I had chosen to love might be, and asking myself why I lied when questioned if all was right with my unfit feeling. The narrator of the story is hampered and hassled; he harangues and henpecks out of longing and knows he has nowhere to go except into more of it:

> There's little hand-in-hand here . . . not in B. No one touches except
> in rage. Occasionally girls will twine their arms about each other and
> lurch along, school out, toward home and play. I dreamed my lips
> would drift down your back like a skiff on a river. I'd follow a vein with
> the point of my finger, hold your bare feet in my naked hands.

As Gass himself once said, one does not read a masterwork the first time
in order to read it, but to ready oneself to read it. On subsequent re-read-
ings, I could smell the stain life had made in my psyche more freely, setting my stare on those trees outside my reading window which had once
meant something very different to find them still the same trees—it was
my stare that had succumbed, had learned to see with skills that once
had no public course to prove themselves but were now myriad inside
one (myself) who had tripped while trying to circle a star with a square.
The sentences ("haze turns the summer sky milky, and the air muffles
your head and shoulders like a sweater you've got caught in") clung to
me like cob-webs—Gass being the trusted Medicine Man who knew I
should not remove them but glory their steely beauty into clusters, as I
would have to oversee my own sentences with a discerning eye and realize my own fullness of vision sorely lacking in the lackluster, minimalista
prose that had been my primary practice.

After having readied myself to read *The Tunnel* by reading it once, I
saw and felt more not only in Gass' text but also in the words of James,
Stein, Rilke, Stevens, Woolf, Joyce, Beckett, Gaddis, Hawkes, and Elkin.
In life, as well. As they pushed him to push further, Gass reflectively
painted their glories in poetic essays, and I could clearly see, by string-
ing myself out on the works of these masters, how my writing took its
shape beyond the easy hand from which it came. I had grown an intricate palm, creased skin on knuckles—sundowns on all fingernails, not
just the thumb. I discovered the nerve endings always there, though I'd
treated them like they weren't alive. Influence can stop a crack as well
as start one.

Three Lives, Molloy, The Recognitions, and *The Tunnel* are works
drowning in images and tropes. There is no recipe for vivid prose—the
kind that gets into the body, the kind that makes you forget you have to
pee—except hard work. A piece of magisterial art: this is ultimately what
we are after. If the reader thinks his or her time will be served better in
another way and puts the book down, then what is there is not enough
to suck one out of the workaday world. If, as Gass and Rilke counseled,

art is for the creation of *Ding an sich*, things in themselves, then those things created will be understood to be living, and the discerning reader will think twice about abandoning such presences for life elsewhere.

A Year with Wallace Stevens

SOME YEARS AGO, I returned to Eugene, Oregon, a town I'd once lived in for six years. The pragmatic but cold and sterile university library named Knight, one of my favorite haunts for its quietude, stands on a slope, straightened onto earth that rises over the damp soil of a small, nearby cemetery maintained since 1873. Douglas firs dot this rectangular plot of death, while chatty crows fling themselves off branches and strut on a grassy field, just west of the reposed souls, which dominates the back of the big library's view.

Upon entering, many times I went directly to the fourth floor's literary holdings, where I could look out through the high windows onto this green scene. Angling my chair so the beige carpet and all those upright books, impenetrable and otherwise, could not stare me down, I mused upon the landscape, where from the ground up I saw a field, a music school, and finally a verdant butte named Spencer's a few miles in the distance. In seeing into space, I could reflect space into the fiction I inscribed on the pages of the artist's book I balanced on my lap—space in story and character, but not in sentence. Though in the midst of studying literature, that gargantuan or miniature unit called the sentence had not been inked into my consciousness as the crucial crux it is. Lines of verse were isolated in poetry classes, but fiction studies were more centered around character, theme, and the often pained circumstances of the author's life. Why was this author writing like this? Well, her husband used to cavort with thick-legged women and her legs, while long, were not large. Yes, that would certainly screw a person up. What? Did you say "screw"?

One afternoon I visited my poetry professor and triumphantly exited heartened and envy-proof. She covered her smoker's breath with a slurp of coffee before taking up my most recent work and telling me how different I was from other students. "You can actually write," she said, in an uncelebratory tone. My paper on Gwendolyn Brooks chose that moment to droop in her small hands, my flabby sentences embarrassed at her edict. Though my quiver of critical words was evidently apt, I tirelessly pursued the muses of fiction so that mine would float, too, kneeling at the altars of James Salter and John Berger, wizened men birthed in the 1920s, while many others swayed to the delights of Don DeLillo and David Foster Wallace.

In the years since that day, what have I done? I've often wasted my energy on unmeaningful games or hectoring my soul to enjoy the women my wiles and fortune have contrived to place close to my face, delighting in their bodies of dialed up colors or a videoed haze—the simulacrum of reality without commitment. Though I wrote throughout all this time, I had no concept of form and maybe this helped. Following my endearment with elders, I swallowed a sea of Cormac McCarthy and J. M. Coetzee. These lodestars led me to others, to minimalism and then to maximalism, and then, weaving in and out of poetry, I crept through the pages of Wallace Stevens and Hart Crane. Crane awed and his verse led back to Emily Dickinson via his iron sonnet of tribute. In sampling Stevens, I mostly hung around *Harmonium* and those early poems of fancy, composed by a mind both addled and delighted by colors and repetition in such lines as: "A red bird flies across the golden floor," "Beholding all these green sides / And gold sides of green sides," and, in a combination of the two, the harmonized opening of 'Tea at the Palaz of Hoon':

> Not less because in purple I descended
> The western day through what you called
> The loneliest air, not less was I myself.

Here was a poet enfolded enough to know logic is anathema to a startling image, as in 'Metaphors of a Magnifico':

> Twenty men crossing a bridge,
> Into a village,
> Are twenty men crossing twenty bridges,
> Into twenty villages,
> Or one man
> Crossing a single bridge into a village.

He was also able to assemble a breadth of space around his verse as evidenced in the dollop of stanza XII in 'Thirteen Ways of Looking at a Blackbird':

> The river is moving.
> The blackbird must be flying.

When I couldn't write much that winter I stayed with Stevens, checking into his babble in an effort to replace or at least hijack my own language overgrown with keen and neat metaphors, pedestrian locution, and sentences speaking of verve but not vivacious themselves. My odes to Raymond Carver, Alice Munro, and other exemplars of the plain style were now deeply unfulfilling.

And for a good year, a rather unproductive but mind-deepening one, Stevens informed me. His answers were not easy—they weren't even answers, but patterns, conquests of thought, of tomfoolery, with music and word motion contained inside ideas both raw and cooked. Stevens was a seer seeing as if stationed in outer space, seeing beyond any kingdom, into the dark infinite. He became the glorious mentor I never met, the father who only begot verse upon verse of beauty. What he could be and remain, for everyone and not just me, was his own prescription: "The dauntless master, as he starts the human tale." Did I deserve him? He made me happy to have his words list themselves into focus over my bent head, more so than many other authors I had taken to my internal ear before combat with Stevens' word-war. "Deserve" is perhaps the wrong stratagem where Stevens is concerned. He can be friendly to every reader who comes to his table. Can initiates reply in kind? Let him lead—one cannot change him or staunch the flow. He goes on, he goes around. A poet, in the guise of a blackbird or river, always moving.

On a cool August day, I visited the Knight Library—that building of books serving as a steel and brick bubble to many pained and quixotic emotions I could only bear to spill when no-one but those closed carriers of consciousness dwelt in my ken. I had examined a few first editions of Stevens' poetry books at the New York Public Library in the high-ceilinged reading room on Fifth Avenue, slapping down request slips to the cavalcade of collegian-aged desk jockeys. Yet not *Harmonium*. To my shock the University of Oregon had the 1931 edition—a first edition of the second version Knopf put out eight years after the original publication, with fourteen new poems and three older ones deleted. It was in a special box, yet it was stationed in the stacks—anyone could take it out for three weeks.

When I pulled up a fat chair to those same high, south-facing windows overlooking the empty grass, across from the graves, and took the book in hand, I caressed its hard contours, opening as I opened it, and reveled in its craft: the heavy, expensive pages, the alluring title page with the title, the author, and the publisher's emblem (including the leaping borzoi) surrounded by swirls of cranberry lines. Inside the book, a linotypeface called Estienne made up the words and was described on the last page thus: "The limpid, flowing grace and charm of the lower-case letters with their tall ascenders and long descenders makes reading easy . . ." This was a strong improvement over the darkened twelve-point Electra typeface of Knopf's *Collected Poems* and the ten-point Liontron Galliard of the Modern Library's *Collected Prose and Poetry*. Here was a book released on July 24, 1931 (with a new dedication to both wife *and* daughter), where each poem was given its proper space with none trailing into the page of another—all set on their own, as Stevens originally wanted it.

I held the book, I smelled its age, I turned the pages, and, fixating on the easeful type of the most indelible line in 'Anecdote of the Jar'—"Like nothing else in Tennessee"—I wept.

It is strange to say, but I badly believed everything in my life had happened in order to bring me back to that library, quaking before this book. While memorializing Yeats, W. H. Auden wrote, "poetry makes nothing happen," a notion that only feels true now, out of chagrin at the way poetry is treated by the popular culture. It's viewed as arcane, difficult, effeminate, and as useless as some humanities people regard geometry. Poetry, for those who appreciate it, makes things happen off-camera. One reads it on a sofa and a line overwhelms and one's regard for life is colored by a burnishing of the words and sounds. Stevens and his poetry brought me to that point, but the rest of the cause surely lay beyond the barrel-chested man and his blue words.

To live with books, with cats, with women was necessary, but none could fully compute my coercions, my drip-dry emotional pandering, and other ploys which ailed my not going deeper into creation. Something else had to intrude to make art that fully represented me. My purpose was to scrape out all the gunk and foggy ideas and words that make a piece of writing blur in the hands of the reader, but where I went wasn't where I thought I'd be going. Book as object had become book as traducer—what seemed like epiphany sat repulsed and I sat still in the same chair warmed by the sun, my same brand of isolation winking, circumscribed and faultless, signaling from its prominent tower that, no, I was the same person as yesterday and pretty close to the guy who thought of a yesterday ten years earlier or at age ten, when memories were thin as twigs and time took its time rather than racing to cap the day with night. I stayed the same, but the way I ordered and produced words would have to change.

When reading Stevens' essay 'The Noble Rider and the Sound of Words,' I had no choice but to concur that the function of the poet was not to lead people out of confusion or to comfort them, but "to make his imagination theirs and that he fulfills himself only as he sees his imagination become the light in the minds of others." From the other side of the page, I could assure Stevens this was happening to me and I could also admit other benefits, as I was surely more thorough and better capable of evincing a burr, berry, or blandishment in my own vocabulary, instead of the same old treats. I became better able to see objects in isolation, to pull focus like an adept cinematographer with a Cézanne tint to the lens, enabling me to make out the most furious crag in the sleepiest mountain. After coming close to masterworks, I've always thought I could place myself better and lean toward the colder side of life with more compassion and a greater honesty, believing I could handhold the most challenging people I so easily loathe, but who often display aspects of myself I haven't deigned to contemplate, much less admit.

The world of Stevens and other masters is often the world I wish existed, and so I attempted to expand it by sharing these differing climes with friends and family. Sycophantic though it might be, I consider it my duty to bring others into these realms, even at the cost of hampering the relationship. As much as I stuffed my mother with the films of Kubrick and Bergman, my girlfriends with Bishop, Glück, Sebald, and the more that miniature nine-line poem in *Harmonium*, 'Life is Motion,' played its abbreviated music in a friend's ear—

> In Oklahoma,
> Bonnie and Josie,
> Dressed in calico,
> Danced around a stump.
> They cried,
> "Ohoyaho,
> Ohoo" . . .
> Celebrating the marriage
> Of flesh and air

—the more greater culture reigned; with reflection and color and the reflections of color and sound superseding the unlovely emotions distributed by TV networks and the sad funk of people pulverized by jobs

and by others, who had merely loved them to the letter of their own ag-
grandized ego. If life is motion (on the plank, I would always contend it
to be and never otherwise), then celebrating the marriage of flesh and
air must be primary, no matter if Stevens meant the flesh of backs and
breasts or the flesh of imagination. The clear or contaminated thoughts
that train one to persuade beauty to make a bed at the base of a chapel
or cesspool, whether in Oklahoma or Oahu, are born of such alchemy.

A week after returning to Stevens in Eugene, I drove south to San
Francisco, fortunate to meet my future wife at the airport and enjoy the
Edenic environs of Big Sur with her. Fog-drenched hills—sometimes
green, sometimes golden—and sheared cliffs overlooking a sea stretching far away; at that height it could only be majestic because so out of
touch. When we were able, we stayed in the sunnier spots where the
sky dyed the ocean blue. At a famous waterfall we climbed south of the
tourists onto cliffs obscured by brittle coastal trees. Into the high dirt not
yet eroded, they must have sprouted from scattered seeds while often in
contact with the great gales and gusts of the Pacific, which fashioned the
growing wood, and then its branches, to trail eastward like the tresses of
a nymph caught by the wind and frozen. There we merrily ate lunch with
only the boom of sea slamming rocks below, where large green swirls of
seaweed clogged the shore.

Is late afternoon the best time for poetry? With a sinking sun and the
stories of our lives in repose after the often fitful midday, aren't the siesta
hours most befitting to an artform so benighted by dreams, the sleep of
dreams, and dreamlike imagery? With nothing to remind us that civilization still existed, except the cheese and crackers we ate and the sleek and
sporty clothes we wore, I brought out Stevens' *Collected Poems*. With
permission, I skipped a few pages into the thick paperback and read
aloud 'Le Monocle de Mon Oncle,' the haunting, twelve-part poem (the
eleventh poem in *Harmonium* and its second-longest), and unwittingly,
perhaps, the most imitated. Why read a poem about sloughing off love
to someone one is in love with? Why dwell on the rusty thoughts feelings
can become? Why? Riddle me only slant rhymes because the only surety
thirty-seven years of living had taught me was that we knew nothing,
except how unpredictable life could be:

> Is it for nothing, then, that old Chinese
> Sat tittivating by their mountain pools
> Or in the Yangtse studied out their beards?
> I shall not play the flat historic scale.
> You know how Utamaro's beauties sought

The end of love in their all-speaking braids.
You know the mountainous coiffures of Bath.
Alas! Have all the barbers lived in vain
That not one curl in nature has survived?
Why, without pity on these studious ghosts,
Do you come dripping in your hair from sleep?

This saucy third canto ends with a last question busky enough to make Frank Kermode wax: "its last two lines are among the most beautiful in Stevens and I do not know what they mean." The hair canto. The smell of barbershops could not make me weep after reading these twisters, because the lines left hair stuck in my nose and mouth. Hair. Hair to some heads, including mine, is sex. It is its own weapon and Stevens knew what power lurked and, to great effect, drained its awing honeycomb.

Three of the six questions in the poem occur in this third canto, but Stevens' questions have no answers and they aren't truly questions, more glories of thought and form capable of the right weight of nudge or scintillating perversion. Later, Stevens even titled a poem 'Questions are Remarks.' "Why . . . [d]o you come dripping in your hair from sleep?" might just be Mon Oncle's way of querying "What are we doing with our lives?" but with a more celestial and somnolent reckoning—including the slake for a surrealism that the Renaissance sonneteer in Stevens would have to patch over, freeing the eerily familiar romantic imagery into a handsome deck of cards fully shuffled, yet parsimoniously dealt.

As I read on, I read relaxed, though concerned that the offertory of this verse might not sway or bombard as it did to me while I sat in a lonely corner of a library a year before, passion punctured by loss of love, endlessly micturating a morose blight, while seeking people who had endured greater endings and torment—poets who made life in the margins miraculous while leveling their abiding lusts. 'Le Monocle de Mon Oncle' is the perfect credo for the philosophically crestfallen. The "I" of this poem "mocks," "wishes," "uncrumples," "greets," "beholds," "quizzes," "finds," "knows," "observes," "pursues," but also "never knows" and shall "not play." Easy enough—we're talking love. Reading again the sonorous retro-flexing words, I heard how Stevens' exclamations have been echoed in the work of many who have followed him, even if they knew him not, even if Stevens himself echoed Shakespeare and Wordsworth, among others. "Like a dull scholar, I behold, in love / An ancient aspect touching a new mind" is an example of verse showing its face in everyone from Hart Crane to Kurt Cobain.

As the sea remained blue with sun-filled sky, my lover and I stayed together on that broken cliff with Stevens' music. My eyes were on her reception of the work, and hers were adrift as she focused inwardly on my vocal interpretation, because, hearing it for the first time, I could not spin words accurately enough to gather meaning. The first time with Stevens is like that other "first time"—nothing prepares you.

Where do certain apexes of emotion burn? Does what moves us have to grow or does it appear with a pop? If it proclaims fittingly and enters one's bloodstream—one sinks, opting to go all olive under the skin, with outward dandy decimated in a flash. Words dart about, and for this reason they are often associated with water; saliva builds the more we speak. From Stevens inditing the lines in 1918, to the book, to off the book, into my eyes, out of my mouth, and into her ears, with any leftover syllables floating out unguarded on the bald Pacific—this train of sound had a fanciful but roughened journey to any understanding.

Did what we wanted to do to each other after the experience of Stevens resemble the simple unbuckling of a belt? In reading this poetic tale of hot and cold, hard and soft, mind and body, though we slowed ourselves to find Stevens, but of course we were still stuck on ourselves. 'Le Monocle de Mon Oncle'—it's French, *le français*.

> If sex were all, then every trembling hand
> Could make us squeak, like dolls, the wished-for words.

Were our "wished-for" words, or the words of Stevens' poem, making a change? Changing our relationship or our relationship to the poem? Or were we fomenting the promise of desire dying? With language, does one settle the self in the world with ideas of order inside sweetened syllables, or does one rear to rush back to silence, because the sound of words frightens with promises of what might be and what is? Whatever the structure, his imagination was now ours—fulfilling the ultimate aim. But if a curtain is drawn in real life (or even in Vermeer's Delft) and a view is revealed, the structure will glisten for a time and go out. What the poet had given I carried like the song I had to keep humming.

After I read, I felt all my sins, real or imagined—everything about myself alert and well past summoned. My memories had been drained—the archness I carried like a bludgeon ceased—and I touched only what I saw, smelling a future finally falling into the now. Living by Stevens for a few moments made me up to myself, and Mon Oncle stood gamely about, but almost immediately I broke the blue of the Stevens moment by asking what she thought of the poem—to fulfill myself, I had to know. There reigned quiet and sea, all these scapes like so many poems and scenes in fiction and film: sun, sea, spume, and the bare skin of bodies gone grainy from intimacy. I don't remember what she said (I do) but it became immediately unimportant, like time spent waiting for the ones who mean the most to us.

If she or I come dripping in our hair from sleep or not, neither case will disqualify us from longings to burn over the ancient and the revolutionary of our time. How we regard color and motion won't impede the delicate horror of one's allegiance to another's soul. On starry nights or sunny afternoons, I can't but believe I will be removed from the earth only to live again and already am, and that however many more turns I take reading 'Le Monocle de Mon Oncle,' or however many times I feel the tingle in my back at the sight of her or at the sound of poetry, I am reminded to regard living as only a joy; and if hallowed love hoists itself only to get shadowed into an irreal, unkempt creation, no matter then—the globe cannot be so haunted by realities apart from art. We are at home in the parlor of dreams. Felicitations, Mr. Stevens.

'A Rabbit as King of the Ghosts'

THE RABBIT POEM. Any mention of Wallace Stevens will pique my
interest and when Adam Plunkett wrote in *n+1* that David Foster Wallace had this poem on his mind in the last month of his life, I immediately investigated. Soon I realized I had passed over it in my initial
meanderings through Stevens' poems. It also appeared in the collection
Parts of a World, which has mostly received scant notice from critics
and scholars, and then myself, but is just as much a major part of the
bedrock that made the man as was *Harmonium*. Aside from an intriguing title, the verse of the poem mirrors and expands its meanings or lack
of them. In a letter, Stevens said he was very pleased with the work.
Harold Bloom goes into some detail on it in his book *Wallace Stevens:
The Poems of Our Climate*. I believe that what makes it stand out, and
even classic, is its inscrutability for a time until it "humps" the reader up
higher and higher with its language:

> The difficulty to think at the end of day,
> When the shapeless shadow covers the sun
> And nothing is left except light on your fur—
>
> There was the cat slopping its milk all day,
> Fat cat, red tongue, green mind, white milk
> And August the most peaceful month.
>
> To be, in the grass, in the peacefullest time,
> Without that monument of cat,
> The cat forgotten in the moon;

And to feel that the light is a rabbit-light,
In which everything is meant for you
And nothing need be explained;

Then there is nothing to think of. It comes of itself;
And east rushes west and west rushes down,
No matter. The grass is full

And full of yourself. The trees around are for you,
The whole of the wideness of night is for you,
A self that touches all edges,

You become a self that fills the four corners of night.
The red cat hides away in the fur-light
And there you are humped high, humped up,

You are humped higher and higher, black as stone—
You sit with your head like a carving in space
And the little green cat is a bug in the grass.

There is narrative to the poem. It has two characters: a rabbit and a cat. The speaker of the poem sides with the rabbit and initially gestures at him with the words "your fur." But almost immediately, in the second stanza, the speaker introduces the cat in its summer malaise, though it is draped in Christmas colors: "Fat cat, red tongue, green mind, white milk." The rabbit must be weary of the cat and so the speaker creates another reality for it, "without that monument of cat," and a brief but beautiful trip away from the feline proffers nirvana:

And to feel that the light is a rabbit-light
In which everything is meant for you
And nothing need be explained;
Then there is nothing to think of.

A few stanzas on, there's an occurrence of that infamous flying dream some humans are afflicted with: "And there you are humped high, humped up, / You are humped higher and higher."

Suddenly, it's a beautiful world. How couldn't it be when everything is "for you"? Bloom says that this refrain, beginning in stanza four and twice-repeated in six, echoes lines in Ralph Waldo Emerson's 'Nature'; and four years before Bloom published his book, Bruce Springsteen wrote a ballad with the same refrain, titled 'For You,' about a woman who has attempted suicide. If it was a romantic sentiment one hundred years before the poem and forty years after, in Stevens it is posited more as a pep-talk to get higher—for the rabbit needs these realizations to ascend to a crown high in the sky, a trip that not only brings about a title but an end to thought. The only romance resides in the way the steely gray of the mind goes blank as it finds the blackness of outer space, leaving the earth to its colors.

Because the rabbit is so high, the light is "rabbit-light," and parts of the rabbit including its "fur-light" end up concealing the cat. While the rabbit journeys, the cat's Christmas colors flicker. "The red cat hides away," then "the little green cat is a bug in the grass." On the rabbit's ascent the alliteration builds, with the repetition of "you" in seven of the last nine lines, and then, later, three instances of "humped," three of "high," and two more h-words, "hides" and "head." All these *h*- breaths blast out the hot air that makes this rabbit rise.

One can argue that the music of the language is what makes poetry meaningful, and one can say that any aesthetic sense Stevens' words make is owing to their musical qualities. As Stevens writes in his most important essay, 'The Noble Rider and the Sound of Words':

> The deepening need for words to express our thoughts and feelings which, we are sure, are all the truth that we shall ever experience, having no illusions, makes us listen to words when we hear them, loving them and feeling them, makes us search the sound of them for a finality, a perfection, an unalterable vibration, which it is only within the power of the acutest poet to give them.

Why the trope of the rabbit? Animals have been among poets' greatest companions, from John Keats' 'Ode to a Nightingale' to Rainer Maria Rilke's 'The Panther,' up to Marianne Moore's 'The Pangolin' and Elizabeth Bishop's 'The Fish.' But in all art and kitsch, animals have always been a more pregnant form of iconography, from cave paintings to YouTube cat videos. 'A Rabbit as King of the Ghosts' was published in the fifty-first issue of *Poetry Magazine* in October 1937; several months earlier, in May of that year, Stevens had written a very curious passage in a letter to Ronald Lane Latimer, the founder and publisher of Alcestis Press, who published two of Stevens' books in short form. It gives a good view of Stevens at age fifty-eight:

> I expect to do very little writing until autumn. This is the time of year

for exercise, for cheering oneself up, sitting down to dinner at 8 and going to bed at 9. Last night, after I had gone upstairs, I changed everything in my room so that when the family came up they were flabbergasted. One side of my bed there is nothing but windows; when I lie in bed I can see nothing but trees. But there has been a rabbit digging out bulbs: instead of lying in bed in the mornings listening to everything that is going on, I spend the time worrying about the rabbit and wondering what particular thing he is having for breakfast.

Why wouldn't poets write about what they think? Stevens had a sedentary life after a certain age, though he reveled in walks during early life: "I have always walked a great deal, mostly alone, and mostly on the hill, rambling along the side of the mountain," he wrote, in 1909, to his future wife. He enjoyed looking at art (and owned lithographs by Kandinsky and Braque), listening to classical music, and tending his garden. He did think a great deal about faraway places (and placed them in his poetry) such as the tropics, Europe, Africa, and China. One of his most cherished correspondents was José Rodriguez Feo, a Cuban editor, translator, and critic nearly forty years younger than him. He often asked the young man for details of his native country, probably to sate his imagination. Feo once said, of meeting Stevens, "I realized then that to him a piece of fruit was more than something to eat. . . . It was good enough for him to look at it and think about it." The experiences of such encounters were filtered into the ornaments Stevens brought into his verse. Birds, rabbits, food, and flowers enlivened him. No wonder he wrote a poem called 'Someone Puts a Pineapple Together.'

The year before writing the rabbit poem, he wrote to Latimer:

> I think that I should continue to write poetry whether or not anybody ever saw it, and certainly I write lots of it that nobody ever sees. We are all busy thinking things that nobody ever knows about. If a woman in her room is such an exciting subject of speculation, a man in his thoughts is equally exciting.

"A man in his thoughts" is an apt picture of Stevens' poetry. His poems speak with the stillness and color splashes of the paintings he ogled, even if at times they speak in surreal tones, like when he begins a poem with "A sunny day's complete Poussiniana," making the French painter's classical visions an intricately amalgamated adjective fused by myriad vowel sounds. His world was his poetry, made by a vibrant and diffusing imagination and a philosophy of sound, as one of his earliest speakers, a small bantam, declares to a chief cock in a barnyard:

Fat! Fat! Fat! Fat! I am the personal.
Your world is you. I am my world.

Doses of Medicine

I ONCE HIT Louise Glück after one of her readings, oddly enough with her own books. Of course, I did so unwittingly. During the post-reading mingle, I kept trying to place my book bag on my shoulder, but it kept bumping against something and wouldn't stay. That something was her, and when my embarrassment met her surprised eyes, any alarm disappeared. We could see the mistake—the mutual understanding was very clean, almost surgically so, like a line of her verse.

I've often read Louise Glück with enthusiasm. Her poems are doses of medication. Her work has always "spoken" to me more than many poets because she examines the concerns I have about being in the world: loneliness and being alone, searching for happiness, and desiring to have my feelings validated, though they often aren't. Her poetry is both direct and indirect, as she will talk through a feeling but sometimes dress the speaker of the poem in a mythical mask, using many Ancient Greek deities and characters in collections such as *The Wild Iris*, *Meadowlands*, and *Vita Nova*. Her first book of essays, *Proofs and Theories*, provides insight to her artistic philosophy. The last essay, 'On Impoverishment,' has a few tempered lines on Glück's major theme, despair:

> Despair in our culture tends to produce wild activity: change the job, change the partner, replace the faltering ambition instantly. We fear passivity and prize action, meaning the action we initiate. But the self cannot be willed back. And flight from despair forfeits whatever benefit may arise in the encounter with despair.

There is something therapeutic to Glück's inquiries, and these words almost serve as a mantra to embolden her to not shy away from what she finds most frightening.

In my my late twenties I was seeking epiphany, and the epiphanies concocted by Glück, those ending points and moments of ultimate response, were similar to the ending of many an Ingmar Bergman film—abrupt, cruel in its truth, but spectacular. Take 'The Silver Lily' from Glück's most prized collection, *The Wild Iris*. The speaker of the poem, maybe God or some other creator, asks another presence, a woman, "Will speech disturb you?" and then implores her to look at the bounty of nature and the universe, in particular the moon:

> In spring, when the moon rose, it meant
> time was endless. Snowdrops
> opened and closed, the clustered
> seeds of the maples fell in pale drifts.

Finally, the being offers:

> We have come too far together toward the end now
> to fear the end. These nights, I am no longer even certain
> I know what the end means. And you, who've been with a man—
>
> after the first cries,
> doesn't joy, like fear, make no sound?

Here, Glück attacks the normal configurations of despair produced by a life of pain. So that the woman doesn't feel sad at the end of their connection, which will also be the end of the poem, the being reminds her of sex she has had and how joy and fear end in the same silence. The consolation of nature is fractured as the being tells the pained woman how all feelings are born from the same stream in which they will also die. There is a good deal of white space on the page, including the gap after the em dash, and there one can imagine the ghosts of words that Glück doesn't use to fight this force. The final question cancels out any response from the woman and nature, both devoid of speech—the world remains mystifying to the humans who depend on it to renew their belief in the lives they live.

Once I showed my uncle, who had originally piqued my interest in Glück, the poem 'Purple Bathing Suit,' in which a woman speaks to a man in such a suit. After its suckerpunch—"your back is my favorite part of you, / the part furthest away from your mouth"—my uncle said, "Boy, she really hates men." And men can hate women, because the book is a documentation of both hatreds, the complete war. But by the end of most Glück poems, there is insight and disturbance—and, for some, maybe even the majority of people who seek poetry, disturbance is as alluring as sunset, because that sensation is what drives them to clasp poetry to their heart and often what drives poets to write it. In Glück's world, to be ultra-conscious is to be conscious of pain, and the words that best delineate that indelicacy are the simplest. Like Emily Dickinson before her, Glück's ideas and questions act as deep pools, and inhabit everyday words while often arranged in short lines. When, in 'The Silver Lily,' she asks, "doesn't joy, like fear, make no sound?" she brings together words from a very basic lexicon. Two of them, "joy" and "fear," are lively, hot. The others—"doesn't," "like," "make," "no," and "sound"—are words that we use to get through most days. Like T. S. Eliot, Glück reorders familiar expressions musically (that last line is iambic) to train the reader to trust her words and isolate them, slowing down life.

One night, while I read again each of Glück's books in the original slim hardbacks, I sat in a car taking an hour-long break from my home-less outreach job in Manhattan. My co-worker and I were parked just off 41st Street between 9th and 10th Avenues, near a hotspot of homeless ac-tivity. It's a dirty street, one of the many garbage dumping areas in Hell's Kitchen, where people set up lean-tos and shanties out of industrial cardboard boxes to sleep among rats crawling about for food. While my co-worker tried to nap, I re-read Glück's 1988 collection *Ararat*. When she couldn't sleep, she thumbed through the Instagram feed on her phone. "Can I read you a poem?" I asked her. She quickly agreed, almost as if she longed for a reason to quit the endless stream of information, welcoming any distraction from distraction. I read the last poem, 'First Memory,' because it was short and powerful, the way I remembered it from when I carried *Ararat* like a Bible, with its final lines,

> . . .from the beginning of time,
> in childhood, I thought
> that pain meant
> I was not loved.
> It meant I loved.

It is an apt summary of the dredging and loosening in that book. All those years ago, it seemed I didn't read poems, but readouts from a heart cooked by memories, impatient to re-season them with a semblance of order and clarity. The message still held, though the word "loved" carried very different meanings from its first use to the next, beyond the passive and active tenses. It meant that in the span of ten years I had loved and been loved and now I loved differently because of time. The speaker of the poem can only come to her sweet conclusion from a distance of years, and only with the experience of ten more—of loves lost and gained—could the startling already past tense of "love" trigger a charge for me and a recognition of the beauty of responsibility.

I read the poem to my co-worker slowly, in a voice I thought the speaker of the poem would adopt if the speaker's voice could be heard. After I finished, she immediately popped up, turned the car light on, and told me to hold the book still. She took a picture of 'First Memory' with her phone and then shared it.

Holy Hill

Poetry is a strange angel. And has very little to do with enjoyment, actually. Great deal to do with joy, not with enjoyment. Enjoyment is patronizing and possessive, like the old archaic euphemism of a man sexually enjoying a woman's body. So when you enjoy a poem, you say, *You are mine. And you please me in my current mood.* And the Angel of Poetry says, *Sod off. Sod off!*

— Geoffrey Hill, 2009 poetry reading

THE LAST OF the fifteen Oxford lectures Geoffrey Hill gave during his five-year tenure as Poetry Professor (works not yet published, but online, as sound files), is called "Words, Words, Words." Hill spends the first moments introducing the poet and critic Charles Williams, before using the last two-thirds (forty-five minutes) to critique Philip Larkin's well-known poem "Church Going" by putting a hot poker to Larkin's word choices, repeatedly checking his softball language (for Hill) against the *Oxford English Dictionary* and how he "poetically employ[s] colloquial ambiguity," branding the line "what remains when disbelief has gone?" as "an act of blundering self-therapy." These lectures are hour-long meteorites demonstrative of what is so missing in today's literary weather— a passion for form where one consistently thinks of oneself secondarily and, in the process, abandons the late-twentieth-century dependence, according to Hill, on "the quotidian and how it has been, with significant exceptions, overvalued as the authenticating factor in works of the imagination. The poem itself, assessed in this way, becomes the author's promise to pay on demand, to provide real and substantial evidence of a suffering life for which the poem itself is merely a kind of tictac or flyer." And indeed, Hill reveals in the final minutes of the lecture that one may take all five years' worth of the lectures and reduce them to one quote he came upon in a *Guardian* interview of choreographer Mark Morris: "I'm not interested in self-expression, but in expressiveness." So how do we go beyond and make art that will resonate over years and centuries? Hill would say it starts with knowing the history of our art, especially in the light of its current dimming.

If we are living in "end-times," and most of the world's scientists so aver, it seems incumbent to think about our place in history; to ask, as we always should, What's worth doing? I don't mean to parse our collective body weight with a certain twenty-first-century technology-finessed truculence, something leading one of the more conscientious fiction critics, Mark Athitakis, to write a "think-piece" for the *Washington Post* with the title "Where is the great millennial novel?" A few weeks later, Henrik Bering, a critic writing in *The New Criterion* about his reading habits, observed: ". . . I seem to lack the patience to read about high-strung millennials with partnership issues." Glib, yes, but it holds a few strains of truth. Many people in the "writing world" often salt their criticisms of someone's work with the old sangfroidian saw "What is at stake?" And if you have to ask, it's usually not there. "What's worth doing?" and "What is at stake?" sit in the same section of the ballpark, but they probably don't like each other. Still, our "moment" consistently demands answers to many other queries that leapfrog the question of the work itself.

As in Athitakis's gambit, there is much perturbation these days about writers finding their place, something like a niche. Though such a position is ideally recognized by others and not self-appointed—to do so tests the last vestiges of compunction and most writers would not risk such a foolishness. But finding a place might be exactly where we don't want to be. Shouldn't a true artist fight against any consumer packaging and the sorry relegation to the flavor-of-the-moment box—one often not of one's own choosing? Besides social media, or in spite of it, authors are expected to promote themselves to puppet-like degrees. Guy Davenport saw the writing on the wall in 1998 when he wrote:

> The idea persists that writing is an activity of thoughtful, idealistic, moral people called authors and that they are committed to protecting certain values vital to a well-ordered society. . . . To this assumption there has been added . . . the image of the author as a celebrity, someone worth hearing at a reading or lecture even if you have no intention of parting with a dime for one of the author's books.

The anxiety around the recognition race is an endless cacophony of wea-sel words. The author, Justin E. Smith, got it too right when he recently wrote, "I am struck by how much, at this point, what we still call 'books' are no longer physical objects so much as they are multi-platform cam-paigns in which the physical object is only a sort of promotional tie-in." Why, yes, the book now *is* a promotional tie-in; at The Strand you pay the price of one to get into an event to see the author read from it, but, in more cases, to divulge their "opinions" and other superficialities, like the time of day he or she writes. Yet, "campaign" is perhaps the most important word in that sentence. Obviously, a writer's ideas or rip-offs and their lyrical beauty in prose or verse are no substitute for "getting your book out there."

During one spate of gray winter months, my taste for fictional prose, as happens every few years, dried up and I began to run in the fields of posey, visiting old friends before reading one of the best American po-etry critics of our day, William Logan. Arch and acerbic, but dignified, he is often undeniably correct in many of his assessments. In his many "Verse Chronicles" (reviewing five or so books at a time), I saw a name repeated again and again—Geoffrey Hill, who had died just two years before. Hill had written sixteen books in the last twenty years of his life, dwarfing the first five books in nearly forty. On-line, there were many murmurs of his agon with the prosified poetry of the moment, and of his own poetry's "difficulty." On first reading the poems, I recognized those "radiant node[s] and cluster[s]" of Ezra Pound, who so defined a poetic image. Pound was famous for his ideograms, a term, according to Davenport, meaning "a pattern of images, which is read as the sum of its components, as in the Chinese written character, which is built up of radicals," with radicals defined as root parts. So an ideogram is a pattern of these radiant nodes or clusters where the verse electrifies as it fossil-izes, becoming a permanent relic in the ongoing scree-pile of Western Art. Hill himself would have called them "fields of force" (a term taken from Pound and Hugh Kenner), and here is one from Hill, the beginning of Canto XX in his *Orchards of Syon*:

> Two nights' and three days' rain, with the Hodder
> well up, over its alder roots; tumblings
> of shaly late storm light; the despised
> ragwort, luminous, standing out,
> stereoscopically, across twenty yards,
> on the farther bank. The congregants
> of air and water, of swift reflection,

vanish between the brightness and shadow.
Mortal beauty is alienation; or not,
as I see it. The rest passagework,
settled beforehand, variable, to be lived through
as far as one can, with uncertain
tenure.

It is nature, pure and not so simple, being parsed through the speaker's mind: "congregants" (a word full of religious connotations) of air and water give off a "swift reflection." The act of seeing gives way to a glorious expanse, with a commentator piping hidden lyricisms into one's innards: the "tumblings" are of not just light, but "late storm light," which is colored by the colorless color of "shaly." Eight lines of atmosphere before the guillotine of old-fogey judgment bears down and hacks out, "Mortal beauty is alienation." There follows a dialed-back mantra for existence, taking to task the platitude of life being very difficult and mysterious, but never saying it; instead, life is our "passagework" (and between the words "rest" and "passagework" is a caesura where "is" would detract from and muss the rhythm), while "with uncertain tenure" blows its second surly word through more hidebound circumstances.

I found myself nodding at nearly every overture of Hill's on poetry in his lectures and the *Collected Critical Writings*, taking them as copacetic with prose, especially how the latter should obey at least some lyrical and acoustic strictures to guide its lines (sentences) to make its verse (prose) more immortal. I'm very tempted to list the nuggets or aperçus in no great discursive enfoldment, à la David Shields's *Reality Hunger* or the forlorn Twitter quotage, where something eerily stands as deity to be kneed to, a morning affirmation forgotten during teeth brushing, but then I'd be only a celebrant, a fanboy not engaged with the form. Maybe nothing more typifies Hill's stance than the way creativity is bastardized by the pop logic of the current age versus the more diverse and rigorous views of the past. In the "Democracy of the Dead" lecture, Hill breaks down his own view of authorship by beginning with an F. R. Leavis quote: "All that we can fairly ask of the poet is that he shall show himself to have been fully alive in our time. The evidence will be in the very texture of the poetry." Thereafter, he adds:

> This moral affirmation of an intellectual concept, that the intrinsic value of a poem is finally determined not by inspiration, or vision, or teaching, or self-expression, but by semantic and rhythmic texture—context—was to affect radically the teaching of poetry . . . for the next

thirty years. Success in this context, equals intrinsic validity of the text itself. Associative pleasure, such as being reminded of a summer holiday, is not only irrelevant, it is vicious . . .

Hill then boomerangs back to the primary source of these directives, T. S. Eliot, who wrote: "The emotion of art is impersonal. And the poet cannot reach this impersonality without surrendering himself wholly to the work to be done." With Hill calling for "the extinction of mere self-expression," and in propping up a more craft-centered type of poet, he highlights Ezra Pound's metaphor in Canto LXXIV: "Hast 'ou seen the rose in the steel dust," a reference to the latter's own critical writing in *Guide to Kulchur*; wherein the artwork's "concept [or] dynamic form . . . is like the rose pattern driven into the dead iron-filings by the magnet, not by material contact with the magnet itself . . . [and] the dust and filings rise and spring into order . . . the concept rises from death . . ." Here is how art is made. Creation of a thing itself, not a simple journal entry on how one felt about something. In citing an obituary in his college newsletter of a man distinguished in another field, but who was said to have written poetry and enjoyed romance novels, Hill testily rejoins, "If you have a hobby, you're a hobbyist, and you ride a hobby horse." True authorship is so much more. Biography and self-biographical pronouncements lessen, and the work stands in for the person—just a name and then their books.

All this comes up dry in the watery world of today's literary culture, but it can be no coincidence that the most serious artists produced their greatest work when embroiled in these questions of form. Hill's own work abhors "mere self-expression." All through the lectures and critical writings, this "difficult" poet is constantly reminding us, as he quotes the early twentieth-century critic Charles Williams, that ". . . the chief impulse of a poet is, not to communicate a thing to others, but to shape a thing, to make an immortality for its own sake." The end is always the work and not the campaign to canonize the person who wrote it, an act that is surely an aspect of the current cultural and language crises Hill often alludes to and many of us feel. Hill called it "anarchical plutocracy," meaning a system, headed by the wealthy, which "destroys memory and dissipates attention," where too many succumb to consumerism and are "self-satisfied with the offer of total solipsistic pleasure in the self"— social media's bane. There may be glints and glitters of Hill's life in his poetry, but often we don't know whom his speaker is really talking about; his own life is just about the least important thing to glom on to. Take the lines at the beginning of Hill's "In Ipsley Church Lane I":

More than ever I see through painters' eyes.
The white hedge-parsleys pall, the soot is on them.
Clogged thorn-blossom sticks, like burnt cauliflower,
to the festered hedge-rim. More than I care to think
I am *as one* coarsened by feckless grief.
Storm cloud and sun together bring out the yellow of stone.

Well, possibly the speaker is talking about Hill himself, or at least an aspect of him (the "I" is as tempting as a suitcase full of money), but it's what the "eye" sees: "Clogged thorn-blossom sticks, like burnt cauliflower." This vignette is more about the quotidian man who began his life in one fashion and has "coarsened" into a very different story—the long journey in a few lines. No wonder he stated, flippantly, in an interview: "All my poems are love poems . . . either about particular women or about language. . . . All my poems are acts of coitus with the English language." As for his view on confessional poetry, it is full of expected opprobrium: ". . . the so-called 'confessional' movement in post-modern art and literature is mainly a mating-display clumsily performed." All writing is autobiographical, but in vertiginous ways and often indirectly, as one scouts the strata for the motherlode. Hill metaphorically suggests that when we look at a table or any other piece of furniture, we don't think about the biography of the person or persons who made it and this should hold the same for a work of literature. It's the only art where verbal criticism is apt—and to react with silence is as scornful as a critical shellacking.

But what is Hill's major concern? Words, with the *Oxford English Dictionary* being "the quarry of [his] distinctions and definitions." Not just anyone would attempt a fifteen-page review of the *OED*, which he did in 1989, or deliver the annual T. S. Eliot lecture with the title "Word Value in F. H. Bradley and T. S. Eliot," or write in a *TLS* review, aptly titled "The Weight of the Word," that "the distance between grace and sentiment may be the breath of a syllable," or deliver this little ditty from the Oxford lectures: "The sonnets by Shakespeare that encounter the double betrayal . . . are delivered with what we call a 'shit-eating' grin—sense 1b, of course, of 'shit-eating' grin: ingratiating, embarrassed, or uncomfortable expression of someone undergoing a humiliating experience." This all leads to one of his main concepts, turned from a precept of Coleridge in the latter's nearly forgotten *Aids for Reflection*—"living powers"—a term so obsessive to Hill that it shows up in his late poetry. Coleridge: "For if words are not THINGS, they are LIVING POWERS, by which the things of most importance to mankind are actuated, combined, and humanized." And how delightful it is to know we have "living powers"— that is, the God-like practice of "naming" and "coinage," which is to say pieces of verse and prose are very goddamned serious things. Any words we use, even those to the deliveryman and the salesgirl, are really "living powers" and we must use our powers to their utmost. Every time we press air to issue in sound, it would be helpful if we gave a little thought to our ripostes, since most of our talk is response, with too many tawdry collegiate innuendos, like "That's what she said" and, more recently, the stripped-down, ballyhooed "LOL" or even just the lonely tower of the exclamation point (!) in texting and messaging. The quality of our texting can maybe tell us more than we'd like about our lives. Our relationship with words determines all of our other relationships. Words enhance and complicate how we see life, how we love; words are our undoing—words people pretend not to hear, those they long for but never find, those they'll never forget.

Hill claims, "Any poem that is seriously good is weird," meaning that the best is not so easily apprehended. This thought is further enhanced by his description of language: "Language, whatever else it is and is not, can be understood historically as a form of seismograph: registering and retaining the myriad shocks of humanity's interested and disinterested passions." He also details how tender and tensile poetry can be, "Poetry is one of the multifarious forms of self-consciousness. It is a consciousness of self, a consciousness to, and in, itself; and an embarrassment to itself and others." Again "living powers," though when Hill says it's an "embarrassment to itself and others," he may mean bad poetry (and bad poetry overheard), but I still take it, throbbingly, in a very personal vein, more as the power of words to cause certain unseen pain since some can't or won't allow themselves to feel anything, even to feel lost, which is hardly ever the poet's intention. The greats often teach you how to read them.

"The modern poem," Hill writes, "is not a public occasion," but so is much of the modern appreciation of poetry. It is a deep and probably inextinguishable, but elementary, tragedy when you can't talk about the things you love with the people you love. Relationships with poets, and more so with their poems, can be very personal, and as healing as connection to a father, a friend. Associative pleasure is often there because artworks act as time machines to many feelings at different points of one's growth.

Falling this far for words had a strange birth. Amid the anodyne smell of the University of Oregon's Knight Library—dust on old books, new books getting quickly older—I was defrocked by each subsequent loan. I often read beyond the syllabi and where, among the tacit stacks, I experienced what Hill explains in one lecture: "The book which is to change your life stands next on the shelf to the book that you'd come to take out from the library." Some kind of trial started in those stacks; courtship proceeded, but by abnormal means. To make it work, I had to accept that unconditional love would never come my way; latter days would contain more magisterial estrangements, leading me to toss out Ashbery and much of Merwin for all of Stevens, all of Pound. As Hill says, "Whatever strange relationship we have with the poem, it is not one of enjoyment. It is more like being brushed past, or aside, by an alien being." Anything great, remaining fully loaded throughout the years, has often first had this effect on me.

The eros of language gets keener as the appetite opens. I can still hear Hill rereading certain poems and prose in the lectures, certain passages—something a person who attended some lectures at the time called "tendentious," but what I would consider the key to understanding. How else do you appreciate a poem?—you hear it and read it again and again. You devote hours. Hill stresses repetitions of lines and phrases, the sounds of combinations, as in Shakespeare's Sonnet 137:

> If eyes corrupt by over-partial looks
> Be anchor'd in the bay where all men ride,
> Why of eyes' falsehood hast thou forged hooks,
> Where to the judgment of my heart is tied?

It is a quatrain from the heavens, as Hill uncharacteristically dotes, "My God how wonderful that is." He once wrote, "Eros is the power that can be felt in language when a word or half-finished phrase awaits its consummation." Ensnared in the harmonics of the quatrain above is a moment when the reader gets to "hooks" at the third line's end and, questing after termination, she enters something like the third turn of an oval racetrack, knowing she is shortly powering to the tie of "ride"—a word still lying on the veranda, waiting to be ravished by rhyme—and zooming across the finish line, she is awarded "tied."

The reader feels these cinchings, blossoms, and ruptures of language occur in a very private arena that tries to get called out in duplicitous terms and half-truths in social media, tamping down literature from a way of life to a bulletin for one's personal political propaganda. When literature is so counterfeited, everyone loses. When seemingly so few can take pure joy in literature without a spotlight of shame focusing to find fault, it is good to be reminded how ninety years ago another generation felt differently about the strange art, as Charles Williams wrote:

> Poetry, one way or another, is 'about' human experience; there is nothing else that it can be about. But to whatever particular human experience it alludes, it is not that experience. Love poetry is poetry, not love; patriotic poetry is poetry, not patriotism; religious poetry is poetry, not religion. But good poetry does something more than allude to its subjects; it is related to it, and it relates us to it.

And, in ninety years more (time permitting), we might feel differently again.

The further glimmering is how the past informs and teaches, as Hugh Kenner wrote to Ezra Pound: "What the next generation knows of the past is what this generation tells it, plus what they find out for themselves by chance; and chance is too random to trust." Maybe the greatest current hinderance to society and literature is the increasingly bewildering unalloyed judgments of the past—how wrong people of ancient generations and, most especially, those of five minutes ago, were to think in such a way and how right we are, because we are alive to now know best. A literary counterfeiter will leave the history of art out in the cold because he is frightened of the authority amassed in thousands of books that have stood the test of time. His time is always the present, reflection and nuance being poisons to his brand of bullying.

Years teach, and let's hope, they teach reverence for the thickets of language we pass through and sometimes pass over us. What stands out with Hill is not only the reverence for literature but that for language and words, down to the origins of their etymology and their continuing grammatical dexterity. Call it "sacred," call it "holy"—you don't have to believe in God to know how those haloed words coax a respectful human attitude to such erudition. As the adage goes, whatever's worth doing at all is worth doing well. For Hill, "what's worth doing" is only the ectoplasm of "what's worth knowing." The past is the fuel—every artistic renaissance, especially the one with the big -R, is about the rebirth and revival of ancient arts. T. S. Eliot wrote: "Someone said: 'The dead writers are remote from us because we *know* so much more than they did.' Precisely, and they are that which we know." Hill is now among them. What a mind to know.

Stylized Despair

TO MY MIND Henry James is a master of terror. Without bloodshed, or the threat of guns, germs, or steel, James' microscope fixes on the motivations that kill the human spirit. At the apex of the first half of his writing life is *The Portrait of a Lady*, a grand and pulsating work of art on the order of Leonardo, Shakespeare, and Beethoven—a novel about what James called "a certain young woman affronting her destiny." Two versions exist: the original version of 1881 and the revised New York Edition of 1907. Both circulate freely today. How could this 130-year-old book slay me? How could its wisdom impact like a detonation? Not just with story, not just with character, but with sentences as stately as Dante's terza rima in *The Divine Comedy*—lines like: "She rested her weariness upon things that had crumbled for centuries and yet were still upright; she dropped her secret sadness into the silence of lonely places . . ." "She" is Isabel Archer, the heroine, and she is looking at the ruins of Rome. James' style flares and flowers out, compounding the story and sending each character into a unique motion and awareness with every ornate sentence.

Along with the singular syntactical sensations he generates throughout six hundred pages, James demonstrates how we become who we are as perhaps no other novelist I have read. He accomplishes this mainly by way of his forensic examination of Isabel. We meet her first as a young woman, fresh off the boat from America, looking askance at England, in search of experience but not knowing the rules or the local customs of the Old World. Her insolence feeds off the sporting scene of high-stakes living as she feels the compassionate but still calculating and wanton eyes of her cousin, Ralph, and those of Lord Warburton, a man fully positioned and full of an endless supply of money. Isabel fends for herself well; every "i" is dotted as she holds up cautionary hands to the on-slaught of men and women who wish to influence her until she is met by Madame Merle, a woman of uncanny intellect and taste who brings the widower Osmond and his daughter Pansy into her trusting ken. These are the figures who will bring about Isabel's downfall.

Most of what occurs in the novel passes in light of Isabel and her destiny, affronted or not. She is everywhere (the characters are in service of her) and James doesn't let much happen without invoking her thoughts and perceptions. The supporting cast wants to see her succeed—some only too well—as when Ralph convinces his dying father, Mr. Touchett, to leave sixty thousand pounds to Isabel in his will, "to put it into her power to do some of the things she wants." Though Ralph makes his gesture with good intentions, he cannot conceive the unhappiness Isabel will grow into after she marries Osmond, enduring her husband's suf-focating lifestyle as the book hurtles toward its unforgiving ending. The heart of the story is, of course, money. Most of the characters, except Isabel at the beginning and to a degree Madame Merle, are very well off—even Osmond, an art collector, who, though he yearns for Isabel's money, has enough to be comfortable when the reader first encounters him in Florence. Money changes the world as it changes lives. Money makes the most vicious cactus attractive to the healthiest hand and Os-mond seduces Isabel to ensure he will have hers.

Life is flawed. That much is clear from James' illustration of the ways in which money complicates the human soul. We are fallible people and one of the reasons we read fiction is to read about other flawed persons, to see how they deal with their lot. All the characters in *The Portrait of a Lady* contain idiosyncrasies and imperfections, rounding them into quietly intricate spheres, so each is a fleshy being with, say, a specific number of hairs growing on their heads and a memory full of all the years lived, including experiences of both happiness and confrontation. The characters on James' pages give off scents the reader can distinctly smell—odors that come by vertiginous thought patterns, as demonstrat-ed in the famous forty-second chapter in which Isabel meditates on her troubled marriage, finding her life and her husband shameful:

> Instead of leading to the high places of happiness, from which the world would seem to lie below one, so that one could look down with a sense of exaltation and advantage, and judge and choose and pity, it led rather downward and earthward, into realms of restriction and depression, where the sound of other lives, easier and freer, was heard as from above, and served to deepen the feelings of failure. It was

her deep distrust of her husband—this was what darkened the world. That is a sentiment easily indicated, but not so easily explained, and so composite in its character that much time and still more suffering had been needed to bring it to its actual perfection.

In this excerpt, James' architectonic sentences heighten Isabel's devastating discovery. The repetition of d-words (three in both the first and second sentences ["deep distrust"]), drives Isabel down into a dungeon of sorrow. But all around, alliteration strikes as in "high places of happiness," "feeling of failure," "easily explained," and "composite in its character," as well as the matched endings of "downward and earthward" and "restriction and depression." While Isabel's twisting emotions prefigure the coming tragedies, the ugliness of lost love is rendered in such poetic and vivid terms that its beauty makes what happens that much more harrowing.

Later in the same chapter, there is another searing section of self-discovery, while Isabel continues to fight her once eager love for her slippery husband. She tries to see how he charmed her, but she feels she cannot blame him too much for their difficulties as she built up the wrong picture of him in her mind:

> Ah, she had him immensely under the charm! It had not passed away; it was still; she knew perfectly what it was that made Osmond delightful when he chose to be. He had wished to be when he made love to her, and as she had wished to be charmed it was not wonderful that he succeeded. He succeeded because he was sincere; it never occurred to her to deny him that. . . . She had a vision of him—she had not read him right. A certain combination of features had touched her, and in them she had seen the most striking of portraits. That he was poor and lonely, and yet that somehow he was noble—that was what interested her and seemed to give her opportunity. There was an indefinable beauty about him—in his situation, in his mind, in his face. She had felt at the same time that he was helpless and ineffectual, but the feeling had taken the form of a tenderness which was the very flower of respect. He was like a skeptical voyager, strolling on the beach while he waited for the tide, looking seaward yet not putting to sea.

Osmond is a man who can't feel himself. As much as he controls his life, he still attempts to command the world's air not to enter his body—steeling himself into a damaged, damaging, and despairing wall of greed who does not surrender to love, or let anyone around him feel it. As Isabel sees this, James sees all, but then why does Isabel go on? Why does she let herself be squashed? This great unanswerable question is held over her as it hovers over the reader and I can't find any more satisfactory response to it than James' own, in his *Notebooks*:

> The obvious criticism . . . will be that it is not finished—that I have not seen the heroine to the end of her situation. . . . This is both true and false. The whole of anything is never told; you can only take what groups together. What I have done has that unity—it groups together. It is complete in itself—and the rest may be taken up or not, later.

In real life, the need for money presses people into self-deception for the sake of gain. But how do people deal with their problems? Often they speak of something or someone in lieu of discussing themselves—the vicarious metaphor—yet these other people's concerns are keenly reflected in their own. Because in *The Portrait* so many people's interests are wrapped up with others', the action of living vicariously has never had a better handbook. One supreme example of this appears toward the end, while Madame Merle and Isabel speak of Pansy's marriage. Madame Merle is upset that Lord Warburton has left the city and will not pursue a marriage with Pansy any further. Isabel suggests Madame Merle discuss it with Osmond, to which she replies:

> It isn't information I want. At bottom, it's sympathy. I had set my heart on that marriage; the idea did what so few things do—it satisfied the imagination.

Madame Merle had her heart set on a few marriages, most of all that of Osmond and Isabel. Even if she didn't ever really care what happened to Osmond, she knew that marrying the two would put her daughter Pansy in a privileged position—the money in Isabel's bank would fund Pansy's future. As to the words above, Madame Merle, through ample deceptions, possesses more information than anyone else in the novel, so when she says that it isn't information she wants, she is speaking honestly. Her life has been a lie and she wants comfort. For a person to pretend that her child does not exist, especially given how often she speaks to Pansy, is an awful life. The notion of "satisfying the imagination" is also intriguing. On one level, Madame Merle is easing her conscience concerning Pansy and the hopes she discreetly generated. And, for all of her flaws she touches on a larger truth. "So few things" do satisfy our imagination. The constant striving and struggle to succeed is our lot in life. No matter how much one accrues, one will ultimately want more, in order to guarantee a time that no-one has control over: the future. Ralph, Madame Merle, and Osmond all interfere on behalf of that evanescent, distant *durée*. Ralph's machinations, along with Madame Merle's, and Osmond's overriding of ethical bounds to satisfy their whims, conspire to destroy a young woman.

As William H. Gass says in *Fiction and the Figures of Life*:

> [James'] moral anger is directed at all those who infringe human freedom, who make pawns of people, who feast on the poor, the naive, or the powerless, who use love to *use* . . . and in those sentences which mark the movement of his mind, his steady shift of position and deepening of view, we ourselves can complain of being caught—caged—victimized.

The beauty of James' sentences victimizes us. The sinuous souls of humans trapped are dramatized by James with a grand and clear perception. Words in every part of the text boil and set us smoldering, ashamed of what we do to each other, as in the middle of the book, when Pansy listens to Madame Merle's call for her to obey:

> Pansy stared, disappointed, but not protesting. She was evidently impregnated with the idea of submission, which was due to any one who took the tone of authority; and she was a passive spectator of the operation of her fate.

This ghostly impregnation mirrors Pansy's own half-acknowledged existence, as "evidently" becomes the triggering word, an adverb so wide and slick, a saint would have trouble keeping upright on its icy surface. Would James have it any other way?

Going Steady with Gertrude

I'M QUITE SURE that if I'd lived when Gertrude Stein did, I would not have enjoyed her person—the pronouncements, the relentless self-promotion, the blatant self-absorption ("I am a genius"). If I'd lived in her time, I, probably, like so many others, would not have enjoyed her writing either—the repetitions, the lack of story, the blatant self-absorption ("I am I because my little dog knows me").

What would Gertrude have made of the internet? She probably would have done with it all there is to do before anyone would have thought to make web pages, profiles, and accounts into altars for each profile who screams for attention like some importunate shade forever ensconced in a backwards/forwards accretion of information.

The sunny truth is that Gertrude Stein created herself and her persona decades before anyone was given electronic access to do so, and she did it because she was smart, because her family moved around a great deal, because her brother knew art and a hell of a lot else and the two siblings engaged in healthy competition, because she went to medical school, because she studied under William James, and because she was finally, fantastically, a genius.

1932 to 1935 were pivotal years for Gertrude. She wrote *The Autobiography of Alice B. Toklas* in six weeks for the money, and although the eponymous Alice—her lover and the cipher through whom she really wrote about Gertrude Stein—thought the work would come to nothing, it was a bestseller and suddenly the two women had more money than ever before. After returning to America and embarking on a lecture circuit, the famous exile began work on a text whose title constituted her other grand obsession besides the capacities of sentences: America and Americans. She called it *The Geographical History of America or The*

Relation of Human Nature to the Human Mind, and she wrote it after having already completed her 1,000-page novel *The Making of Americans*, as well as *Four in America* and *Lectures in America*.

There is much braying about experimental writing today. What is truly experimental? Does such writing even exist? The more fitting question might be: who has read Gertrude Stein beyond *Three Lives* and *The Autobiography*? Whenever someone goes Duchamping about with language, she is there. *The Geographical History of America* is the ultimate thinkpiece, because the thought is raw—it sits on the page newborn, squirming in blood, with its American placenta very warm. Stein's greatest commentator, William H. Gass, had this to say of the book:

> We not only repeat when we see, stand, communicate; we repeat when we think. There's no other way to hold a thought long enough to examine it except to say its words over and over, and the advance of our mind from one notion to another is similarly filled with backs and forths, erasures and crossings-out. The style of *The Geographical History of America* is often a reflection of this mental condition.

There are many chapter IV's in the book, and a chapter III follows a chapter I, and so on. Here, some pages into the text, Stein anticipates and addresses her critics:

> Chapter IV
> They say I am not right when I say that what you say is not the same as what you write but anybody try to write and they will say that this is so.
> When you write well when you write anybody try to write and they will say that I am right.
> What you say has nothing to do with what you write.
> Does it rain in America oh yes and there is snow. High up and
> low down there is snow, snow snow really beautiful snow.

She wasn't into the comma thing: "commas are servile and they have no life of their own," she wrote in *Poetry and Grammar*, "a comma by helping you along holding your coat for you and putting on your shoes keeps you from living your life as actively as you should lead it." Commas conspire—they point the head in the wrong direction, like our eyes taken to the empty space of a plane's sound when the aircraft has already crossed the sky. Stein's music already had its tone, and as the crackling words contained a child's jabberwocky, her common sense mixed with no sense and came out crisply baked. And so her philosophy today seems wrong in all the right ways, because the head does squawk centuries removed from how the hands spell the sentences. She explicitly warns against trusting what she says, but this history isn't oral; it's written. Who are we to say she is right? Sentences composed in the head have to pass the checkpoint of the heart before the hands write or type them.

As Stein proceeds, her alliterations and repetitions pack the ideas so full of stuffing they eventually explode into epiphany:

> You may say I think you may say that no one can really give anything to anybody but anybody can sell something to somebody. This is what makes the human mind and not human nature although a great many one might say anybody can say something about this not being so. But it is so.
>
> And the human mind can live does live by anybody being able to sell something to somebody. That is what money is.

The tussle between the human mind and human nature is the more capricious theme in the book. A rancorous bout—which side can be taken? Without either one, we aren't whole. This farrago into ontology is the perfect complement to Stein's lexical devolutions. See the ways of the first sentence quoted above. "May say" repeats, and Stein plays with the *anys* and *somes* on "things" and "bodies," with the sibilance of "sell something to somebody" repeated as an unfriendly refrain. The last line of comedy is the ye olde punch-line and when she puts that leafy tender at the end—a tender that is the current God, begetter, and begotten—everyone chillingly remembers what really directs our lives. Later, Stein introduces a seeming dead end of information:

> Part fifteen.
> Four things that having nothing to do with this.
> 1. That when anybody is elected to anything although he has never done it before he begins to do that.
> 2. I said to Upton Sinclair what would you have done if you had been elected and he said thank god I was not elected.
> I used to wonder when I saw boys who had just been boys and they went into an office to work and they came out with a handful of papers and I said to them how since you never had anything to do with papers before business papers how do you know what to do with them. They just did. They knew what to do with them.

She never gets to numbers three or four, by the way. Since her book is a geographical history of America, one needs Americans in the cast and so enter Upton. And because it's a history it has to be political, even if human nature is political and the human mind is not. The "boys" grow out of the "What is the use of being a little boy if you are going to grow up to be a man," which she bats about like a tiger with a duckling at the beginning of the piece—a mantra and a process that puts the reader in a Wilde mood. These boys, however, aren't British. They go into an office, get their papers, and suddenly they are men—slipstream. Gertrude wrote in every genre.

As the book goes on, she more and more weaves her philosophy into her country's flag:

> Part X
> I think that if you announce what you see nobody can say no.
> Everybody does
> everybody does say no but nobody can nobody can say so, that is no.
> That is the reason that you can say what you see
> And so you see.
> That is what the national hymn says the star spangled banner.
> Oh say can you see.

Gertrude made use of what most abuses us, but turns the pain into laughter. To go steady and read her is the same as going outside to play catch, but the reader only catches. She throws, throws some *sees* and some *says*, and sees if you can see.

Later in the *History* a pivotal word is introduced over which Gertrude pivots all ways: "master-pieces":

> But to accustom oneself to the problem the problem of why if human nature is not interesting are master-pieces supposed to be interesting because of the subject of human nature in them . . . Human nature is not interesting and what the master-pieces tell about human nature in them is not what makes them everlastingly interesting, no it is not.

In a companion essay, 'What Are Master-pieces and Why Are There So Few of Them,' written the same year as the *History*, Gertude said:

> There are so few of them because mostly people live in identity and memory that is when they think. They know they are they because their little dog knows them, and so they are not an entity but an iden-

tity. And being so memory is necessary to make them exist and so they cannot create master-pieces.

Though a "History" of the West, Gertrude's dissecting of modes of being verges on Eastern, as she packs koans like "they are they because their little dog knows them" into the groundwork for her metaphysics of morals. In the *History*, she adds:

> You see the only thing about government and governing that is interesting is money. Everything else in governing and propaganda is human nature and as such it is not interesting.

This assertion talks back to the essay and points toward its culminating dismissal of ego and history itself:

> If there was no identity no one could be governed, but everybody is governed by everybody and that is why they make no masterpieces, and also why governing has nothing to do with masterpieces it has completely to do with identity but it has nothing to do with masterpieces. And that is why governing is occupying but not interesting, governments are occupying but not interesting because master-pieces are exactly what they are not.

Is this why old newspaper articles are not interesting? The same government issues—the only difference is the amount of money involved. Perhaps no-one has stated in so straight-laced a way why politics has no place in art—and this was before the second war Gertrude was to see. If she had an interest it was to turn the world on its head, and although she is still yoked and yodeled about unwittingly and disingenuously as prolix—a prominent history professor says of her: "She was not a radical feminist. She was Jewish and anti-Semitic, lesbian and contemptuous of women, ignorant about economics and hostile to socialism"—she remains America's best statesman, ahead of economists, self-help gurus, creative writing professors, ahead of everyone except her little dog. She owned a portrait of Mme. Cézanne, painted by Mme. Cézanne's husband, and she stared at it while working on *Three Lives*. The blurred colors she meditated on assaulted a mind that had read Shakespeare continuously and, later, Henry James. Gertrude's revolutionizing of the English language had to be based on the previous paragons and her prose piece called 'Henry James,' from *Four in America*, is more about enunciating the difference between Shakespeare's sonnets and plays than it is about the American exile who lived in England, one of the few other writers she would stoop to call a "genius."

Why aren't we writing like Gertrude? Because we are writing like Hemingway, who was taught by Gertrude how to write better. She clipped his sentences and he won the Nobel Prize—certainly a chain of events reminding us how this has always been a man's world. Two eccentrics, Gertrude and Ezra Pound, took English-language literature into the modern age, but the writers they shepherded, collected the gold. Not only Hemingway. Eliot, too.

Gertrude Stein created individual works, including poetry, plays, lectures, and two more autobiographies, but they were all part of one giant book with many gradations. Her *History*, supported and composed out of the ideas in many of her lectures on method, is a hinge in her grand design. Her mind turned in the wake of the success of *The Autobiography*—she was confounded by it, and eventually saddened. The *History* is a fittingly proud book because, in taking "the oldest country in the world" and attempting to give it a geographical past, Gertrude finally turned away from writing out of an extrinsic need, and returned to "writ[ing] for herself and strangers."

How to Live, What to Read

BOTH OF THESE QUESTIONS often occupy me, fanning my flames more than the food I eat or the merriment I make. Shall I bend an eye and singe an ear over Dickinson or Stevens? Hop into bed with Bishop or Borges? Yet, when one starts reading essays pointing to other works one should read, one compounds an already compelling problem. Often some force will intervene with an answer, possibly signaling a caesura to my yen for other books to fondle while carrying three or four master-works in my bag at a time, daily stealing kisses from each. Sluttish, yes, but also tremulous—I need only wink at Rilke or Valéry in order to gain affection I know will be good for me, a guarantee anything with a heart would scoff at.

Coming home on the subway one evening, I sat sprawled on the curved orange seat of the 2 train, reading William H. Gass. His essay 'Narrative Sentences,' in his book *Life Sentences*, contains examinations of twelve sentences of the narrative nature. Owing to the fractured structure of the essay, I read those sentences of writers who interested me most (James and Joyce and Beckett), before turning to those I had never read seriously (Ford Madox Ford and George Eliot). Gass' last example, and the most ornate, is from Henry James' *Italian Hours*, a travel book. A sentence over two hundred words long, its sinuousness touches on the tensions between city life and country life. In Gass' spindle diagram of the sentence, revealing the threads around which James' fat phrases and clauses turn, one delights in the gorgeous way the unit builds up one's fast-paced experience in the city only to laze into the easeful nature of the country, before reconnoitering and returning to the shuffle of the city. It is an all-time sentence, a sentence teeming with twenty rever-berations, a sentence more beautiful than any one-name supermodel. By mapping this sentence's architecture with the spindle, Gass impressed upon me how James' Italian journey should find its way next onto my discriminating list of books to shag.

The train rumbled under lower Manhattan, screeching by the hairpin turns at Park Place, and then on toward Brooklyn. It was eight o'clock at night, but many people were only just shuttling home from work. A few were reading.

After briefly glorying about acquiring *Italian Hours*, I paged back to the beginning of Gass' essay, taking in his readings of Daniel Defoe and Sir Walter Scott, before reading what I did not know, but could subtly feel, were the last three sentences of George Eliot's *Middlemarch*—another cornerstone missing from my mansion. "The growing good of the world is partly dependent on unhistoric acts . . ." Yes, George, yes—but then that title. *Middlemarch*. Hadn't I just seen that somewhere? And wasn't it a somewhere that my hands were still holding? I flipped to the sentence from *Italian Hours* and indeed, at its end, as the narrator returns to the city, James decrees:

> . . . to come back through one of the great gates and a couple of hours later find yourself in the "world," dressed, introduced, entertained, inquiring, talking about *Middlemarch* to a young English lady or listening to Neapolitan songs from a gentleman in a very low-cut shirt . . .

Yes, *Middlemarch*, I hear you, I cried to the voices in my head while staring in wonder at my shrunken world—my eyes glazed with good humor, possibly good will. Some of the people on the seats facing me did not reflect my inner joy. They nodded off, punched at or swiped the screens of their phones as if scraping frosting from a cooling cake. An older woman, with the hard angles of an Eastern European face and short hair recently clipped at a salon, sat hunched with a thick book. Always curious about the inclinations of others, I tipped my head to make out the cover. By the insignia I could tell it was a Barnes and Noble classic and when the woman turned a page, bringing it slightly closer to her eyes, the title revealed upside down to me was the m-endowed, three-syllable word keenly in my consciousness: *Middlemarch*.

This could have made things easy, but the difficulty is that I'm a person who won't accept "yes" as an answer. Is there any mischief-making in assigning *Middlemarch* a lower place in my to-read pile? The situation on the train was too obvious for me to give much credence to the signs, signals, or imprecations of a book baying to be read, a patch of soft pages to finger. There are no English ladies in my life to talk about *Middle-*

march with. Today, hooked on text and email, people are lucky to talk at all, much less munch a slice of biscotti and tackle Eliot or toil about in James. *What is a sentence!? What is your problem?*

What is my problem? It's what to read next and my committee of one strives to answer this, even as I'm stroking the spines of a few new books I've just bought, while sitting safely in my city, clothed or naked, but certainly sequestered. I am always entertaining the promise of what will be, dreaming of inquiry, a heady man with the syntax to split me from identifying too closely with myself or a quiet stranger.

The Sound Is the Story

WILLIAM H. GASS' story collection *Eyes* contains two stalwart novellas (his self-proclaimed natural breath of prose writing), 'In Camera' and 'Charity'—of which the novel, *Middle C*, would have been (what else?) the middle piece of the three, had it not grown into a novel published in 2013—as well as four short fictions, Gass' shortest since 'The Order of Insects,' in the landmark collection *In the Heart of the Heart of the Country* from 1968. As is customary for Gass, these fictions have exemplary sentences: long and short, full of metaphor, rich sound, syncopation, intelligence, gravity, and comedy—architectural wonders as intricate and unbridled as Gaudí's buildings, as grand and severe as Serra's steel. They are treats both for the mind whose mouth speaks them aloud and the mind with an inner ear to the sound of thought philosophical, lyrical, and holy hewn. Sound before story? Guts before glory? Maybe, but in Gass the sound is the story. One leads the other like wind gusting up a kite, but the wind is also the story because it gives the tale good weight, though it can sometimes be invisible, just like Gass' famed metaphor in a public debate with John Gardner about fiction. Gardner said: "What I think is beautiful, he [Gass] would not yet think is sufficiently ornate. The difference is that my 707 will fly and his is too encrusted with gold to get off the ground." Gass replied: "There is always that danger. But what I really want is to have it sit there solid as a rock and have everybody think it is flying." What about the *form equals content* dispute? That's another debate that may have more interest to diagnosticians of art than artists themselves, since so much of art is the unconscious gabardined as order.

'In Camera' features Mr. Gab, who loves certain photographs and has a rare print shop where he moons over his valuables as Gass' narrator describes an August Sander photograph of a hotel-keeper and wife:

> . . . the innkeeper's arms clasped behind him so that the swell of his stomach would suggest to a hesitant guest hearty fare; well, they were both girthy and full-fleshed folk as far as that goes, her eyes in a bit of a squint, his like raisins drowning in the plump of his cheeks.

Such a metaphor does not grow a branch in the reader's mind but inaugurates a sweet gooey sensation, so that this photograph is worth these fifty words transferring the Sander to the modern mind even though the image remains unseen. And in 'The Man Who Spoke with His Hands,' that man is described thus:

> And despite all of this nearly continuous motion, the Professors hardly noticed them; took little heed of this habit; were not distracted as much by the fingers as by the light which rollicked from their owner's bald head, pale as paper. He was a man, compact and even slight, whom one could nevertheless pick out of a crowd as one would the most attractive piece of fruit from a bin. His hair would have been brown had he had any.

Again, metaphor and harmony—six out of ten words in the last sentence start with h- and four out of those six begin ha-. Short sentences with few clauses, showing not telling. But, really, the story is being told—*related* might be a better word—so the reader knows who they are hearing about. The way Gass writes is a show, and yet, supra-ironically, in the showiest time of human civilization, show-women and -men are taken to task for showing off: *Not being very Alice Munro-like, are they?* the current gatekeepers wag their fingers.

Once, a youngish novelist published a diatribe in *Dissent* on many illustrious and popular writers of English prose—essentially a thumbs-up/thumbs-down appraisal, but all his thumbs, with caveats, pointed south and he seemed to ask for literature that is not too knowledgeable, not too in love with itself, but pleasurable for the reader. Gass (though called a genius) and his late friend, William Gaddis, were bandied about as both mean and snide, though only Gaddis was disparaged for being smug and classist. The piece is symptomatic of much paper-thin criticism, codifying people or art into one's favorites list, like asking one's internet date to fit all the nitpicky criteria before agreeing to meet. Gass' interest in decrepit characters has often drawn rebuke, from the nasty history professor William Fredrick Kohler in *The Tunnel* (*A professor! It's just*

Gass, some critics cried, forgetting that there is the poet, the poem, and the speaker of the poem—even in fiction) to the phantom and phony Joseph Skizzen in *Middle C*, who poses as a music professor (*Gass!*). And don't forget "Mrs. Mean" or the narrator of 'In the Heart of the Heart of the Country,' who "want[s] to rise so high that when I shit I won't miss anybody," nor the abusive families in 'The Pedersen Kid' and 'Emma Enters a Sentence of Elizabeth Bishop's.' In the two novellas, 'In Camera' and 'Charity,' there are two more uncharming men to add to the heap, though the former's Mr. Gab has u-Stu (short for "you stupid kid"), the deformed son of a former wife, but not Gab's issue, as counterpoint. 'Charity' only has Hugh Hamilton Hardy, a repugnant lawyer who is sick of strangers asking him for money in all the ways people do, though he eventually confronts his miserliness with help from the past in this kaleidoscopic seventy-page opera that often shifts space and time. For this character there is little sympathy, the modern yardstick for connecting to the reader, but as the words accrete there is a unique sense of the cur, who sucks a woman's toes and has her stand on him. He is "the other" who admittedly no-one aspires to be, but maybe at this hate-filled time more than ever before, we need to put ourselves into the soul of this other to learn how to get along. No matter the extent of our selective reading and viewing or our surgical friendships (*I only do this with him, I'll never do that with her*), we surely all inhabit the same planet. The book, as Gass has said, is a container of consciousness, and as Gass has also averred,

> The world is not simply good and bad on different weekends like an inconsistent pitcher; we devour what we savor and what sustains us; out of ruins more ruins will later, in their polished towers, rise; lust is the muscle of love: its strength, its coarseness, its brutality; the heart beats and is beaten by its beating; not a shadow falls without the sun's shine and the sun sears what it saves.

People have been uncomfortably identifying themselves and running scared from Richard III, Othello, Macbeth for four hundred years. What makes this time an exception? How does Gass come to describe such a sot? Here is one 115-word sentence:

> Hardy's passivity was perfect, he'd been told—although it hadn't gotten him a raise in two years due to tough times, he'd been also told— because it was not subservient or cautious or lacking in oomph, but gave off an aura of calm confidence and certainty about the legal, if

not the moral, superiority of his position, a nimbus which could have come from nothing but a clear and steady we'll-wheel-you-into-suicide point of view, accompanied by a softly polished face, a cuff and color odor as seductively alluring as perfume from a scratch patch, yet a posture exhibited by the suit that resembled, in representing the claimant's attitude, a volcanic cone only momentarily covered with cooling snow.

Hardy's passivity was perfect, he'd been told—The subject of the sentence is Hardy's passivity—the point-of-view of his attitude in life, a key ingredient of his shtick. He doesn't judge it to be so—others do.

although it hadn't gotten him a raise in two years due to tough times, he'd been also told—because it was not subservient or cautious or lacking in oomph,—But in this first clause there is comedy because his way of living doesn't translate into more money. Still the passivity was perfect because it was ostentatious.

but gave off an aura of calm confidence and certainty about the legal, if not the moral, superiority of his position,—But because his passivity is level-headed and a reminder to others of his business, the legal, as "off an aura of," becomes a saucy sauce of vowels with a diphthong dropped in the middle like a dab of butter.

a nimbus which could have come from nothing but a clear and steady we'll-wheel-you-into-suicide point of view,—What is that aura? Now the narrator says it's a "nimbus" and the metaphor grows with "could have come" being the sweet music that sends it on, and "clear" completing the trio of hard c- sounds.

accompanied by a softly polished face,—But the nimbus is pulled inside-out, back to his physical being, his face, so sight unseen to seen and then smell—Hardy's passivity is really being expressed; it's not a small thing—qualities that make the character live in a reader's mind.

a cuff and color odor as seductively alluring as perfume from a scratch patch,—And now his passivity is also accompanied by more hard c-'s, "a cuff and color odor," ("odor" slant rhymes with "aura" and "moral") but the odor has its own double simile, "as seductively alluring as perfume from a scratch patch," with double p-'s.

yet a posture exhibited by the suit that resembled, in representing the
claimant's attitude, a volcanic cone only momentarily covered with cool-
ing snow—But Hardy isn't that easy because he also has a posture that
goes along with his face and odor, a posture that takes the cake, because
his haberdashery resembles, like his client's force (he is a lawyer, but
something of a hired gun), "a volcanic cone only momentarily covered
with cooling snow." Two more hard c-'s, and one grand metaphor for his
real power and success, his posture that threatens by sight with a little
gloss—"They that have power to hurt but will do none"—proving that
the man's stance in life mirrors the anger in his mind.

Gass, like many before him, but few who have followed, examines characters who are flops and successful hypocrites because flaws interest
him more than luck, but also because his fictional universe is not that of
making the right moral choices (those have already been made or not),
more the result of civilization's one-step-forward, three-steps-back build.
He wears his rue with a difference. In 'The Toy Chest,' the final story
in *Eyes*, and the last to have been written, a man remembers his youth,
his toys, and the toys that women would present, eventually taking over
for the trains that couldn't: "We were sitting right here alongside the toy
chest. She said hers composed the toy chest now . . . I never again had a
happiness so brief, so intense, so scared."

    Gass, a former philosophy professor, but more appropriately a phi-
losopher of the word and the sentence, devoted his life to showing how
the world is within the word and how a sentence has a soul and is its
own story. He developed spindle diagrams of countless sentences, which
he débuted when speaking of the work of Gertrude Stein in the 1970s.
In more recent years, there has been renewed interest in Gordon Lish
and his theory of consecution, writing sentence upon sentence by means
of repetition of what came before, be it word or sound, built from the
work of Harold Bloom, Denis Donoghue, and Julia Kristeva. Gass and
Lish are squarely in the same tradition—if you don't have music, no-one
will listen, or at least they won't listen very hard. This tradition stretches
back to Joyce, Stein, James, Dickinson, Melville, and Emerson, and over
the ocean to the authors of Baroque prose, Shakespeare, to the nameless
bards of the Bible, and to Homer. It has nothing to do with the moralizing
realism that has come to dominate contemporary American literature, or
the epiphany moment, whether in prose or in verse. Some ask for fiction
to show us how to live. Some ask for entertainment. Absent religion,
the pagan Walter Pater says, "art comes to you proposing frankly to give
nothing but the highest quality to your moments as they pass, and simply

for those moments' sake." Politicians pander, but parents, teachers, and friends, or some combination of the three, are those consistent pitchers who help us learn how to live and what to do. Literary language communicates something ineffable. Even parables work by metaphor. Rilke, Gass' talisman, had the gumption to end a poem thus: "You must change your life." Yet art is not usually as easy as self-help. It presents alternative realities that may be accepted, reviled, or ignored. So sentences come to us giving nothing but the beauty of their words—more than enough. Or, as Gass said, "a consciousness electrified by beauty—is that not the aim and emblem and the ending of all finely made love?"

Remembering William H. Gass

HE GREW UP in the worst of times and died in end times. The Great Depression colored his mind's eye, and President Tweetledum and our "tweet is mightier than the truth" zeitgeist recently told him, *Yes, the language can be more perverted and debased than anything heretofore.* No matter. For William H. Gass, the world was within the word, the soul inside the sentence, the great texts together made a temple, and he added overly qualified artistry and highly poetic explication to the great chain of wordmaking spanning the Bible to Beckett.

Born in Fargo, he grew up in Ohio, before spending three-and-a-half years in the navy during the Second World War. A PhD in philosophy at Cornell and then life at a lectern and days in a chair, sometimes as a chair, at the College of Wooster, Purdue, and then at Washington University in St. Louis. *Omensetter's Luck* in 1966 was his first book, although, before the novel's publication, there had been a long apprenticeship. We who now publish instantly shall be chagrined to hear he began the novella 'The Pedersen Kid' around 1951. It was published in a journal in 1961 and finally appeared in book form in 1968. He also suffered a writer's greatest nightmare: at Purdue, a conman colleague stole his only copy of the manuscript of *Omensetter's Luck*, forcing him to basically rewrite it from older drafts and notes. Undoubtedly, this tragedy made it better.

1995's *The Tunnel* is much ballyhooed for its twenty-seven years in the making, but the truth is that Gass wrote many things during this stretch of time: a few of the best books of American essays ever produced (*Fiction and the Figures of Life, On Being Blue, Habitations of the Word*), many introductions and reviews, and some novellas that would eventually appear in *Cartesian Sonata*. A good chunk of his haunting tome was written when he was a research fellow at L.A.'s Getty Museum in the early 1990s: "I wrote half the book there in one year," he told me once, "because the circumstances were just marvelous. No distractions." Fourteen-hour days. The Oklahoma City bombing occurred on the day *The Tunnel* was released, perhaps foreshadowing the novel's seditious reception, though that also had to be owed to the book's narrator, William Kohler, a hard-hearted German history professor who seemingly holds Nazi sympathies. A Third Reich specialist, Kohler has just finished a book on the period and tries to write its preface, but when he finds himself blocked he writes what becomes *The Tunnel* instead. He hates his life, i.e. wife, and kills her cat as he digs a tunnel under their house.

Most critics were angered, and conflated the character with Gass himself on the basis of the many similarities between the author and his creation: teacher, tough Midwestern childhood, and, principally, the first name. The great Michael Silverblatt asked point-blank why Gass "provoked" such an identification, to which Gass replied: "It's a *It Can't Happen Here* book. . . . To say, 'Well, that's those people' is to cop out. It's us. . . . You praise even the most awful things by trying to render them as eloquently, clearly, as perceptibly as you're capable. . . . The whole world, which is constantly flowing, has to be perceived and saved and redeemed, even if it's awful . . . because that's what we want to forget." The critic Robert Kelly wrote of *The Tunnel* that "it will be years before we know what to make of it," and, of late, it has gained more followers, alongside the U.S. political and red-state idealogues, embodied in its the oft-quoted line: "I suspect that the first dictator of this country will be called coach."

I came to Gass through my best writing professor. One on one, he gave me things to read and he once handed me the eponymous novella 'In the Heart of the Heart of the Country,' the title a nod to one of Gass' masters, Gertrude Stein. There followed a decade without much further involvement, though I saw Gass speak at the Housing Works Bookstore in 2006 on the release of his audio version of *The Tunnel*. Four years on, a co-religionist re-piqued my interest as he read the entirety of Gass in preparation for interviewing him in St. Louis. When he told those in the know what he would be doing, they said, "Oh, you're going to see the Master." I began to ingest it all, every line, over and over. There was beauty, erudition, cunning, and something unreconcilable. Here was a writer who dictated his own terms and saw into the schema of our most wordy art with a crystalized vision, like a surgeon taking apart words (there is a long essay on the word "and") and sentences (he made spindle diagrams of great sentences to map their structure and notate their music), while also creating fictions in which characters try to find their way amid inhumanity and where language honors the horror and the beauty of life equally. Who else would compose a novella titled 'Emma Enters a Sentence of Elizabeth Bishop's'?

I met Gass a few times in New York, helping to get him a Bishop book on a high shelf at the Strand, as he then researched an article on her for *Harper's*—uncollected at this time. What do you say to a Master? One should just listen. And though I went to see him in St. Louis in the fall of 2011, armed with thousands of questioning words, I asked only a third of what I'd prepared, for his high-calorie answers obliterated the need. That day Bill and his wife, Mary, showed me the greatest kindness. After a morning session at home in his kitchen, we repaired James-style to the American fiction room for the afternoon. There he revealed things I had not espied in any printed matter pertaining to him. He had been ushered out of Purdue (and West Lafayette) in the late sixties due to his protesting stance, as well as the nudity and language in *Willie Master's Lonesome Wife*. One question about animism garnered a head-spinning mini-lecture on Gaston Bachelard, leading to a lengthy discussion of positivism and rationalism. It did dawn on me that I sat with a man who'd interacted with Wittgenstein, who'd counted William Gaddis as a great friend. Even more significantly, I sat with the man who wrote *The Tunnel*. He'd been tetchy about going through with the interview, saying, before the recorders recorded, "Being interviewed isn't good for the soul." I now know what he meant, or at least, I wholeheartedly agree with him. Don't think about what you do, do it—reward enough. Afterward, we drank wine in the backyard, as the city was blessed with an Indian summer. He relaxed more, recalling the two greatest highlights of his writing life: seeing *In the Heart of the Heart of the Country* translated and for sale at the Sorbonne bookstore, and dancing with Severo Sarduy, the Cuban writer, on the continental divide in Colorado (they were being driven around after a conference and Sarduy asked the driver to stop so he could dance with Gass). The St. Louis Cardinals were in the World Series that year, and after a fine dinner and more conversation (I filled them in on Occupy Wall Street—Zuccotti Park still being occupied at the time) we watched the ninth inning of game five.

We shared a few more emails over the years but I didn't want to bother him; I knew his time was better spent on something we'd all be better for. Is it surprising that some people don't realize someone on the order of Henry James and Virginia Woolf has left us? Out of two acclaimed novelist friends, one gushes about the fiction and hasn't really read the non-, while the other is all about the essays and less enthusiastic about the three novels and three collections of shorter prose. Why did Gass write? What does he leave behind? What to make of his passing? Perhaps the frayed Kohler, sometimes given to beauty, said it best: "The greatest gift you can give another human being is to let them warm you till, in passing beyond pleasure, your defenses fall, your ego surrenders, its structure melts, its towers topple, lies, fancies, vanities, blow away in no wind, and you return, not to the clay you came from—the unfired vessel—but to the original moment of inspiration, when you were the unabbreviated breath of God."

The Self that Did So Much

BIOGRAPHERS OF AUTHORS have a long history of soaking their subjects in a chemical bath of hagiography—often offering an epic five-hundred-page or longer account of admiration, maybe two books, or even the colossal Leon Edel and Joseph Frank five-volume sets on Henry James and Dostoevsky. Many biographies are painstakingly researched and cantilevered with a conservative equipoise, building drama where there is often none (a showdown with a blank page?), and sketching in anecdotes that create a too moderate picture of a legendary figure in the face of his or her often immoderate workings. These stories are told in very historically temperate terms: where the great-grandparents came from, what the grandfather did for a living, how the parents of the special one met. It's well-meaning information, but often unimportant to the making of art. William Gaddis spent his life in production, writing hefty novels satirizing the American individual's struggle against the state—increasingly known as the corporate world—and the question of ownership. His novels from *The Recognitions* to *A Frolic of His Own* ask: when forgeries and lawsuits make more than artworks themselves, what is worth doing?

Of course, people's lives do contain drama and, in retrospect, William Gaddis' has a bit more than most. Gaddis enters Harvard twice and twice leaves with long travels and odd jobs bookending both experiences; the years 1947–1951 are mostly spent overseas, traveling to and from Central America, Europe, and North Africa, and gathering experiences that propel *The Recognitions*. Then: marriage, children, becoming a provider, followed by a spell in the corporate world; then bitterness and divorce, remarriage, *JR*; another divorce, teaching positions, some acclaim; *Carpenter's Gothic*, more acclaim, first interviews given; *A Frolic of His*

Own, an end to a long-term relationship, and death. A full life, a life he
made more and more transparent in his fictions, which, after the bounty
of *The Recognitions* (956 pages with almost a dozen main characters),
grew dialogue-centric, minimizing any narrative voice so that speakers
would dig their own graves with their scintillating and sloppy language.
To make art is to risk failure, and though Gaddis' first book had only
failed commercially, its marginalization reinforced its own idea that forg-
ers and people on the make are more revered than artists in his native
country. As Bast, the failed composer in *JR*, says:

> I was thinking there's so much that's not worth doing suddenly I
> thought maybe I'll never do anything. That's what scared me I always
> thought I'd be, this music I always thought I had to write music all
> of a sudden I thought what if I don't, maybe I don't have to I'd never
> thought of that maybe I don't! I mean maybe that's what's been wrong
> with everything . . . just doing what's there to be done as though it's
> worth doing or you never would have done anything you wouldn't be
> anybody . . .

Joseph Tabbi's accomplishment in *Nobody Grew but the Business* is his
winnowing of laborious details. At just over 200 pages, this biography is
shorter than each of Gaddis' own books with the exception of the post-
humously published novella *Agapē Agape*. Yet it is not just a critical biography or a work of literary criticism, but also a prolegomenon on how
to persist in the creative world. It's a portrait of an artist who struggled
with the little attention his large efforts received (scant royalty checks
for *The Recognitions* haunted him), and whose works still seem ahead of
their time: Tabbi considers 1975's *JR*, about an eleven-year-old who turns
his penny stocks into a fortune in the midst of hapless adults, to have
captured the spirit of the "corporate life world" of our present day more
effectively than any contemporary fiction.

   Tabbi's book also serves as a critique of the current creative writing
system, dominated by MFA programs in which community-building is,
he claims, "secondary to the need for self-advancement within an insti-
tution devoted precisely to cultivating individual talents." Although Tabbi is firmly seated in the academy, he forwards Gaddis' hard-edged views
against these programs. When Gaddis taught, he preferred to teach "creative reading," and he saw creative writing programs as emphasizing individual identity and branding, producing "the chance to make a living
'not by poetry' or novel writing but by 'being a poet.'" The author Chris
Mazza remembers Gaddis dismissing NEA fiction applicants because

"the author purposely wrote as though the piece was memoir . . . to make it feel 'real' and . . . gain more audience interest and/or sympathy." In contrast, Tabbi says, in each of his books Gaddis used highly autobiographical material to construct a "compositional self . . . specific to the aesthetic and technical problems" he encountered during the writing. As Gaddis said in a 1985 interview with *Publishers Weekly*, this self endures in "the real work . . . the thought and the rewriting and the crossing-out and the attempt to get it right"—one's creation is about what happens to the writer involved in this process, but is framed with a parable of his choosing, the way the old masters put themselves into their every depiction of the Madonna and Child or the crucifixion. Artists are the primary characters in each of Gaddis' books: painters, novelists, science writers, playwrights, musicians. Gaddis did speak through these characters, but the compositional self held it all together—the poet as opposed to the speaker of the poem. Their drama of failure was the writer's own drama. The novel, as an artform, is an act, a performance, and Gaddis' work encourages us both to watch the show and to consider the man behind the curtain, the life that both exceeds and requires the novel. *JR* is not really "about" an eleven-year-old who dupes everyone; it is about the outrage of a larger consciousness at the dehumanization of corporate life—Gaddis' primary theme.

Tabbi accomplishes the difficult task of bringing us close to Gaddis' "compositional self": not a magician or a saint, but the "self that could do more" (a phrase in every Gaddis novel)—the aggregate of the hard work, the hours, days, and years of throwing away, revising, rethinking, and making the object, the art, and the drama better. This is exemplified by a photograph of Gaddis' writing desk (in a garage converted into a study) in Piermont, New York, where he wrote *JR* in the early 1970s. Books line the walls, and on the long desk is a typewriter with pages laid out around it—pages that Gaddis added to by typing inserts and affixing them to other pages with Scotch tape, developing a manual method of accretion that lends *JR* its bounty of leitmotifs. This quiet, ennobling picture is where the maelstrom of creativity occurred.

Gaddis' letters, published by Dalkey Archive in 2013 and edited by Steven Moore, Gaddis' main scholar aside from Tabbi, provide insight into his last relationships—his second marriage to Judith Gaddis, his sixteen-year-long co-habitation with socialite Muriel Oxenburg Murphy—and show us how he transformed his everyday world into words. *JR*'s characters are stuck talking to each other in a series of rooms, while *Carpenter's Gothic* and *A Frolic of His Own* are each essentially set in one house that resembles two he lived in during his last thirty-odd years. As Tabbi says, *Frolic* is a critique of the country, "through PR and legal manoeuverings, in the sphere of power and influence that Gaddis himself now could know from the inside." His traveling days were over and he wanted to be settled, but he would need to complete his work because the compositional self took on primacy. His second wife left in the late seventies, leaving him aimless—"Still a terribly quiet house & somehow a chilly one," he wrote to a friend; "wash out one's shirts, cook for 1, nobody to share the small great things of life with like the turning of the leaves"—and leaving him bitter as well: "I'm a bit sick & tired of people stepping out to 'find themselves' coming up at last with too often, in Cyril Connolly's exquisitely harsh phrase, 'a cheap sentimental humanism at someone else's expense.'" These emotions were carried forward into *Carpenter's Gothic*, a book that nearly had the first four words of Shakespeare's seventy-third sonnet as a title. The book is a paean to Shakespeare's intricate fourteen lines of feeling, as T. S. Eliot's *Four Quartets* was a touchstone for *The Recognitions*: the novel is set in autumn ("a burst of half yellowed leaves"—one of twenty-seven times the word "leaves" is used) among those same changeable leaves of the Bard, "That time of year thou mayst in me behold, / When yellow leaves, or none, or few, do hang."

Books are made out of other books, said Cormac McCarthy, a writer Gaddis nodded to approvingly. How else could the compositional self become the self that could do more? When he was a sickly child, Gaddis had more than enough time to pore over the classics, and later sought out Robert Graves in Spain and Katherine Anne Porter by post to further find the author in himself. Maybe instead of any of Gaddis' own novels, Tabbi's biography is the best place to start with Gaddis because Tabbi isolates some of those works' exquisite passages and their many themes. And maybe the book is also best for the artist or for anyone who wants to do something with his or her life—no matter if it isn't writing. Gaddis' story impels one to get going, even when few people recognize art as worthy work, when one can't make a living at it, and when many believe it's all been done before, so why try.

William Gaddis and American Justice

"JUSTICE?—YOU GET JUSTICE in the next world, in this world you have the law." I went around quoting the opening line of William Gaddis' *A Frolic of His Own* before I'd even read all those following. As a homeless outreach worker in Manhattan, I'd have occasion to transport people to shelters, and in a ten-minute car ride I'd often get an earful of their lives and their problems. One particularly gruff man raged about the legal system and all the mess it had made of his life. I didn't know if he would whack me or the driver in his fulminations, so I threw out the line to redirect him. He laughed and settled, saying, "Whoever wrote that knew what the fuck I'm talking about."

One summer, I suggested to my wife, a criminal defense attorney in Brooklyn, that we read the book concurrently. We'd both represented and tried to help the most helpless in our society, but we saw the legal system in different ways—even though we could both admit it was, of course, skewed in favor of the rich. She saw her job as manoeuvring around district attorneys, judges, and laws that often support mass incarceration in the United States. The homeless essentially have no rights, so the legal system is a hindrance for them. I brought more skepticism to our reading of the situation. The year after high school graduation, I delivered mail for a cadre of mainly male lawyers, handing it to their agitated secretaries who gave me copy jobs galore. I made all the coffee. I stocked beer and soda in diverse refrigerators. These loud and lusty men who came to work in $30,000 cars were not like me, my father, or my grandfather, and they were not what I wanted to become. Most were ungrateful, taunting, and impatient, ready to embargo any joy that did not ultimately shine on or derive from them. To be fair, a few of them did treat other people like the human beings they are. But it was easy to see the well-off were persons never to emulate.

Gaddis' novel is a satire of the legal system, full of frivolous lawsuits, including *Szyrk v. Village of Tatamount et al.* In this suit, the artist of a huge outdoor public sculpture (Cyclone Seven) sues a small city after a seven-year-old's dog, Spot, becomes trapped in it, leading to rescue operations that damage the work. Then there are the two lawsuits of the protagonist, Oscar Crease. The smaller one, ostensibly against himself, springs from an attempt to hotwire his Japanese car (a Sosumi made by Isuyu) which ends with the vehicle running him over. The main action is against a film company that has produced a Civil War epic, *The Blood in the Red, White, and Blue*; Oscar believes that the film is derived from an unproduced and unpublished play, *Once at Antietam*, which he wrote some seventeen years earlier and submitted to the film's producer—though he can't locate the rejection slip.

Reading together, my wife and I found ourselves taking the book and its dips—from narrative, to legal decision, to further dramatic scenes, to a deposition, to play excerpts, to legal opinions, to implosions of hilarious dialogue—in a certain stride. In the news that summer was a despicable lawsuit taken as seriously as Oscar's: Manhattanite Jennifer Connell sued her eight-year-old nephew for jumping into her arms because she broke her wrist in the subsequent fall—on his birthday. The case went to a jury but was dismissed. Another iteration of this obtuse use of legalese was the case of the New England Patriots fans who sued the NFL after their team lost draft picks in the Deflategate debacle. Thankfully, a judge dismissed that one, too. "Why do you think people sue?" I asked my wife. "Because we have been told by society that this is how we solve problems, plus everyone wants money," she answered, putting her in mind of the old commercial from *Saturday Night Live* where a person in the street responds to a law firm advertising cutthroat tactics: "I'd love to sue somebody, but don't I need a reason?"

In a 2016 issue of *Harper's*, Ralph Nader argued that lawsuits, certainly commonsense ones, are good for America. Deregulation reigns as more and more corporations and politicians become bedfellows, repealing laws that once protected "the rights of injured people to recover adequate compensation for harm inflicted." Nader added that "multimillion dollar advertising campaigns, heavily funded by the insurance industry, made wild accusations about outlandish jury awards assessed against innocent companies, even clergy and obstetricians, in order to raise the public temper." Gaddis' book could be used as propaganda by the corporate/political forces in this battle, but it would also indict them as having a pioneering spirit of greed, power, and profit. And although Oscar eventually wins the movie suit, the money awarded is meager because, as Nader points out, multi-million dollar corporate law firms are beasts that can rarely lose. When lawyers start suing other lawyers, loopholes are everywhere.

The 586-page novel (the last to be published in Gaddis' lifetime) is set in New York City and on Long Island, though it takes place mainly in Oscar's house in the Hamptons. *Frolic* is full of a neurotic vernacular of Americana that purls and perfectly personifies the sue-happy, media-soaked period during which Gaddis constructed it: 1986 to 1993. Those years saw the rapid growth of cable TV and the cultural acceptance of its obsession with scandal, culminating in the intense media coverage of the Clintons and one of the first pitiful tabloid "stories" worthy of the national news: the violent interaction between John Wayne Bobbitt and his wife Lorena. In a scene from the middle of *Frolic*, there is a miniature rendition of the type of satire Gaddis often favors: people getting uncomfortable with other people. The Crease household is visited by Trish, a rich friend of Oscar's sister, Christina. Much to Oscar's chagrin, the visitor brings her dog, Pookie, and when Pookie has an accident on the floor, Oscar characteristically finds a sinister motive: "It was not an accident Christina, I saw him, he did it deliberately . . ."

Oscar's high-pitched hysteria typifies how unserious and childish he can be, complicating his "creative" character with his tendency to blame others for his mistakes; he also makes a maid who can't speak or read English look for the missing rejection slip and he continues to sit and watch TV after his girlfriend asks him to examine a lump in her breast. There is a great laziness to this "artist," now a history professor at a community college. The question my wife and I kept coming back to while reading *A Frolic of His Own* was: Does Oscar seriously believe the studio plagiarized his play, or is he after a handout? His impetus is called into question when he staggeringly chides the producers for stealing certain parts of his script, while also being disappointed that they didn't use others. Perhaps our question is best answered when, after Oscar temporarily wins his case and is granted an injunction, the studio shows the film on television in order to make money and the main characters watch it together. At first Oscar complains about its crude opening, but the battle scene at the heart of the film mesmerizes him, and he becomes as bloodthirsty as the producers who insist on such gore. He celebrates how they pictorially replicated the century-old skirmish: "unbelievable, it's unbelievable look at that! Half the regiment wiped out at thirty feet . . ."

I HAD BEEN turning into a Gaddis freak since I interviewed the author William H. Gass, a friend of Gaddis' and one with whom Gaddis was often confused in literary circles. I read my wife snippets of *The Recognitions* and *JR* in order to bring her into the fold. A *Frolic of His Own* is a book that has become a lost classic. Usually an author becomes synonymous with one or two of his or her titles, while the titans are allowed three to five. It hasn't taken people so long in years to come around to Gaddis. It started happening in his lifetime, but, despite the fact that *Frolic* won the National Book Award, there has been no new edition of the novel since the paperback was published in 1995, and Brooklyn's main library at Grand Army Plaza doesn't include it in the stacks. There's not a chapter or page break in the book, which might go towards explaining its obscurity compared to the gobs of white space and other breaks *de rigueur* in many current novels. Gaddis' body of work, since 1975's *JR*, is one long gush where everything happens on top of something else— where everything interrupts, including Gaddis' favorite stage prop, the telephone.

Gaddis took the book's title from *The Handbook of the Law of Torts*, which he found during his voluminous research on the legal system, including obtaining all eighty-four volumes of *American Jurisprudence* (the encyclopedia of U.S. law) while corresponding with lawyers and clerks about the validity of his fictionalized judicial opinions and one long deposition. During that fifty-page exchange (in legal transcript form and font), the studio's lawyer attacks Oscar's lawyers, badgering them because Oscar's play only shares a few ideas with the studio's movie (another lawyer says, "You can't copyright the Civil War") and then connecting William Shakespeare's practice of taking material from familiar sources to Oscar's own ways of borrowing:

Q In other words . . . it was all just there for the taking, wasn't it? . . . Whether you were Shakespeare or Joe Blow, you could turn any of it into a play if you wanted to, couldn't you?

A Well not the, if Joe Blow could write a play?

Q Do you mean it would depend on the execution of the idea?

A Well, yes. Yes of course.

Q Not the idea, but the way it was expressed by the playwright? Isn't that what makes Shakespeare's King Lear tower above Joe Blow's King Lear?

Gaddis' propulsive style of writing blends the chilling admonitions of the great Russian novelists and T. S. Eliot with the evaporating social order of late-twentieth-century America. Gathering up the detritus of our age (TV and radio commercials, print ads, etc.), Gaddis churned it about in his outraged mind, and delivered an art as timeless as the ancients while obeying the oft-quoted dictum: good artists copy, great artists steal. Gaddis eventually came to the point where he had to steal from himself, as the excerpts of Oscar Crease's play, *Once at Antietam*, are verbatim bits of Gaddis' unproduced play (same title), written around 1960. In his own brooding intensity, he found the right profile to insert himself and exorcise his ghost self: the failed artist who, Faust-like, sells his soul to earn a living while shirking his moral responsibility towards his art, something Gaddis never succumbed to but observed all around him. Perhaps if Oscar had stolen from Shakespeare, his play might have been produced all those years back.

After living forty some years, and being all too cognizant of the hype-driven galleons, it's apparent to me that the novel comments on our culture's incredible jealousy at other people getting what we think they don't deserve—a truism since Alexis de Tocqueville. Whether it is entitlement in all forms, or simply the result of sticking our noses into other people's business and taking offense where there is none, these very hypocritical acts are the basis for many laughable lawsuits, including Oscar's pursuit of a handout. But Americans don't necessarily need a lawyer to intimidate someone. As Lionel Trilling writes, in 'The Meaning of the Literary Idea,' we are "the people of ideology." A furor and gusto similar to the Salem witch trials, but without the physicality, is put to use by viral internet campaigns to bully and shame people—the hysteria of doctrinal vindictiveness is all too easily a click away from actually ruining someone's life. But this consequence gives few people pause before sallying, on social media, a reactionary "fuck you."

This free play of opposites is pointed to in Gaddis' epigraph, care of Henry David Thoreau, the epitome of American individualism, who said to Ralph Waldo Emerson: "What you seek in vain for, half your life, one day you come full upon, all the family at dinner. You seek it like a dream, and as soon as you find it you become its prey." Oscar seeks fame and fortune, but he receives only a token payment, and all his other ridiculous lawsuits garner him nothing.

The book speaks to our current moment, post-9/11, post-financial crisis, not only in terms of authorship, entitlement, and an oligarchy created by the corporate-political police state, but also because we are still the same people of ideology that we were when Gaddis was writing. And the difference between then and today? Now that we are armed with the technology to more easily harass and destroy each other, even Gaddis couldn't anticipate how easily we would cede our humanity for fame and fortune at other people's expense.

William Gaddis' Compositional Self

THERE ARE STOLEN MOMENTS when raising a young child, the let-up during nap-time being a prime example. In one of these recent pauses, I read to my wife the beginning of the fifth chapter or section (they are unnumbered) of William Gaddis' 1985 novel *Carpenter's Gothic*, a book most seasoned readers of the author would place behind *The Recognitions* (1955), *JR* (1975), and *A Frolic of His Own* (1994). As I age, I've been letting go of the impulse to rank. *Carpenter's Gothic* fits perfectly with the other three novels as one long scroll of words.

I chose the section to read randomly. In it, the main character, Elizabeth (Liz) Booth, is in bed with McCandless, the man who owns the house that she rents with her aggro Vietnam vet husband, who is involved in shadowy religious and political scheming and away on a "business" trip. McCandless, who has some checkered CIA connections in his past (fitting him for the Gothic template of "the mysterious stranger"), keeps a locked room in the house, which is up near the Hudson River, about an hour from New York City, and is built in the style referenced in the title. This house is the book's only setting. McCandless had encountered Liz in two previous scenes, in which one could sense an attraction developing between them. The passage I read commences with the couple pillow-talking either before or after sex. In fact, they are dishing about quite important matters, like Liz's memories of her dead father, which she recounts while McCandless suckles her breasts: "he used to read out loud to me and I thought all the books were about him, [but] he wasn't really reading to me at all. *Huckleberry Finn, The Call of the Wild* . . . He was just turning the pages and telling the story the way he wanted." Then Liz delves into the meaning of life in a quilted paragraph where their dialogue is combined, the narrator briefly interposing to handicap the exchange:

> I mean if you could get this tremendously powerful telescope? and then if you could get far enough away out on a star someplace, out on this distant star, and you could watch things on the earth that happened a long time ago really happening? Far enough away, he said, you could see history, Agincourt, Omdurman, Crécy . . . How far were they she wanted to know, what were they, stars? constellations? Battles he told her, but she didn't mean battles, she didn't want to see battles,—I mean seeing yourself . . . Well as far as that goes he said, get a strong enough telescope you could see the back of your own head, you could—That's not what I meant. You make fun of me don't you.

And thus we are presented with another battle in the war between men and women, a theme central to his final three novels. Generally, Gaddis' men favor the grandeur of impersonal history—and sex. His women, by contrast, seek to communicate, they want to grasp their own history. The labyrinthine complexity of Gaddis' novels is constructed out of such minute, one-on-one scenes, the delicacy of chamber music braided into symphonic structures.

As the scene goes on, Gaddis continues to broadcast information and emotions from his own life, manipulated into fiction. He extends his well-known views on writing, ascribing them to McCandless: "They think if something happened to them that it's interesting because it happened to them . . ." McCandless denies being a writer to the woman he is sleeping with, though he did write a novel—or at least a novelization—about his time working as a geologist for the CIA. Gaddis' book was written in the early 1980s, after the author had taught at Bard for a few years. The constrained 250 pages of Carpenter's Gothic are filled with discourses about "writing" and types of fiction in vogue at the time. Liz herself, coping with the two other crazed men in her life, her husband and her ne'er-do-well brother, clandestinely thinks up phrases and then writes them down, hopeful they will become passages in her own novel.

In bed, Liz continues to seek emotional intimacy, speaking of her and her brother's relationship with their father: "when we started to say things he thought were critical and he sort of drew away and he got those dogs, those hateful little Jack Russell terriers they just adored him, they followed him everywhere they'd do anything to please him and we never could." Meanwhile, McCandless continues to stroke and probe her body, but when this heavy petting goes nowhere, he relents and begins to speak of his own past, revisiting why things went wrong with his ex-wife: "that fear of disappointing each other and those inadvertent little betrayals that poison everything else, isn't that it?" This leads to her musings about procreation ("it's really children that choose their parents just so they can get born?"), then a rant by him about the afterlife ("coming back as the Dalai Lama choosing his parents in some Tibetan dung heap"), before settling into more crosstalk about creativity and fiction-making from Liz: "I mean I don't know if I've read Faulkner much either. Except The Heart of Darkness, I think I read that once." The phone interrupts (it's a man looking for McCandless' ex-wife), which provokes a squabble with Liz, before, finally, the couple has sex. The next morning, all of this intimacy, whether triggered by lust or anger at someone else, is neutralized when, after her brother shows up, McCandless refers to her blandly as "Mrs. Booth."

Such is life, such are the games people play. Gaddis' novelistic art involves the dramatization of these small tragedies, which slowly add up, ending in an apocalyptic meltdown. As Cynthia Ozick said in a perceptive review of the novel: "It isn't 'theme' Mr. Gaddis deals in (his themes are plain) so much as a theory of organism and disease. In *Carpenter's Gothic* the world is a poisonous organism, humankind dying by itself."

In his classic 1961 study *The Rhetoric of Fiction*, Wayne Booth argues that "[t]he author creates . . . an image of himself and another image of his reader; he makes his reader, as he makes his second self, and the most successful reading is one in which the created selves, author and reader, can find complete agreement." Gaddis once gave a name to this "second self": the compositional self. The compositional self is the nightside of writing, which all the so-called glamor of being a writer can never touch upon; this labor cannot be understood by those outside the inner circle. That's why any film about writing or writers fails—you can't see this internal combustion; it's password-protected.

As V. S. Naipaul (whose work will later appear in *Carpenter's Gothic*) commented in an interview on *Charlie Rose*:

> A writer has—he's going to do something. He'll do one thing; he'll do two things; he'll do three things. Probably there are three levels of consciousness. But in the writing, there are many more levels if the writing is any good, and this is where the reader starts reading his own book because the better the writer, the more he's sunk into his material, the more there are things in it that he's not aware of at the moment of writing.

This experience of being "sunk into his material" is the state Gaddis sought in his most fruitful hours.

The compositional self is the supreme metafiction. To say that *Carpenter's Gothic* is Gaddis' most personal novel is to miss the point. Yes, Gaddis lived in Piermont, New York, in a similarly styled house. Life may imitate art, but what about the reverse? How did Gaddis take his life and parse it, put it through a sieve, and then craft it into an organic work of art? An artist's letters can give a glimpse into method, and Gaddis' certainly do (at least for his last two novels). In a missive where he first mentions what will become *Carpenter's Gothic*—from October 1977, sent just after his second wife had left him—Gaddis goes on a full roar to a trusted old friend:

> In fact Judith's been away for so damned long by this time (since the end of February) that she's rapidly becoming rather an idea than a person. Still a terribly quiet house & somehow a chilly one, wash out one's shirts, cook for 1, nobody to share the small great things of life with like the turning of the leaves, nobody but the fool cat stamping about & shouting for his supper while the porch steps collapse & I add that project to my list of things undone, invitations to stylish openings unattended in favor of sitting here with a glass of whisky & wishing I could write a maudlin popular song . . .

Later, he adds:

> really worse that I have no work of my own & haven't for a year so the 4th or 5th whisky doesn't get that down since it's not there, simply not one damned idea after the terminal obsession of J R that holds enough interest, enough passion, for me to sit down to it with any sense of sustaining these things for long enough to complete it, to resolve it. Though perhaps looking back up the lines of words I've dumped upon you here there may be something, a latter-day American version of Waugh's *Handful of Dust* perhaps which I've always admired & may now be mean enough to try to write.

"Perhaps" would turn into "sure enough," though it took three more years. As he told William Gass just before the 1980 presidential election: "the only thing that rouses me these days are all these God damned born-agains & evangelicals"—a politico-religious context that would come to form the backdrop of *Carpenter's Gothic*. Drafting commenced soon after, and a few months later he had the first fifty pages. In March

1985, he sent his daughter, a novelist in her own right, the final revised page proofs, adding:

> in fact the whole passage where Liz talks about seeing herself as a child through a telescope light-years away . . . grew out of my remembrance of the story of yours that of course touched me closest about the girl watching her father going down the walk at Fire Island.

The Mysterious Stranger turns out not to be so mysterious. He is the lustful, destructive figure whom "Mrs. Booth" aptly sticks a knife in later ("you're the one who wants Apocalypse . . . because you despise their, not their stupidity no, their hopes because you haven't any"). Six months before he finished writing it, Gaddis told literary critic Steven Moore that he himself was McCandless.

In the scene just before his bedding of Liz, this ruined man—who can still seduce women, and shortly will—walks around his Carpenter Gothic home. (Later he will detail the history of it to Liz: "It was built that way yes, it was built to be seen from outside it was, that was the style.") Now he goes about burning papers, including the information for which an ex-associate has just offered him $20,000. Then he puts an old stew on the stove, and turns on the radio, "which eagerly informed him that a group of handicapped mountainclimbers had carried an American flag and a bag of jellybeans to the summit of Mount Rainier . . ." Then he burns more things in the fire, a passport and an address book, before opening a "slight book's paper covers to page 207"—Naipaul's 1967 novel *The Mimic Men*—to find "a slip of paper, a list in an open and generous hand, milk, paper towels, Tampax, tulip bulbs," a guide for shopping written by his ex-wife, which he also burns. Then he reads out a passage from the book until the narrative voice returns: "while from the kitchen, the chords of Bach's D major concerto heaved into the room around him and settled like furniture." This is how we live when we are alone—artfully detailed with pathos, satire, and intrigue, echoing the powerful confession of loneliness made in the letter to his friend.

What most impelled Gaddis's prose was a sense of calling out personal responsibility—exposing how people persist or give in to vice in the face of corporate or political forces. Liz may pick the wrong men to be attracted to, but the males in this book are the prime problem. They represent those legions of today who are fascinated with violence and the ways people literally destroy each other. Cloistered, they dutifully read towering, scrupulously researched books on the Nazis and the Holocaust, watch the second plane going into the South Tower from all forty-three known angles, and then take the family to Gettysburg, as if serving under some obsolete flag. The world in all its cruel particularity churns on, and we live in modest houses often slightly off their foundations, cleaning out our past to reduce what weighs down our present— but not by too much, for otherwise we would lose some of the relation, the sustaining memory. *Carpenter's Gothic* deserves to be read—and re-read—because if we are all "humankind dying by itself," we need a little beauty as the collective ship goes down.

Envy, the Unsuccessful Writer's Friend

WHAT IF PEOPLE fell into themselves? I don't mean to restrict this query in any sense. Think of those falling into love and subsuming each other. It feels good—there is bliss. When we're inside, we're there—darkening in the dark. But can we as happily live inside ourselves? How do we eat? What about sex? Can we talk to others?

It seems we fall into ourselves for some moments every day. No-one else can be with us then and only a practiced phrenologist performing a tactful surveillance could tell there has been a change. We are the truth of our lives, and with or without Freud and Jung we carry this pledge like the child we can never lose. All that is is light and all that we are accrues until the heart cannot so much as murmur, experience being a delicious pain. Some of the time we are only us, completely capable of being solipsistic in everything we do. How easy and simple that no-one else's needs impose—though, of course, they will continually interfere. We are our own mystery—no-one else can solve us but ourselves. Who said life was complicated? They must have been poking into other people's mysteries instead of staying self-registered.

In Edward Yang's film Yi Yi, a woman, who has gone on a retreat after her mother has fallen into a coma and her husband succumbs to disregard, returns home and tells her spouse: "I've come to realize things aren't really so complicated. Why did they ever seem so?" Life may be simple but because of the agendas of many around us, difficulties and emotional encounters dominate our time, whether shared or not.

For twenty years the literary world has been designing a new being made up of three unpleasantries: the internet junkie, the disgruntled commenter, and the unsuccessful writer (the last a catch-all moniker for the trifecta). This new unsuccessful writer, whose life might be the most despairing of all, does want to write, but by instantly producing his comment, he sacrifices the future for the present, eschews the possibility of a reverberating work for a trickle of reactionary babble. Most scribblers are incredibly insular; if someone blinks at them the wrong way they will have a story of revenge, with the blinker as butt, fashioned in four seconds. Yet many people like us would rather only contaminate ourselves with these germs than relish a future in which the objects of our scrutiny read the published text and recognize themselves as *treacherous* but *sloppy*, adjectives that don't accurately describe them, except that *tall* and *from Toledo* are too telling to dismiss.

Such a future rarely occurs. The myth that people the writer knows populate his stories has been too often perpetuated to be seen for the type of truth it is—useless. Sure, our mothers get in there, first lays and enemies, too, but so does the mother of a friend we met once, as well as the mother of Balzac, pictures of Hiroshima, Paul McCartney's voice in 'Yesterday,' and the taste of fried plantains. Living gets and gives itself to us every second and everything adheres and anticipates—as our noses near the smell of smoke, our heads bargain with our bellies about what sweet treats could be cooking.

The goo of life grows fat with our age, our internet era. Everyone has a comment ready, and most everyone has to tell their story, but for the unsuccessful writer to tarry toward this programmed cult of culture is a grand misstep. On the internet, the quack and the curiosity get the most attention, though they gain little but ignominy in exchange for their souls being plucked. By avoiding this vicious interchange, the unsuccessful writer might find himself bending to a more unilateral strike and pressing his screeds into parable form or a more endowed *précis*. One's duty should not be to the lethargic comment, but to the aptitude of one's anger. Troubles dominate our thoughts and those who have not weathered have no book to write nor need to read one. Who better than the unsuccessful writer to squawk about the indignities of the more fêted in the world? Being the dismissed provides a greater perspective—it humbles.

A relative once said to me, "I don't want to read a book about a normal person in an extraordinary situation. I want to read a book about a great person." But my blood unwittingly spoke of the same thing, and if he had ever ogled E. M. Cioran, the crotchety Romanian, master of despair, champion of the unsuccessful writer and artist ("To venture upon an undertaking of any kind, even the most insignificant, is to sacrifice to envy"), he'd see that the dispossessed often make more intriguing characters, with Melville's Captain Ahab, Beckett's batty Molloy and Krapp, and Nabokov's Humbert Humbert atop this dastardly pyramid. And so the unsuccessful writer can be a hardy weapon who has no end as device or character because he is very willing to persist in the vacuum. Though ham-handed in handling words, this writer can make a clearing in others' consciences—telling them it is all right to be alone, afraid, and awkward. He has his rightful place in the pantheon as the mirror of the artist—the extremity that doesn't fit, the body repelled by other bodies, other minds.

Cioran was only too prescient in his bolstering of this quicksilver emotion before the age of the anonymous internet graffiti artist. Envy doesn't carry the unsuccessful writer to a right success, but it points him to the more correct form. He doesn't so much acquire envy as garner it in installments. When he comes into a more crucial understanding of the term, it attaches its spirit to him as a burr to a woolen sock. The unsuccessful writer won't know how precious this emotion will be until he's lived through a night in which he could not write one sentence. Seen without its imprimatur of a routine shit smear, envy becomes an indubitable object on the toolbelt—valued and weighted as much as hate, sadness, joy, and exhilaration. If we'll always remember what it was to be happy, our envy will not be so accommodating—the verges of the mind become very adept at scrambling data as ordered by our egos.

Envy lurks. Out of the many writers I've met, there's not even three who haven't told of some others who get too much attention. When we envy, we empower ourselves, though it can be sand to hold and fire to touch. Like love, envy connects and repels, and those who serve it often don't know how much they cherish its invisible temple.

The Patrick White Experience

I DON'T KNOW when I developed the habit of veering in and out of multiple books at the same time, but for at least as long, I've been inclined to deride the practice. I'd just come down from *Swann's Way* and a long season given over mostly to poetry and essays when I slapped down an injunction—I should really get back to Patrick White, maybe the most under-read and underrated English-language novelist of our time. So I began his 1973 novel, *The Eye of the Storm*. Yet, I read slowly—more than just a "page-hugger," as Gary Lutz would say, I grasp the page for an uncomfortably long time, checking the texture of the paper and the number of sailboaty y's per line, hovering over the author's punctuation and other word choices proceeding.

The next morning, on my way to a doctor's appointment, I passed an old building being gutted and a resident bringing out armfuls of, mainly, good books. I grabbed a couple of Don DeLillo's, including *Cosmopolis*, and read the first pages on the subway home. *The Eye of the Storm* and *Cosmopolis* began to jockey for my attention. In my free hours, I read them in tandem, though thirty years and many nautical miles separated the two enterprises. Eventually, their two styles rose up like bleeds of color and then separated into diamonds and rhomboids like in *2001*'s Star Gate sequence, before trailing away from each other. I would read a sentence of DeLillo and then stop—huffing with bluster at their twenty-first-century powerlifting poses. The post-*Underworld* novels are of a lesser detail—not as many brushstrokes and in some places only an odd monochrome, white drowning out the bedrock color, with blurs and blears of cracked, rilled, and crevassed gray tincturing parts of the canvas, just like in Gerhard Richter's series of five so-colored 2009 abstracts, displayed that winter at the Marian Goodman Gallery. I took

Richter to be DeLillo's favorite painter even before I read of his paintings detailed in the short story "Baader–Meinhof." Many of these late
narratives portray people looking at or contemplating art. The subject
of *Cosmopolis* is a young billionaire who thinks of buying more of it
(why not the whole Rothko Chapel?) as he is driven across Midtown
Manhattan in a stretch limo. Not a relatable character, but he is like
nearly all of DeLillo's protagonists from *The Body Artist* onward—that
is, not so much a character as a series of moods and morose anthems
typifying our rampant egomania, which lets us not take things, like the
destruction of the earth, too seriously. The prose bespeaks doing more
with less, but one constant remains from the most honored books of the
eighties and nineties—the tone of the narrator in nearly all these works
is fairly consistent, with a kind of husky, neo-Hemingwayesque way of
relating: "He watched her. He didn't think he wanted to be surprised,
even by a woman, this woman, who'd taught him how to look, how to
feel enchantment damp on his face, the melt of pleasure inside a brush-
stroke or band of color." Grand gestures in the sweep of a few syllables
with the occasional fuzziness like "enchantment damp on his face." That
layered sheen of Richter's spreads all over DeLillo's late works, which
themselves seem sickly, contained in the gauge-controlled atmosphere of
a museum or high class gallery. Such prose is for the reader, it's adorned
and it is refined, but it isn't exactly ennobled, and so it resembles Richter's vaguely-colored bedrock—an art of line and color with little room
for narrative; an art that skirts the issue of what it means to have a soul
trapped in a body.

   The canyon walls of late DeLillo had narrowed around me and I
couldn't see enough of the many-faceted world, where the vistas let the
imagination stretch, in the space provided. In Patrick White, as in Virginia Woolf, James Joyce, and William Gass, there is a feeling of reple-
ness. One gets to the heart of the sensation, whether awe-inspiring or
foul, not through winks and nudges but through full orchestration—the
Sistine ceiling in person, not a postage-stamp-size .gif on the internet.
By some synchronicity, White's book is also about a character, Elizabeth
Hunter, who has a good load of cash, though she lives in Sydney, and is
old and dying. The place of the book in the author's *oeuvre* is also similar
to that of *Cosmopolis* in DeLillo's. Many people, even an admirer like
David Malouf, view *The Eye of the Storm* and the novel before it, *The
Vivisector*, as "overwrought, excessive, unlikeable books, full of larger-
than-life (theatrical) characters and grotesque, lurid situations, and an
oddly old-fashioned view of the artist as sacred monster." To Malouf, they
are some galaxies from White's expansive style in his early books of the

fifties and sixties: *Tree of Man, Voss,* and *Riders in the Chariot*—though I prefer *The Solid Mandala,* as do White and J. M. Coetzee. In returning to *The Eye,* I began to get caught up, certainly by the language, but also the story—this old woman, who has multiple servants, remembers her life while lying on her deathbed as her grown children are flying in to see her off. I became entrenched in a concentrated, Henry Jamesian way, applauding how every sentence gushed with life—the wisdom of White doled out equally to every character and delivered to us in their distinct terms. Early on, the favored servant, Sister de Santis, passes a portrait of Elizabeth's deceased husband:

> Sister de Santis did not stop to draw the curtains in the dining-room, but hurried through its brown-velvet hush, past the portrait of Alfred Hunter ("Bill" to his friends). Mr Hunter's portrait was smaller than his wife's; it must have cost considerably less: even so, a lot of money, if you read the signature in the corner. For a man of wealth Mr Hunter looked rather diffident: he probably disappointed the painter, except by writing out his cheque. The nurse moderated her pace, walking with the reverence accorded to those you have not known in their lifetime, but might have. Out of respect, she endowed Mr Hunter with virtues she could remember in her father.

When I re-read that paragraph aloud, I could not suppress a force that, with a minor screech, turned on the waterworks in my left eye. We garner our wisdom through parables because advice or the self-help cliché is as distancing and antiseptic as the white-and-pastel jackets such books demand from publishers. Consequently, the parabolic deftly scorches and sends us through time, letting us talk back to our parents, our lovers, and that dope on the street we won't deign to call a stranger. White's nuggets—koan-like pronouncements and sculpted judgments on character—carry a strange, propulsive magic for the reader and have a secret but simple recipe: enough of this, but just enough of that. It's a very raw feeling, an acid bath, when you're drawn so tightly into a story that eventually you're reading your own book, as V. S. Naipaul said in an interview—you are the character or observer in the dream (the book) unfolding in your mind.

In the course of John Hawkes's novel *The Lime Twig* a gang member beats a woman with a wet newspaper, a scene William Gass described as "stunning, and it is so beautiful, but, does that make it in a sense, less horrible? No, it makes it a monument to horror and you know what is going on in a way you never would otherwise." This is what I want to enter, a monument built for me, the reader, to experience all of life's sensations and reverberations, like how Elizabeth remembers sex with her late husband. White brings us inside her character, and I mean through the body cavity and up into the brainpan:

> She only realized how small he was as he lay wilted and sweating, rather fatty about the shoulders, his exhausted lungs still battering at her practically pulverized breasts. At his most masterful his toes would be gripping the sheets on either side of her long legs, as though he had found the purchase to impress her more deeply than ever before. Once, she remembered, she had felt, not his sweat, his tears trickling down the side of her neck, till he started coughing, and tore himself away from her: their skins sounded like sticking plaster. She tried to make herself, and finally did, ask what had upset him. His 'luck', in everything, was more than he deserved; however indistinct the answer, that was what it amounted to.

I don't exactly know what women feel about men when they have sex with them—I've certainly tried to find out—but I do trust Patrick White's vision of this character, and only for the reason that every sentence I've read of his has demanded my attention and pushed me to read the next. I know I give him too much credit, but I would go to the mat for White—I have to, because my reading life depends on it. Certainly the staunching of male tears is relatable, I did it just the night before reading this, because I didn't want to make a fuss while I remembered my dead father. "Fatty about the shoulders . . ." and "At his most masterful his toes would be gripping the sheets on either side of her long legs"—White's prose puts one in the bed better than any Hollywood sex scene does, which, thanks to the passage's sturdy entablature, briefly flash-pointed my past (my toes too have had memorable cranings) and became my sex scene—I'm the craven fool atop a woman I use for sport, but I didn't bury my head after wilting, did I? I'll have to read more to find out.

White's book did have a famous admirer, Shirley Hazzard, who wrote:

> Imputing "inspiration" to novelists is as dangerous as discoursing on Nature with farmers: but each of White's novels has been blessed and quickened with a center of narrative power—large meaning in which the author seeks to create our belief. Without at least some measure of this mysterious ignition, which is utterly distinct from "content," the most diligently wrought book remains stationary and merely professional. White has always been able to command it in abundance: his

novels, plays and stories are irradiations from related central themes in which the author participates no less intensely than his characters.

This answers Malouf's critique of "overwrought, excessive, unlikeable books"—an analysis mainly aimed at the "content" Hazzard doesn't prize, as she bids its bloviated pop sensibilities to return to the chintzy window dressing it almost always is. She also judges *Cosmopolis* and many other books as "stationary and merely professional"; without that narrative power, as when the author is not steeped in their material (DeLillo from *The Body Artist* on), the rudderless reading experience is perplexing—it might make us put down the book.

I went to the Met with my uncle a few years ago and we stood at the far side of the Vermeer room to watch how people flocked to the four assembled paintings. After some moments of silence, he asked how it is that there is Vermeer and then there are the rest of the Dutch Baroque painters, and that nothing, not even Rembrandt, comes close to Vermeer's endless sublime beauty, which might be defined as "an expression of the fullest possible range of human capabilities within the circumstances of a given narrative or situation," per Daniel Davis Wood. This is how White, Woolf, Faulkner, and James, along with DeLillo in *Libra* and *Underworld*, light up my imagination—runway markers in a dark night. Another master, Marianne Moore, offered a telling example when detailing her own sentence structure: ". . . you don't devise a rhythm, the rhythm is the person, and the sentence but a radiograph of personality." This might imbricate Hazzard's contention that White participates in themes "no less intensely than his characters," for if the themes and the sentences are the writer's "personality," at the same time they are those twin forces shooting through our consciousness, their powerful confluence building the sublime. But it's sublime and egalitarian and human at the same instant, like Joyce's mention of Bloom and Stephen comparing their piss streams at the end of a long night together, or when Elizabeth Hunter "wonder[s] momentarily whether she should give Mrs. Badgery something from her jewel box; it was easier to give presents than to waste emotions you were storing up against some possible cataclysm: as time ran on you did not know what you might have to face." This art is not "like" life; much as us, it is as alive and breathing and blood-filled.

An Adultery

SOME WORKS OF great art come, as Walter Pater wrote, to give the highest quality to our "moments as they pass, and simply for those moments' sake." But there is a bastard mode of great art, a tripwire type that takes us simultaneously downward and upward, as we can't remain on its quicksand embankments bordering volatile seismic ground. The epic curmudgeon Edward Dahlberg, loined in burly prosody, was a major literary practitioner of this: "I know sage, wormwood, and hyssop, but I can't smell character unless it stinks," along with Stanley Elkin's stand-up: "The peculiar dignity of men seen eating alone in restaurants on national holidays." On the visual side, there is Stanley Kubrick after *2001*, reflecting civilization's incredible disregard for humanity, while tinged with the blackest of humor, and in a more Poundian way, Jean Luc-Godard's strafing of narrative cinema and western art into shards, exposing the hypocrisies that sustain us. Relentlessly vivid, these works can sneak up on our equipoise and bludgeon us into uncomfortable states. They go beyond our threshold terribly, ingratiating as they eviscerate. Alexander Theroux belongs to this select group.

"Hate" is a much ballyhooed word of the zeitgeist:, We lob softballs like "I hate tofu," "I hate Knausgård," or "I hate Bernie Bros." Theroux didn't write the book on hatred, but he wrote four novels where the emotion coruscates, first through the Baroque sentences in *Three Wogs* and *Darconville's Cat*, and then in the more late-twentieth-century syntactical *An Adultery*, which Steven Moore, his closest critic, describes as "a neo-Jamesian style that recalls the Master's inexhaustible fascination with the subtleties of manners and morals, as well as Proust's exhaustive analyses of character and culture"—*Laura Warholic*, his last, is a quasi-return to the amplitude of the first two. In these books, Theroux makes

today's purveyors of the emotion (ideologues all, who will eat their own)
seem like they are playing in a little league to his major. Is it nihilism?
Or is it just a pitch dark routine á la Bill Hicks, with Theroux deploying
well-oiled barbs and epigrams to filigree his literary enterprise? These
are the types of jolts which Roland Barthes wrote are "like an insect's
thorax; like an insect, too, the maxim possesses a sting, that hook of
sharp-pointed words which concludes and crowns it. . . ." Early on in *An
Adultery*, the narrator, a painter named Kit, pulverizes the state of New
Hampshire, where he teaches art at a prep school:

> New Hampshire has always been cheap, mean, rural, small-minded,
> and reactionary. It's one of the few states in the nation with neither
> a sales tax nor an income tax. Social services are totally inadequate
> there, it ranks at the bottom in state aid to education—the state is
> literally shaped like a dunce cap—and its medical assistance program
> is virtually nonexistent. Expecting aid for the poor there is like look-
> ing for an egg under a basilisk. . . . Mud season is long, frost heaves
> are everywhere, and black flies should be denominated the state bird.

I'm not sure the experience of this is so much literary as redolent of sitting beside a bombastic man verbally shooting everyone in sight like they
were unevolving skeet. There are plenty of people like this in the world,
who want to overrun our souls with their brusque perturbations to see
what we are made of.

To treat the text in a neo-autobiographical manner, Marianne Moore
wrote: "style is a radiograph of the personality." Theroux concurs, writing
(in his essay "Theroux Metaphrastes"): "Where there is no style, there is
in effect no point of view. There is, essentially, no anger, no conviction,
no self. Style is opinion, hung washing, the caliber of a bullet, teething
beads." Challenging oneself to read Theroux, darkly serious and seriously funny, does gives one the street smarts and blush of experience, rather
than the teething beads often offered with the latest literary bestseller.

An Adultery begins bleeding, almost as soon as it starts, opening as
Kit's ignoble diary, before becoming a case study of Farol Colorado, with
whom he has an affair. This soon-to-be hated woman constantly keeps
things from him; eventually he finds out she had been cheating on him
and her husband with others. The prison of Kit initially has three cells:
two for the principals and one for the reader, who becomes chained to
their dysfunction, but as the pages go on, the book unsplinters with Kit's
admittance that, "People like us didn't want advice. We wanted approval." He assumes responsibility in the action, which is more complex than

the dance of intimacy between unfit people, more like the parsed-over
betrayals in Shakespeare:

> If eyes corrupt by over-partial looks
> Be anchor'd in the bay where all men ride,
> Why of eyes' falsehood hast thou forged hooks,
> Where to the judgment of my heart is tied?

Here is desire, the being in heat, the erring of eye and heart during
days of intertwining—this miniature from Sonnet 137 is stretched to
symphonic lengths in *An Adultery*, as the forensic report on Farol Colorado swells into as thorough a search (from the outside) into a wounded
psyche as there is in late-twentieth-century literature. And it is to be
trusted only because Kit indicts himself in the madness, and, in the end,
gets what he deserves. Instead of working deductively, the narrator keeps
refining his viewpoint of Farol's manic existence, first with high attitu-
dinal proclamations: "She was in competition with herself. She wanted
success in the person she married but simultaneously loathed the role
it imposed on her," and lower ones, "She acted exactly as she had been
raised and gave herself away in the small thoughtless ways people do
who never hang up a towel or replace water in ice-cube trays or rinse out
a bathtub after using it," and finally, synthesized with Kit's own addiction
to painful relations (he grew up in an orphanage after his parents died in
his early years), producing the emptiness of the "moment's" superficial
payoff: "Nothing in adultery is additive or cumulative. No one wins, all
the time. And nothing can stem the torment of what is by what could
be. . . . You become but two cold copulars lapping frost off each other's
rectitude." Perhaps readers who have endured such tortuous times, who
have let themselves be hurt, or have even gotten messy in the first place,
will cozy to this biblical strain of dereliction demonstrating that they had
as much to do with their hurt as the other person, something Kit later
pronounces: "Each person in a couple does enough bad things in a relationship to feel that when it breaks down he or she is alone responsible."
It's a statement that, if posted on social media, would immediately, like
fresh kill still oozing on the blacktop, draw vicious scavengers. Yes, it is
quarrelsome, and with obvious exceptions. But its able application to
most of humanity hurts—for why would we not want books, as friends,
to challenge, to dare to call what is foul foul? Theroux taps into the
enigma that is relationship—to hell with love.

To say Kit falls for the wrong woman would cheapen what it means
to live and learn. But Farol Colorado is so entirely retrograde, glaucous,

and phlegmatic—she is one of a breed of people who never grow up, who constantly stack the deck in their favor, and who belittle fact, while pathologically lying, including, in this case, about having a disease. She seems the type of person who—age thirty in 1986, and sixty-five now— would have developed into a tyrannical Republican voter, mindlessly lofting a misspelled sign, while hanging out of an F-150, yelling sorry imprecations at the nurses risking their lives to save her friends and neighbors. What's amazing is that people like Farol Colorado exist in nearly every county of our country, with some voting the other way and some not at all. My heart was tied to such a person, and, like Kit, I realized toward our end that I was as much responsible for her aches, lies, and sidelonging feelings, as I had done enough bad things in the relationship—we fall in love with people who help us see our shortcomings, and who we will instruct to best enable them. Late in the book, Kit says, "We make people important by what we feel for them" and perhaps our love lives would be a little less fraught if this admonition had come out of the Oracle at Delphi, with "make" the cunning, laugh-out-loud verb of our undoing. Finally, the couple's whole affair gets bitterly simonized with, "It was as if while I was waiting for something to happen she was waiting for something not to."

Sections of the book revel in the negative capability of knowing another where the reader might be slogging through the deep wheel ruts made by Theroux's prose—part and parcel of its gloomy New England setting. Kit constantly describes Farol's body (and those of other women in the novel) and her defects (some of which she professes), like the size of her head and hips, her changing hairstyles, and her "pencil-thin calves"—something symptomatic of greater inner ugliness—and one is reminded that, yes, others will judge us much more harshly than we ever could imagine. The book was written during the time of the burgeoning self-help industry in the early eighties, along with shows like *Donahue* that pushed a certain pastel self-composure the narrator finds hideous: "You heard things like 'I'm just beginning to feel good about myself' and 'I have to start learning to say no,'" mantras soon merging with Farol's narrow-minded notions that everyone can be an artist, as she flailingly tries sculpting and woodcarving: "She didn't want to make, but strived to compete. . . ." But just when you've had enough of the grousing, after a few runs of pages that stain, there comes a chapter of inner reflections, like midway through, where the weather transfuses his Venus to Medusa:

We ate lunch in silence. She eventrated the afternoon. It was not the same day at all but a different one, a pale solution of sunlight coloring the sides of things that were now unalike, the sky a diluted blue without distance, neither near nor far. A streak of alizarin crimson across the sky reminded me in its synthetic hue of her.

These sentences (Theroux's bullets) are perfectly calibrated—the sounds pass on triumphantly, as sonically balanced as a Wagner opera. Eventrate: that is "to disembowel." The assonance and consonance of "a diluted blue without distance . . ." "Neither near nor far," a play on "Neither Out Far Nor in Deep" by Robert Frost, New England's forever poet laureate, with the lines: "They cannot look out far / They cannot look in deep—"; pointing to Farol's frozen soul. And that "streak of alizarin crimson" that does the reminding, tells us love may make us beautiful, but hate makes the world go around, and here it poisons this painter's purview.

It is an uncompromising book and is fully welcome in an era of soft-serve MFA-diluted works. They often contain an abundance of knee-jerk liberal ideology that can't countenance the many-faceted intricacies that bulwark civilization. Even when our friends are everyone who voted the right way, the strong-arming of "you are with us or against us," employed by both extremes, can lead to the same type of cliff, only on different shores.

There were times when I eyed Theroux's book as something more confounding than comforting, and extra abrasive, as the glimmerings of my own romantic faults overwhelmed my sight, in particular, the recent canard detailing insanity as writ large by Kit: "doing the same thing over and over again, but expecting different results." But Theroux takes the action in an unexpected direction, so that in the final somber pages, reminiscent of *King Lear*'s "great thing of us forgot," one can say without question that this is our lot in life—people pass in and out of our everydays, as the latest editions of magazines and newspapers get a glance before going to the recycling bin, and, more cruelly, as this morning's tweets, full of sweet nothings, pass into a twilight sedation, only to be revived and weaponized when someone decides to "hate" their author.

Return to Enigma

ONCE, IN AN EMAIL, after I'd named W. G. Sebald as the barometer of the novel in our century, a friend wrote to me about V. S. Naipaul's *The Enigma of Arrival* (1987), describing it as "sort of like Sebald before Sebald." Months later I finally put eyes on the pages, but the opening swarm of perceptions about the English countryside threw me. This wasn't a novel (though of course it was) but, at the same time, it was far afield from reportage. Bricolage it was, and the reality of Naipaul's time in the countryside bent and swerved to the extra-literary, to the whims of a narrator plainly him, though self-scalped. Some ten years of experience had been flattened, fractured, and upended to spawn a matrix of narration that had then been desiccated and re-established—a broken mirror autobiography glazed in the modernist mode. I petered out, but knew I'd be back in a better mind.

Another writer friend dubbed him V. S. 'Corrugated Iron' Naipaul. Every book, including fifteen works of fiction and fifteen volumes of non-fiction, contains this phrase, sometimes donning a hyphen, sometimes not. In Trinidad, where he grew up, the use of this building material was widespread, and he would often see more of it on his many journeys into other developing nations. He enjoyed a stardom few writers in America ever achieve, gracing the cover of *Newsweek* four years before he began *Enigma* in 1984. That year, he'd just written about the Republican National Convention in Dallas for the *New York Review of Books*, a periodical that carried much of his travel writing over the years, including the nearly-complete text of a few books. What to say about the world of Reagan only came to him when he was back home in England, responding not to the "staged occasion, but the things around the occasion." He wrote *Enigma* in the same oblique manner, in a continual searching, "finding experience where I thought there had been nothing . . ." Indeed, *Enigma* might be one of the best how-to books on novel writing because the narrative is the process and the veil is rent to show the hard-to-imagine truth of how the writing of a book is the discovery of what it should be, how it evolves in ways never planned until the words flow.

Large portions of *Enigma* appeared in *The New Yorker* prior to its publication, with one section spanning fifty magazine pages. In March of 1987, Knopf released it in hardback. Ostensibly, *The Enigma of Arrival* is the account of the narrator's time in a cottage on an English estate holding a large manor house, until later he purchases his own cottages nearby. Broken into four parts and an epilogue, Naipaul outlines the area and its surroundings, close to Stonehenge, in the manner of the nineteenth-century country writers Richard Jefferies and William Cobbett, the latter receiving a mention in the book. The vivid prose deconstructs the very act of looking that is so central to a novel of perceptions:

> . . . here the rivers of the chalk valleys all around met and ran together, the water always clear, giving an extraordinary brilliance to scattered pieces of litter, the water seeming (like glass paperweights or like photographs) to have the power to isolate ordinary or well-known objects and force their details on the eye.

Given his own Trinidadian background, Naipaul lays out his pseudo-autobiographical, Proustian program very early on:

> That idea of ruin and dereliction, of out-of-placeness, was something I felt about myself: a man from another hemisphere, another background, coming to rest in middle life in the cottage of a half-neglected estate . . . with few connections to the present. . . . I felt that my presence in that old valley was part of something like an upheaval, a change in the course of the history of the country.

He discusses the books he wrote while staying there, especially *In a Free State*, as well as his own health concerns. The most glaring omission is any mention of his wife Pat. She often resided there with him—and when she read the early drafts, she thought about libel.

When one considers Naipaul, the best adjective to encompass both him and his writing is "severity." When I've foisted *Enigma* onto others, I've described it as a pastoral, though it is heavily concerned with severe portraits of neighbors seen through Naipaul's discerning eyes. He thus incorporates into the pastoral the hidden form of autobiography: that is, coloring one's own psychic makeup by detailing others'. The neighbors he portrays often live on the grounds of the estate itself, working in various guises and ranging from a gardener, a car-hire man, a servant, and a caretaker to the invalid landlord whom the narrator only sees twice in his time there. In casting these portraits, Naipaul proceeds by way of deduction, detailing what clothes they wear, their faces, their explicit emotions, and how they use language in what few words they say to him:

> The new dairyman was an ugly man. His wife was also ugly. And there was a pathos about their ugliness. Ugliness had come to ugliness for mutual support; but there had been little comfort as a result.
>
> His sentimentality frightened me. It was the sentimentality of a man who could give himself the best of reasons for doing strange things.

These psychologically pungent miniatures are blunt, even caustic, but they certainly contain as much of Naipaul's soul as those he seizes upon. Naipaul started in radio and the concision of material required to fit into time-slotted "stories" probably helped formulate such tart rejoinders to other people's worlds. His economical style expanded to detail cultures and countries in the travel books, as with his razor-wire nod to Buenos Aires in 'The Return of Eva Peron,' wherein lies "the stupefying nightclub, which enables people who have said everything already to be together for hours without saying anything."

Naipaul said he wrote *Enigma* in the order in which it proceeds. Part two, 'The Journey,' halts what narrative there is—a narrative where things befall the people he describes, where everyday mysteries pile up and implode—to detail his first journey from Trinidad to Britain (and, eventually, Oxford) when he was eighteen. He notes the culture shock in the plane, in Manhattan, on the boat, and in London, as well as describing his first fumblings as a writer. In part three, the book reverts to where the narrative began and continues with his time in the countryside cottage, twenty years after his arrival in England. Without the prior recall of the virgin journey (coupled with the narrator finding a reproduction of *The Enigma of Arrival*, the titular surrealist painting by De Chirico, at the cottage), and without his fleshing out those first green feelings, there would be no sounding board to play off the pastoral and observations of British personality traits surrounding the nearly one hundred pages of part two. If the reader didn't know what the flailing Naipaul details in his account of his premiere voyage, how could she come to see deeper into his perceptions? How could she trust a consciousness that is so imperious as to thresh the psychologies of all those around him? Projected as such a strong, indomitable presence later, the Naipaul of eighteen years old is naïve, untried, but with a tint of the uncompromising nature he will toil so hard to foster. This structuring goes against the prevailing winds of narrative because the typical points of empathy with the narrator are put off for so long.

Revitalized, the book charges on. Many details are now explored with a counterpoise from the past. People who were only gestured at in part one, like the landlord, Pitton the gardener, and Bray the car-hire man, are greatly expanded, again with a pitiless regard: "Both Pitton and his wife were people without the gift for words. . . . But the beauty of Pitton's wife was of such a sort that it overcame her intellectual, which was also her social, disability. . . . Beauty is beauty, though; and beauty is rare; no one who possesses it can be indifferent to it." With this further fleshing-out of other characters, there emerges a clearer intention for the narrator himself:

> I wanted, when I came to the manor, after the pride of ambition, to strip my life down. I wanted to live as far as possible with what I found in the cottage in the manor grounds, to alter as little as possible. I wanted to avoid vanity; and for me then vanity could lie in very small things—like wishing to buy an ashtray.

I believe he wanted to live without vanity, which is to say I believe he is vain and strongly admits it, though with a deflection. His belief is that everything should be in service of the work—things, even wishing for things, would not get his art to where he wanted it to go. Metafictionally speaking, it was just this type of asceticism that led to a drastic change in tone in Naipaul's *oeuvre*, exemplified in his three violent masterpieces— *In a Free State, Guerillas,* and *A Bend in the River*—all written at the cottage in the 1970s.

In a book full of so many perceptions—with its celebration of nature, lamentations of change and decay, and its biting judgment and censure of people—I've often wondered how Naipaul himself might be judged. Or rather, why is he excluded from the judgment he exercises against others? Who watches over him? To answer this question, it helps to look at the Proust he quotes in both his Nobel Lecture and an earlier essay, words that could be etched as an epitaph to *Enigma*:

> . . . a book is the product of a different self from the self we manifest

in our habits, our social life, in our vices . . . it is the secretions of one's innermost self, written in solitude and for oneself alone that one gives to the public. What one bestows on private life—in conversation . . . or in those drawing-room essays that are scarcely more than conversation in print—is the product of a quite superficial self, not of the innermost self which one can only recover by putting aside the world and the self that frequents the world.

Ironically, the two selves—the author's actual self and literary self—are both firmly on display in Enigma. That he speaks often and highly of himself is acceptable because he has enfolded himself into his literature—even though the narrator is Naipaul, it is still Naipaul as the speaker of the novel, just as distinct from the man himself as a poet is distinct from the speaker of a poem. This person is a construct, even though 99% of what he details might align with how the decade bore out. So the grandiosity and large pronouncements continue in the second half of the book. He is a megalomaniac, he is near to paranoid (numerous times while meditating on certain nature scenes in the manor grounds he tries to stave off the emotional letdown of their inevitable change by saying, At least I've had this for a year, at least I've had this for two years . . .), and yet, he is a seer. There is little room for argument with this man, the construct. He tells you who he is (save the women who propped him up—he had a lover at the time) and what he is thinking. Sometimes his perceptions about people are off and he will admit so, but that does not hijack the fact of everyone else being his theatre, those whom he studies in order to strip them down to their final fold of skin.

   In trying to reconcile the megalomaniac with the artist, it's instructive to consider Naipaul's most famous line, the opening of A Bend in the River: "The world is what it is; men who are nothing, who allow themselves to become nothing, have no place in it." It's a line everyone must grapple with, no matter their politics. No one should try to claim the artist as friend, one self is always getting in the way of the other. In Naipaul, the innermost self does flicker off and on as he writes of his breakdowns and fears of death by describing those of others. The apparent superficiality in his loaded and strong-armed remarks is poached, aligning them to his perceptions in an act of looking inside and out at the same time. He constructs hearty truths about the world and its people: how they are often afraid of each other, or say one thing when they mean another. People show their insides to him here because he—the narrator, the writer, the construct, the enigma—is the watcher, the listener, but also the proctor and prodder.

Written in the fifty-second, fifty-third, and fifty-fourth years of Naipaul's life, *Enigma* is more than a meditation on death: it is a reverential treatment of history, civilization, morals, scruples, and compunction. Naipaul supersedes the cliché that we look at others to learn about ourselves, instead making this suggestion: we look at others to define the world, then we are able to make our place in it. Near the end of the book, the narrator says, "The story had become more personal: my journey, the writer's journey, the writer defined by his writing discoveries, his ways of seeing, rather than by his personal adventures." Naipaul, wise and impossible, and probably intolerable, wrote fearlessly and "not always respectably"—a critic's phrase he often cited, holding it as a quite agreeable mantra for his artistic sensibility.

The One and Only Autobiographical Writer

> . . . a book is the product of a different self from the self we manifest in our habits, our social life, in our vices. . . . It is the secretions of one's innermost self, written in solitude and for oneself alone that one gives to the public. What one bestows on private life—in conversation . . . or in those drawing-room essays that are scarcely more than conversation in print—is the product of a quite superficial self, not of the innermost self which one can only recover by putting aside the world and the self that frequents the world.
>
> — Marcel Proust, *Against Sainte-Beuve*

ALL WRITING IS AUTOBIOGRAPHICAL: that's been tossed around so many times in countless iterations, one can't help hearing it as cliché, but a cliché diminished—something from the dustbin of history. The above words from Proust should unsettle in times like these when the "self" has transmogrified, the ego now granted an online persona to go with the public and private one. While pursuing these issues of autobiography, David Attwell's fine, slim "biography," *J. M. Coetzee and the Life of Writing*, is much reliant on the notebooks Coetzee kept during the composition of his novels. According to Attwell, the type of "autobiographical" writing Coetzee practices is tied to the latter's citing T. S. Eliot and Roland Barthes as forebears in the journals: "for all three, impersonality is not what it seems. It is not a simple repudiation of self in the name of art; on the contrary, it involves an instantiation of self, followed by an erasure that leaves traces of the self behind"—a furtherance of Proust's keen vision. As is William Gaddis' ghostly "compositional self," an entity produced through the making of a book.

These quotations I throw about are to be taken together like a cornucopia. They each answer the pettiness of people critically calling out an author for "just writing about herself" and yet they also forward the notion of "writer as magician." So much of that mystique has been quelled by our "everyone is a writer" zeitgeist, and especially the legions of bloggers and self-published commentators who think that just because their sentences have been posted on the infinity of the internet with many "shares" and "likes," or printed on post-industrial paper, they themselves have become successful scribblers.

Who is this different or innermost self? Can he or she co-exist with the superficial self who is often now required to sell the book, primarily through the internet and social media, giving endless interviews and explanations of the motive to write?—a most incriminating, even pedestrian, act these days. By rights, the innermost self is the precious cargo serious writers carry with them. This self is the being or the mode that needs to be switched into or turned on to create the singing that is creation. In different hours, composition is a stropping of the razor to pierce the light, but this slog is a relief for the superficial mind. Here is the time never showing in the cracks of the face but in the gnosis, spread, and harmony of sentences. In the final pages of V. S. Naipaul's *The Enigma of Arrival*, the narrator describes his path to this innermost self: "The story had become more personal: my journey, the writer's journey, the writer defined by his writing discoveries, his ways of seeing, rather than by his personal adventures . . ." His thoughts here blend into Eliot's thinking in 'Tradition and Individual Talent': "Poetry is not a turning loose of emotion, but an escape from emotion. It is not an expression of personality, but an escape from personality. . . . What happens [to the poet] is a continual surrender of himself as he is at the moment to something more valuable. The progress of an artist is a continual self-sacrifice, a continual extinction of personality." It is impossible to demonstrate why one writes, but short of hoisting a book award, writing is probably driven by this act of extinction.

All writing is autobiographical, but in various ways. Naipaul used his travels, and the material he garnered for those acclaimed travel books in mainly third world countries, to inform the narratives of his three bloody masterpieces of the 1970s, all of them set in Africa: *In a Free State, Guerillas*, and *A Bend in the River*. He began to use his journals in his fiction with *In a Free State* and then freely became a character, but not in a meta way, in *The Enigma of Arrival* and *A Way in the World*. Of Coetzee's novels, from 1974's *Dusklands* to 1999's *Disgrace* (eight books), some are set in very distant times: one each in the 1600s and 1700s, two in the late 1800s, and one in the early 1900s, with three having female first-person narrators. Although two of the main characters are professors, the others are very distinct: a housewife, an elderly magistrate, a simpleton with a deformity, a female castaway, Fyodor Dostoevsky, and (for the two novellas of *Dusklands*) a government agent and an explorer. Gaddis, in contrast, uses alter-egos in the guise of failing artists in each of his books, with each also set in places he once lived.

This talk points to the holy grail of all the questions aimed at writers: where do you get your ideas? Probably no answer should be kept more private, especially during composition of the work itself. Many greats, when asked, simply lie. Writing is unique in that the words are the art—they already say something. A William Gaddis character, speaking for his author, extrapolated further, as he wondered what people wanted from the man that they didn't get from his work. Many writers today are unapprehensive to name the source or sources and explain, through reason, why they have made up what they have. It makes good copy but it pushes the act of creativity into the numbing squalor of chic algorithm. Perhaps the most famous American example of this is William Faulkner contending that *The Sound and the Fury* "began with a picture of a little girl with muddy drawers, climbing a tree to look in the parlor window with her brothers who didn't have the courage to climb the tree." Probably not a lie, though Faulkner was famous for them, yet it's a remark that doesn't help countenance the act of writing any better. "Remarks are not literature," as Gertrude Stein averred.

There's no doubt how many long games of the imagination sprout from such saucy triggering visitations, but between the event and the finished product is a tortuous time that can't be recapitulated in any fashion. The real answer to the idea question is: months and years of sitting and scratching things out, about as sexy as working on an assembly line at the factory, with the hands as essentially effectual as the mind. And in the thick of the scratching out, one's ghostly innermost self is created. Where do you get your ideas? One might say, "The only ones that matter in the end come as I write. If I didn't debunk and revise those first ideas, they'd be meaningless." To this end, later in the same essay, T. S. Eliot wrote:

> the poet has, not a 'personality' to express, but a particular medium, which is only a medium and not a personality, in which impressions and experiences combine in peculiar and unexpected ways. Impressions and experiences which are important for the man may take no

place in the poetry, and those which become important in the poetry may play quite a negligible part in the man, the personality.

The innermost self is rarely, if ever, full of didacticism or superficiality—unless it is to rebuke that nasty drawing-room essay self (or social media self) which Proust galvanized to make a world out of and which we, in our times, filleted into a franchise.

Why Write?

AT AN EVENT I once hosted, I asked the assembled writers this question. Besides the "practical ordering of my reality" type of answer, there were also some surprises. One woman had been a classical singer, but failed, and needed to embark on something else having to do with language. One man said, "I write to talk about what I read"—equally unassuming. I began to think that it would be much more stimulating to know why certain writers wrote than to engage with anything they had written, especially fiction or poetry—two ultimate forms needing years of practice. It's debatable who said "everyone has a book in them," yet the second clause of that sentence, as uttered by Christopher Hitchens, is concretely dismissive of the first: "but in most cases, that's where it should stay." Who would have thought there were so many writers, that oodles would have the calling—many thanks to the internet? Now there is no barrier to that fusty adage, but it might be better to say this: everyone has some *opinions* in them.

So many of the famous statements of intent have to do with a sense of outrage at the world. George Orwell put it like this: "I write it because there is some lie that I want to expose, some fact to which I want to draw attention, and my initial concern is to get a hearing." Here's William H. Gass: "I write because I hate. A lot. Hard." But anger doesn't always carry the muse. Flannery O'Connor: "I don't know what I think till it is written, which is as good as the answer, the writing itself." Certainly John McPhee doesn't write out of a sense of outrage, but rather a hope for new discoveries and by not being bored by anything in the world. But if you poll writers not as accomplished as these—those struggling, or even struggling to wring royalty checks out of their small press publishers—many reasons fog up the glass containing them, but the underlying reason they write is a desire for attention. People want to be heard. One writes to be counted, even to be counted higher than others. Outside of gabbing, writing is the most respected and inflammatory pastime, though certainly less well compensated—it generates a conversation between ourselves and others without the need for another person to be there. And if we are writing to be counted, it is inevitable that there is a lot of discounting going on. Society is uneven, a few have too much, and too many have too little. How do we square this? Everyone knows life is unfair, but bringing a little beauty into the world is a small progressive step.

Why write today? Plasticity is at issue. The fakery of life. All the phonies out there—Holden Caufield's famous refrain that so many people identify with. This is perhaps our first biting teenage thought as we start to see significant holes in the people who rule our lives. Phonies still exist, especially with the creation of online personae, which are sometimes completely the opposites of the people who make them. Have we lost our bullshit detectors with the drive toward ego or are we just more deluded than at any other moment in history? Is it now all right to give people a free pass on all hypocrisies as long as they sidle in step with political correctness and celebrity worship, two of contemporary letters' most redoubtable genuflections? Why would people want to write, daring to add to the myriad pap and smear of floppy dramatics and weak sentences? Even some of the world's better-known writers, who are celebrated by reviewers, the bulk of whom function as publicists, have aged to eschew the mark. Of those fiction-making sources I quoted, only Gass lived long enough to see so much more that he amended his "hate" answer, thirty-five years later—though it is never repeated, probably because it wasn't published in the *Paris Review*, but merely spoken on a podcast called *Word Patriots*: "I certainly don't write for money, or for glory. . . . All sorts of writers receive that, but they have written worthless books. I and any other writer who is serious shall die not knowing whether you've wasted that much of your life in a fruitless pursuit or whether you've achieved fame and actual immortality, but you're dead for that." Immortality and death make attention-seekers uncomfortable because each is too immense a concept, dwarfing all the transitory tweets, gibes, gabs, and self-love that wash away with every new wave of the same. Similar to Gass's words is John Berryman's advice to W. S. Merwin, which the latter transformed into the art of a poem:

> I asked how can you ever be sure
> that what you write is really

any good at all and he said you can't

you can't you can never be sure
you die without knowing
whether anything you wrote was any good
if you have to be sure don't write

I think many people write because it is therapeutic and it is used to therapeutic ends, i.e. writing a letter to a dead parent with whom there are unresolved issues. Writing encompasses language, which encompasses our minds, defining everything from our psychology to our morals, answering the question *What do we want?* with our only means: our words. If clothes make the man, words do also, but not always truly, depending on the person interested in them. Many abusers are seducers. Many misspelled and misused sets of words can pop out courtesy of some celebrity, athlete, or politician, yet people will always admire him or her for their "game." If photography, and even "selfies," but really "selfishes," are becoming the new parameter of being human, it still is the case that, deep down, photos of us and photos of beautiful sunsets with us in them say very little about who we are. They are a dime a trillion dozen. Only words are a direct bloodline to our soul, and this is probably the reason for the equivocations of "everyone has a book in them." Everyone has words in them. Many sentences, too. *I love you.* Many of us often say it or write it in different languages. Diaries and forms of diaries are still important, especially the brief entries typed into social media. People kill and commit suicide over words, owing to their content.

Where does all this leave us? There can be no conclusion except that writing, aside from speaking, is the most human activity. It expresses like no other substance can. We need to be heard, and many people, even more now with the plethora of social anxiety disorders (most named in conjunction with the creation of the PC), can't speak to others for fear, embarrassment, or simple isolation. When we answer why we write, we reveal more about ourselves than we know. It is the intimacy available to so many who have no-one, or who have chosen written words to have their say. We write because we hate and love. It is a sacred act connecting us to distant civilizations and all the minds in history. Maybe I should write, "Y rite?" It is a magical act, no matter the misspellings.

REAL LIFE

Paris Doesn't Belong to Us

INVESTIGATIONS DON'T USUALLY begin on a honeymoon. *Honeymoon*—that compound, bloviated word from the sixteenth century, is more apt to be punctuated by pre-Happy Hour debauchery, raucous sex or imaginings of sex, the ribald, the body-centric, or the consumer-centric, buying things of temporary use, or maybe pleasure-boating, looking at clouds or the lack thereof while entwined on sand or the forest floor. All that rather than something signifying learning. *Inquiry*—the word has been fancified out of the French *enquerre*, yet it stinks of old moldy philosophical texts that few care to read, but will perspicaciously name. I wonder if Descartes or Kant or Hume—take your pick—ever began one of their inquiries without knowing what they wanted to accomplish, let alone what they felt.

Arriving in Paris for the third leg of our honeymoon, after Berlin and Amsterdam, I held a special affinity for the mythically named city we stepped into on an overly warm October Saturday. The Gare du Nord had the same hectic feel as the last time I'd visited, twelve years earlier. The Metro still used the same small tickets, and we veered through the same weekend droves populating a station serving as one of the nexuses of the city's train lines. As people ricocheted around, easefully cutting each other off and barrelling onward at light speed, I expressed unease to my new wife with a face straight out of the deck that spelled us in New York—a shared and wordless cocktail of screwy features standing in for cursing at all that is insurmountable.

Airbnb had so graciously garnered us a one-bedroom flat in the 11ᵗʰ Arrondissement, a mile from Père Lachaise and Notre-Dame, complete with a balcony and furnishings, a small metal table and two folding chairs, and we marched there with few presumptions except the desire to eat a real baguette with local brie. The balcony doors opened and there it was—the cherished view. One building looking out on the others, with most of the doors on those facing balconies open to catch the afternoon air. Down the street, greeny Square Maurice-Gardette was flooded with families, and in the alleyway below us a small film crew shot a scene of a woman walking and yelling, then yelling and crying. Magic.

The repast: simple fatty proteins put together from our quick shopping trip, along with a bowl of tomatoes doused in olive oil and spices. As we set to eating on the balcony, the Algerian mother of two next-door came onto her outcropping and saluted me with "Bonjour." I returned the greeting and she teethsmiled. Was this in recognition of her neighbor making a monetary killing or my foreign accent stamped onto the first word everyone learns? Both? Such is the mystery of the city.

Paris has gone through many incarnations. A Celtic tribe named it before the Romans settled the land, transforming the islands in the middle of the Seine into a garrison. After Christianity came, Clovis the Frank, the first Merovingian King, made it his capital in around 510, and by the twelfth century it had become the focal point of the country called "France." Since then, it has evolved to signify *cultus*, the Latin for the sacredness of a place. The monarchy rose so that by the late seventeenth century Louis XIV could say "L'état, c'est moi," but then, one hundred years later, revolt was followed by Napoleon, then more revolt, which led to Impressionism and the birth of cinema. In the early twentieth century, nearly all the important Modernists working in every artform lived or spent some time in Paris. It's called many things: the city of lights, the city of love. New Yorkers think they live at the center of the world, but if you put the land masses back together into a Pangaea, the northern hemisphere's center is Paris.

Soon we reclothed ourselves and walked down east-west streets with the sun's descending autumn angles filling our vision until we entered the Place des Vosges, where the neighborhood locals and a sampling of tourists packed themselves during the golden hour. We circled the white gravel and found an empty green bench. It was anchored near a sandbox where parents watched over children young enough not to be interested in their keepers' phones, but only in basting their hands in something altogether immediate and capable of manipulation.

We sat arms in hands. Apparently the right amount of rigidity and relaxation beamed from our irises and a Frenchman, who lived not in Paris, asked us directions. We didn't live in Paris either, we said with chagrin. Sitting quietly, our skin at ease, streams started. Though I had been in Paris for a good three months on a few different occasions, I'd never been with another—never in love or lust, never kissing. Paris—city of paramours—had always left me distraught amongst all those other lovers hotly conjoined. Every turn of my head in those days brought me a view of the true romance I cherished only because to be in that way seemed like the best way to be happy—incredibly easier than living alone and lying to myself about how I liked being solo so I could do whatever I wanted. No. I wanted to learn what it was like to be two. Sitting on those same benches, reading Proust or a biography of Van Gogh, what a sourpuss I must have seemed, systematically ogling examples of what I really wanted.

My love affair with Paris began with the usual pictures of its terrain through the films shot there. The monuments, the museums, the style. I watched Truffaut, I looked at Godard. *Bleu*, Krzysztof Kieślowski's first film in his *Trois couleurs* trilogy, arrested, as did Juliette Binoche's petite, intellectual, and alluring presence. Also, an uncle had moved to France and lived for some time in Paris. He regaled with stories of its mystique, its art, its nationalistic citizens, the German director Wim Wenders speaking at the Cinémathèque Française, and the quality of the light—how the sun hit the city in an entrancing way, to inspire new ways of seeing, quite unlike the rays cast on North America. Then I read droves of Samuel Beckett, who had lived in Paris most of his life, as well as James Joyce, and many writers of the Lost Generation. In the summer between my first and second semesters at the University of Wisconsin Milwaukee's film program, I wrote a screenplay set in a Paris I'd never visited, titling it *Julianna* by pasting the two main characters' names into one. I wrote it for two actresses I had the hots for, both physically and artistically: Binoche and Jennifer Jason Leigh. I had to see myself in conjunction with stars. I still faithfully watched the Oscars then, gauging success in terms of money and popularity. Shortly afterwards, I looked in on the screenplay game and found Binoche's agent's address and that of Tribeca Films—Robert De Niro's recently formed production company. I printed the ninety pages twice and mailed the two packages to New York, where they fell onto two desks and then promptly into each company's garbage.

In 1997, I went to Paris on a lark with some college friends, but I spent my time solitarily, frightfully clawing my way from site to site. Two years later I passed ten days walking through every nook, getting riveted by the many crannies, and flopping around the city's only campsite (in the Bois de Bologne) to save money. I muddled about with a young man from Poland who had served in the French foreign legion, one amongst the half-dozen other campers with off-kilter buzz cuts and taut muscular bodies who scoured the site for thrills, fools, and trouble. June days were spent going from the Eiffel Tower to Notre-Dame, from St. Eustache to the Centre Pompidou, and once squeezing into the Metro turnstile with this conman who had a thin strip of a moustache like an old-time used car dealer. I followed his lead and saved a few francs, though I nervously guarded the traveler's checks that I thought might interest him if he knew the amount I had to get through almost three months in Europe. He assured me we could go to Nice by train without a ticket—the conductor would simply send a bill to our home address. I lived on another continent, but that was all right. Airmail.

SO I RETURNED TO PARIS betrothed and woozy and weighty with fifteen years of extra living hammered into me. On our first full day there, a blown fuse in the kitchen sent us scampering to the nearby park, where I held my wife's iPhone at askew angles like a new-age necromancer to catch the free wifi and alert the owner to the situation. While waiting for his reply via email, I watched the people of the neighborhood frolicking and laughing. Two Russian men, now living in Paris, took over one ping-pong table, while two young French boys looked on helplessly from another. The boys were barely ten years old and each of their rallies lasted three hits at most. They approached the Russians just a few minutes into their match and asked if they wanted to play doubles. The elders didn't flinch and soon schooled the kids in more correct ways of holding and swinging their paddles. Fifteen minutes later, the much younger children of these men appeared with their mothers. By this time the French boys had left. The men had abandoned their match and tried to involve their real sons in the play. At this goodwill, I seemed to rise out of my seat a bit. It wasn't a major culture shock, but it was shock enough. As much as one can't easily extrapolate larger meanings from such a minor event in a neighborhood park, this, in combination with the contentment experienced at Place des Vosges, had me twisting in appreciation and nodding in censure at the selfish delinquencies I often see in my own country across the ocean—the pickpockets of Paris notwithstanding.

The dream ended later in the day as we walked to a dinner party in the 14th Arrondissement. Even Paris tends to thin out on Sunday evenings. The Jardin du Luxembourg had already closed and we kept walking south into Montparnasse near the Observatory, where we saw tents set up on the sidewalks, spaced every fifty feet or so. In the last light of dusk it was impossible to tell if they had just gone up or if they'd been anchored full-time; the city's homelessness has grown by leaps and bounds since 2008. In Manhattan, where I worked with the homeless, tents are insanely rare, and if one is pitched it's nowhere near a sidewalk. The police instantly confiscate them, especially after the Occupy Wall Street protests, yet throughout the winter of 2014 there was one along the side of the Mid-Manhattan Library, at 40th Street and 5th Avenue. As we weaved about Paris, passing one of the official, guarded entrances to the Observatory, the downtrodden were coming out into what was left of the light as if it was their day's first exposure, transferring materials from one bag to another, readying their necessities so they could garner a modicum of comfort hours on. A few had dogs who clamored wildly during a human disagreement. Misfortune has no borders.

We were on our way to the first and only social outing of the trip, a salon-style dinner given by an American expat and publicized widely enough for my wife to find it and reserve our places in a matter of minutes. We entered through a gate with others of our species, Americans, and followed a chorus of voices crackling uphill to the small yard outside the building where food was being prepared. The participants were from everywhere but France—America, England, Australia, Denmark, Israel. They seemed so happy. I didn't know if it was because they were able to speak more freely in their primary language or because of the free booze. Maybe the word "salon" had a mystifying effect on our souls. We weren't at just any party, but something birthed by tradition, in the city where the tradition started in the seventeenth century. Maybe the fact of Paris, and its international slant, set everyone into incontestable giddiness.

We spoke to four young Danes with Vietnamese blood, two of them brothers. One wanted to be a writer, or he was—he changed his mind mid-sentence—and wanted to know all about my process: what did I write, how much, and where did the inspiration come from? He was bright-eyed and young enough for me not to squash his happiness at being alive. His dreams were blustery and fighting to rise higher as the waters of responsibility rolled off his back. He could sleep or get stoned at a friend's house; he was pliable. After repeated inquiries, I told him to read as much as he could—writing is a long road and only spending years in thrall to it confers any sort of satisfaction with its creation. Answerless, he blinked his eyes and smiled. I think he heard me.

Later, we spoke with a mother and daughter who had come to Paris from England to celebrate the older woman's birthday. Their cheery resemblance was a monument to the process of life begetting life and their stories unfolded in answer to our questions. They both courted a new-age way of living and the mother raised her eyes at my knowledge of her mentor, Byron Katie—a darling of the North American market.

We sipped wine out of plastic cups and bandied about other names and different periods of our lives, breaking off only to refill our containers.

Soon, we lined up for dinner. The server of the chow commented on our marriage's twelve-and-a-half feet of height, and we sent his sugary banter back at him like a cat batting a toy away in order to snag it when nearly out of reach. We found a table outside and were soon joined by a twenty-something woman and a jazz guitarist some years older than her. They were coupled up, or at least courting in the familiar yet sloppy way of one person putting up with another because of his or her precarious place in society. The woman, with eyes as unfocusing as a doll's and a jolly round face, had just moved to Paris from Britain the month before, a fact belaboring her every fifth thought. Things were hard, but the expat host had offered her a place to stay—she alerted us that he not only owned the two-story structure, but also the one to the west of it. She didn't know how she would survive, but many people had her phone number and she checked her device and updated us all on the doings of her existence every few moments. The guitarist, an Israeli, was her foil, flirting and poking at her for the way she carried out plans, for how she spoke and behaved. He condemned her, then squeezed her hand in lieu of her more porcine parts, agitated at our presence, and answered our questions in ponderous, unenthusiastic tones, as no doubt he met loads of people at salons he attended only to be fastened to her. I'd seen it all before, indeed felt it, once holding his point-of-view all too keenly, waiting interminably for the woman to catch up to one's speed. Sadly, I assumed their pull and push would spell doom for any future stability. Once the keys were finally handed over, what then? I knew that answer now. It wasn't something to be communicated to a mere acquaintance, except in knowing looks and double entendres.

When she went away and he sat by himself with no straight person to play to, his voice circled back to its normality. As his shoulders came down, he explained his music and his station in Paris artfully, as a person unbeholden to anything but his self-sufficiency. So the lark of lust was more than an act for him—it was its own tidy unreality. He had so much, he did exactly what he wanted to do wherever he wanted to do it—but the core of him remained unsatisfied. A familiar jingle—one I thought I'd almost perfected throughout many of my forty earthbound years. When I met my wife three years earlier, my movements around cities always brought me to stand palsied on the most deserted street corners because of my "grass is greener" affliction. Would a less concupiscent life save me? Over time, I emptied myself of unease, but vestiges remained, accreting their proteins to rear up again on my more challenging days. I so well matched the jazz guitarist that all my descriptions of his fancy, his stridency, and his ruthless compunction were only poses I had autobiographically filched for fiction-pictures of others, but were, in truth, core aspects of the real me. On lazy days, while sitting on a bench and staring out at the sky over the last twelve seasons, I could uncover what made my blood ooze, what mystifications ruled my brain—what I was. Wallace Stevens stenciled this bleak understanding in his poem 'Tea at Palaz of Hoon':

> Not less because in purple I descended
> The western day through what you called
> The loneliest air, not less was I myself.

> What was the ointment sprinkled on my beard?
> What were the hymns that buzzed beside my ears?
> What was the sea whose tide swept through me there?

> Out of my mind the golden ointment rained,
> And my ears made the blowing hymns they heard.
> I was myself the compass of that sea:

> I was the world in which I walked, and what I saw
> Or heard or felt came not but from myself;
> And there I found myself more truly and more strange.

I could have told him, "Look, it can happen to you," and proffered the ringed finger for evidence. He'd caught our scent and asked after the reason for our European vacation. But five minutes with us and five without her was enough for him; he excused himself to find his lady.

EVEN BEFORE I KNEW the word's full imprimatur, I never wanted to make any trip I took touristic. I'd like to think that tourism is a post-war phenomenon that bloomed in the 1950s, since the 1959 *Webster's Dictionary* defines a tourist as "one who makes a trip for pleasure." Nowhere have I seen the stony, vapid tourist face (in the sense we understand it today) so mercilessly mocked as in Jacques Tati's *Playtime*, from 1967, with its bevy of travelers descending on Paris. Later, in a travel bureau, advertisements for London, the USA, Mexico, Hawaii, and Stockholm are seen placed side by side with their near-identical new-age skyscrapers dwarfing the other geographical characteristics of the various cultures.

I looked to another more recent film to imbue myself with what travel felt like further back in time, at least in the 1930s. Bernardo Berto-lucci's adaption of Paul Bowles' *The Sheltering Sky* shows Americans adrift in North Africa. Monied, the three principals have their heavy valises shipped with them on their boat and then in cars, as they give porters oversized African bills to move them in and out of their hotel rooms. They follow Lao-Tzu's advice: a good traveler has no fixed plans and is not intent on arriving. Being true to that dictum is something to experience at least once in one's life, but a task not easy to duplicate while married and when your source of income awaits a return after two weeks. As we travel these days, most all information and reservations are disseminated through the internet, but lacking a wireless connec-tion outside our apartment, we relied on the ubiquitous *Lonely Planet* to guide us with its *plan de ville*. In a nod to my more whirligig days of yore, we asked the friends of our Airbnb host what they recommended. They had to come to the apartment in order to restart the electricity that had shut down when one of the stove's faulty burners snapped off all the power. A woman named what could be expected: Montmartre, the Eif-fel Tower, and the Louvre. She probably didn't understand that we had visited these places years before, but it was her offhand remark that she lived in quiet, beautiful Bercy that sent us there the next day.

We wandered the two miles from our apartment, passing under the tracks of the Gare de Lyon, choking on car exhaust, and meandering the ins and outs of a highway (le Quai de Bercy) before becoming stranded on its narrow shoulder while vehicles whipped past, rushing north and south. Fortunately, my wife hadn't been beside me in 2001, when I ridicu-lously walked onto the shoulder of the Autobahn to hitchhike some sixty miles to Mannheim, Germany, helplessly watching as cars shot by at speeds of eighty or ninety miles an hour. Soon a ride did slow and stop, but it was a police officer, staunchly pronouncing that hitchhiking on the Autobahn was "verboten." He pointed me towards a steep grass em-bankment, which I was to walk up in order to rejoin the regular streets; there, the S-bahn would legally take me to my destination. I struggled on the ascent with too much weight in my backpack, including a duffel bag, and a much-too-large army regulation sleeping bag—old, moldy, and leaking feathers. This haul raises my eye and ire today, as I write with the hand connected to a slipped disc in my neck, a disc I started to sacrifice through such youthful excesses as these inglorious treks to save money and prolong my time in Europe.

Parc Bercy is one of the least visited parks in Paris, tourist-wise. Cre-ated in the mid-1990s, it was built on the site of some derelict wine ware-houses and now it holds a vineyard, an old railway line, and a menagerie of attractions amongst its three gardens, including fishponds, dunes, and two footbridges. The meandering trails are wide, and during our time there we hardly saw anyone else. Those people we did see were either exercising or pushing strollers. When we entered a fenced-off garden we encountered a few homeless Parisians, cocooned in gray- and nut-colored blankets and surrounded by many crinkly bags, plus a few other solitary souls. An older woman in a red sun hat was reading *un roman*. A younger man with a crew-cut smoked while holding his phone so close to his face he seemed readying to kiss it.

We found a bench facing a long garden leading to the vineyard and made a quiet lunch—cheese and baguette *à la carte*, snapping off the ends of a heavenly bread still fresh after its creation eight hours earlier. My wife is a proverbial foodie, but with too little time to read too deeply into the literature of food or even comment lightly at Yelp or any other gastronomic yardstick. She enjoys the thing itself and all through Amsterdam the promise of French bread and cheese set her swooning. Each morning in Paris, one of us would walk to the neighborhood boulangerie to purchase fresh baguettes and a few yeasty niblets, while the other heated water for tea and set the table, readying butter and cheese to be parsed.

Chic, 1970s confab apartment buildings overlook the park, then abruptly give way to Frank Gehry's silver-scaled Cinémathèque Française. It is probably fitting to watch a David Lynch film in France, especially *Mulholland Drive*. Originally, it was made as a pilot for a television series ultimately not picked up by ABC. That section now comprises about the first ninety minutes of the total one hundred and forty-six— most of the financing to shoot that last hour came from French backers, with Studio Canal distributing. I was also curious to take in the film surrounded by Parisians, who I believed were much more respectful towards the artform they had created and from whose ranks a gang of film nerds, chaperoned by André Bazin and Henri Langlois (founder of the Cinémathèque), and under the ægis of the movement's father figure, Roberto Rossellini, exploded film's possibilities near its golden anniversary—a Nouvelle Vague indeed. No popcorn or other refreshment was sold for consumption, and in my earlier French cinemagoing experiences only beer had been available as a concession to not doing anything but watch the screen. Even on a Monday afternoon, two hundred people showed up, many of them students; our host's friend had told us we'd come during a holiday week. And? Silence throughout, not even one of the cellphone squeaks or squawks that are *de rigueur* in present-day Manhattan and Brooklyn, though nothing trumps the MOMA and its many elderly and inconsiderate members who snore and endlessly sift through plastic bags to munch sustenance while viewing. It was fucking *Mulholland Drive*; if it made you fall asleep, you might not be of this earth. Afterward, I told my wife I didn't feel like we were in Paris while we watched it and, in Lynch-like symmetry, she concurred that she had thought the same thing.

On walking out, we found the capital enveloped in rain. We tottered through the wet streets, backtracking but avoiding the pit under the Gare de Lyon and, instead, examining the main rues of Bercy. Soon, the storm passed and the famous Parisian spectral light that is partly myth, partly continental latitude after millions of years of drift, and partly good publicity, embraced the objects in our vision. There were Claude Lorrain clouds and falling light, no rainbows, no magic hour yet, but something gabardined and imbricated in the sky's physiology, and we ascended to the Promenade plantée, a linear park so grand in its scope and engineering that it makes Chelsea's High Line look like something out of Legoland. Some speak of the French pushing culture and the arts harder than other peoples on the planet, and while walking the Promenade plantée and its nod to the ancient Roman aqueducts in the extended viaducts of the old trainway it is built on, it's hard not to stand in awe and applaud the design, the grandeur, and the beauty of the collective mind.

After sitting at a corner café, enjoying an aperitif, we found the Moroccan restaurant that had been both friend- and *Lonely Planet*-recommended. As it had only just opened, we were one of the first parties to be seated. The waiter, a blithe Moroccan with close-cropped hair and a smile forever not coming to full term, immediately sussed our dithering accents and began to speak simple French, even breaking into playtime English for our cognitive benefit. We were trying to present as thoughtful individuals, not ugly Americans. But our essays only ended us up in the same grimy bucket. My wife had also taken the lead in ordering for us at restaurants, our main interplay with the French, though I was proud of carrying on two volleys of a conversation with three elderly and respectably-dressed Parisians outside the gates to the Cimetière de Montmartre about how the grounds were temporarily closed, repeating their reason with aplomb while nodding my head ignobly—I think they said vandalism, but I couldn't confirm it via the internet.

The large restaurant, bereft of music (an American staple), quickly filled to capacity and the hum and swerve of speech roiled my senses. In between nips of khobz bread, I felt my soul retreat with one excruciating step after another into my favored teenage comatose ground zero. Was it the food? Heartburn? My heart? My wife? Since I had taken

French in college and she in high school, my competitive side judged her taking over the ordering as demeaning. Though I had little love for the tradition of the male species leading the way, I reminded my inner brat that I had married a very upright and outspoken woman, a woman raised by very verbal parents on Manhattan's 86th Street just off River-side Drive in the dangerous eighties and early nineties. She'd been in the shit since consciousness. "Take charge" is one of those insidious cover letter catchphrases most seekers must brand themselves—it's a reflex, a lick of lips to show the disseminators you are human and you have your credential baloney down. She embodies "take charge," and I gladly presume my attraction and affection for her grows out of this vir-tue. Yes, please, someone, do "take charge." For how else do things get done, careers get forged, or money get earned with regular increases, but by a combination of education, wiles, and presence, the accoutrements of an easier citizenship? She is a hero, a role model, and though I have the edge in height, I often look upward, and not always because I am regularly sedentary and she is eminently in motion. If "money" wasn't so scuzzy a term, I would aver love does accrue. As love works, it becomes more knowing and robust. It is a journey, but perhaps it finds its better metaphor in the toils of the mollusca phylum, or slug. At the sight of a slug on the side of a mountain, retrograde upon a manmade trail, two thousand feet up, one wonders: how did it get there? where did it come from? At that speed it had to have been born nearby, never knew sea-level, never knew sea. Its sheen belying its camouflage in certain types of light—it moves imperceptibly toward some more copacetic destination than a denuded strip of ground trod by \$100-to-\$300 water-resistant foot-wear made in China. If one glances, it might not seem so impressive, but linger a little and shards of brilliance occur. This is the love I find myself in. The love that doesn't call itself out routinely, but lives on, born by the intimacy of close encounter, fully satisfied by its regularity.

It can be a tussle to claim such a position after the poison of past years. For a spate of minutes, I can tend to remember all that is not good, or at least all that is dissatisfactory or potentially so. In my forgetting the recently hewn title of courtship turned to marriage, a new magnetic tape of evil aphorisms constituted the din in my head. I'm not a foodie so much as a consumer of food, irreverently mixing cultures and their tra-ditional dishes. I believe I had chicken cartouche, but cartouche is Pal-estinian. It was served at our wedding. Let's just say I had chicken and there was red wine. Potatoes also made an appearance. When I think back on that meal, I keep seeing people occupying tables that had amaz-ingly been empty when I looked up just before. I saw them speaking, I saw their harmony—whether the young couple, the two older (seem-ingly gay) friends, one of them eyeing me every time I resolved in his direction (I had temporarily forgotten, based on years of daily examples, how a person can feel another person, friend or not, looking at them in a certain range of close space). Then there was the family of four, the family of three, and the refined couple with the husband, neck buttoned by a dainty cravat, performing not-too-obsequious exploratories of wine until his pursed lips purled a medium-sized assent to the waiter who was not his favorite. My blinkered analysis of their stations flared and floun-dered, charged by my own delinquent envy, corroded and rusted by years of character assassinations. I wished my table were as talkative as theirs, all I required was a simple pass of hand and I could remove the chronic dust I carried and plant myself in my more pressing engagement. But I told myself I wanted not just my wife and I to coalesce, but everyone to elope with everyone in the restaurant. The end-point of this furious mental activity remained the same—I sat at the table mildly irritable and unable to express anything of substance except directives to pass some-thing or curt comments on the quality of the fare.

The hurdy-gurdy of my perceptions in concert with the one I love is a hard case to argue. I've often thought it better to retain the inner tor-ment and not reveal anything to the other party. This is an antiquated way of compartmentalizing my feelings and surely the reason some of my most important interpersonal relationships have become belabored. I've had many of my most passionate conversations with other people in my head. Their true personas might have been relieved that I didn't supply their responses too often or in too much detail, except for, "'All right,' she said, gingerly." Years of workshops, therapy, and general reparenting have gone toward rectifying this isolationist fetish. Fifty-five minutes into the dinner, I began to string words together—sentences carrying sensations close to those craggy ones that had assaulted me. Like a baby deer goo-ily stepping from the womb, I could walk, I could even awkwardly strut in a language resembling the one I portrayed underneath my brain pan. I could share, I could amuse, I could desiccate my warranted hijinks in favor of face-to-face. With her help, I came back to the atmosphere.

Later that evening, after we ascended the five floors heavily laden with cockroach repellent, we brushed our teeth and laid down. Before separating to our respective sides for sleep, we held each other briefly. I smelled the face of my wife. It is a scent like no other I've encoun-tered in the world. Her soul's dishabille—soapy, sweaty, and sweet—with a smell standing for her large eyes, distinguished nose, and pretty lips more than the sight of them. We stared and then we kissed. Her part of this exchange—for I think it must work this way, but never ask me if I'm right—is her nightly letter to me. It is at once support and counsel saying, *I know you are having some stony feelings and you can't necessarily express them all, but know I love you as you love me. Thank you.*

I quickly thanked her in my mind. We were happy. Tomorrow will be a fun day, I told myself.

ON TUESDAY, RAIN would be interspersed with sun as we embarked on a day dominated by parks. Parc des Buttes-Chaumont—an awing escapade, no matter man-made—was only a few miles away through the nearby neighborhood of Belleville. On the way, we walked the redoubtable Tuesday street fair, a place of farmers and hucksters alike selling fruit, fish, and fashion, including bounties of cheap bras. It wasn't my first choice for an excursion, but does one truly see a culture until one sees its people buying things? As I looked on, I couldn't fool myself—most of the patrons were just like the grabtastic, rushing, snippy types one rubs up against at American flea markets, rummage sales, dollar stores, and discount megaplexes like Walmart. Similarly, they had a makeup two-thirds elderly. We passed women with their fold-up rolling baskets 5% filled and came upon the odd shuffling portly man in a beret and pastel scarf damaging two times as many plums with his hearty squeezes than the three he'd buy. The adrenaline rushes of paying less for a fillet of salmon or garnering a sweatsuit for half the cost of the respective Fnac or JC Penney are unaccountably the same, irrespective of the land or language, since we are all taught what money means before we are four feet high.

With a few clementines for the road, we wended our way uphill, coming across a surprise park before reaching the main attraction. The lower stages of Parc de Belleville begin in what seems a small rhomboid of grass, but, upon climbing, one comes into its expanding bounty and the modernized upper reaches, displaying exquisite Marienbadish shrubbery amidst winding paths, culminating in a large white platform offering a view of Paris comparable to that from Sacré-Coeur in Montmartre. On the overlook, a teenager sat on a bench with no device or distraction in his hands, only a quizzical expression pressed onto his face as if an unfriendly ghost had alerted him to a fact he couldn't comprehend. To play the valiant husband, I moved between him and my wife, readying myself against a more untoward unfolding. Instantly, he proved me right and quickly stood at attention, looking askew at the bright sky. Then, he scratched himself where one wouldn't want to imagine another's hand scrounging, especially in view of a playground. I never alerted my love to the potential pest—once dubbed an "instigator" in my youth, I've turned more coquettish about warnings, including "shoulding" on people, and the "you better's" bespeaking my Midwestern roots. These warts of worrying only aped my parents' hypochondriacal pronouncements, which once so irked me that I wished my fingernails long enough to puncture my arms to the bone. His exposed biceps were as thick as pythons but hungry for exercise, and his eyes made erratic revolutions, equivocating about his presence in the park, and, indeed, in Paris, in Europe, and finally the solar system. He receded behind a white pillar and let his left arm hang loose as he worked on a remedy for his incongruities.

We then traipsed through more winding streets, still fingering the *Lonely Planet* maps, but at times we were unable to decode our exact location until a more detailed *plan* appeared at the head of the stairs to the underground or at a bus shelter. We crept on, absorbing the relative calm of the hilly neighborhood—past a school with closed doors containing the energy of a few hundred children caught in the matrix of learning before the explosion of recess, past a telecom worker on a ladder to the lines, past a patisserie with a window display out of Norman Rockwell. Two young women walked with their bookbags to the nearest university library, their hair spritzed with strawberry-scented sculpting gels, their wrists wet with the daub of perfume the magazines told them would last until well after supper. A yammering black cat eased itself into and out of its owner's fenced-in yard, finally extending like taffy before brushing our legs with its flank.

These couldn't have been the streets of New York because there were no beeping horns or other ugly noises like booming music or jackhammers (these are plentiful in Paris, just elsewhere) and no homeless people with their renowned continuations of conversations they are destined to keep recounting, often tales of umbrage at some unseen other who resembles a father or friend (in spirit, not in body). I mistakenly told my wife that this hilly neighborhood was the one where Jacques Rivette filmed a good portion of *Celine et Julie vont au bateau* in the year of my conception. I added that maybe the incline up which Celine hilariously follows Julie during the film's famous opening scene—a practically wordless chase—was only around the corner. Indeed, my wife had only seen the first five minutes on YouTube because the film is criminally not available on DVD in the United States. In truth, the chase and most other parts were filmed in Montmartre, a place we avoided because of Sacré-Coeur's tourism. Rivette might have delighted in such a distortion, though, since many of his Paris films are overlaid with references to the occult, secret messages, and metaphysical maps, especially *Out 1*,

Duelle, and *Pont du Nord*. But his good friend and my filmmaker obsession of the preceding year, Eric Rohmer, was the man who brought us to
the Parc des Buttes-Chaumont. At least he was half the reason.

Fifteen years before, owing to I know not what, I came upon the park
with an Israeli man I met at a youth hostel. Sela lived in Tel Aviv, where
he'd just completed his two compulsory years in the military. As tall as
me, he had a stoic face, imperial as a Piero Della Francesa, and a mass
of black hair harnessed into an exquisitely braided ponytail. On one occasion he had misunderstood my plans for the day and waited for me at
the hostel, which stranded him from his room because of the midday
closure for cleaning. The confusion wasn't due to a language mishap; it
had more to do with him being a very genuine individual who felt a little
lonely encountering Paris by himself, preferring the company of guys
babbling while sightseeing.

On a hot June day we had walked about the park and followed a
gaggle of Nordic girls to the Temple de la Sibylle, a miniature version
of the famous ancient Roman Temple of Vesta in Tivoli, Italy, a sort of
standalone cupola at the top of the mound of earth, two hundred feet
high in the middle of the park's artificial lake.

Together we performed the clichéd scene of two single, hormonal
men in their early twenties ribbing each other about the scenery and
not that of the park. The inevitable questions were exchanged: "What is
your type?" (both physically and behaviorally—a query part and parcel
of many Rohmer films), "Is there a special someone back home?" and
"What will your life be like once you find 'the one?'" And so we gazed
at milky skin and Maybellined eyes (though I preferred those *sans* accoutrements—living then in Eugene, Oregon, my eyes coveted that city's
ubiquitous "nature girl" look as my desired form of beauty). What we
saw engendered other questions and different expectant and unexpect-
ant moods, and later, on a hill, we relaxed with the knowledge that someday we would fall in love, someday we could cling to a body in public,
and preferably in Paris, where couples kissed more often per hour than
the chorus of "Fuck yous" in the streets surrounding the Port Authority in commensurate time, and, after an exchange of addresses, that we
would toast each other on either side of the ocean when that day came.
"Be sure to visit if you are in . . ." We were so young.

Up there, near the cupola, on a cloudier October day, my wife and I
saw another group of young women who had probably been in the world
for less than three years on the day that Sela and I had made those vows.
They stood under the small dome, handholds making them into a circle,
while laughing and singing some shared paean to their friendship. When

they left we sidled over to the landmark before another tourist could and looked out on the surrounding arrondissement.

We had not yet come to the Rohmer half of the reason for our visit. In our three-and-a-half years of relationship we had made it a practice to visit certain sites ingrained on film. For instance, *Vertigo's* Mission San Juan Bautista in California; we'd tried not to feel too disappointed when we saw that the bell tower from which two different women fall was in fact never really there, only a special effect. Over the last year I'd tracked down as many of Rohmer's films as I could, to the point of illegal downloads and ordering DVDs from Britain. One of those discs was 1980's *La Femme d'Aviator*. Six months earlier we'd watched the grainy copy (Rohmer shot it on 16mm; when blown up to 35mm, grain builds to Seurat-like dots) and we'd been swept up in the long, proto-Hitchcockian Paris chase that contains a Buster Keatonesque shadowing. A young, pimpled postal worker has just found out that a man (an aviator) has been having an affair with his girlfriend. A few hours later, he comes across this man with another woman who may or may not be his wife. The young man follows the couple onto and off a bus and into Parc des Buttes-Chaumont, while a perspicacious young woman from the bus accompanies him. When the first couple reaches the park's lagoon, the young man keeps watch from a distance, and when the young woman figures out who he is spying on, she demands to help and walks over to them. What follows is a hilarious scene in which she approaches a Japanese-American couple and tries to get them to take a Polaroid of her in front of the oblivious couple on the grass behind her—the proof to puzzle out the other woman's identity.

We played detective and tried to find the area in the park where the couples had been, though Rohmer had filmed *La Femme d'Aviator* some thirty-five years earlier. The thing was, the lagoon went around the entire moat, and when we came across the same perspective of the young couple looking at the other couple on the far bank, I snapped a picture of my wife, though no lilypads spread themselves across the surface of the water as they had when first filmed. Soon we walked about and found a bench on which to eat our fruit and then, in a moment that duplicated Rohmer, a torrential rain started to fall and pushed us to find shelter, just as the couples abscond before a storm catches them on their way out of the park.

The rain seemed to pass and we walked on, but when it started again it ushered us into the closest restaurant for a late lunch. Even some Parisian restaurants have succumbed to hanging a large TV ominously in the eating area. Over and over looped stock footage of the chairman of Total

Oil, killed in a plane crash in Moscow, momentarily eclipsing Ebola for the top headline. After eats, we took the elevated 6 train across the Seine into the vicinity of the Eiffel Tower, making a bread stop at the renowned Poilâne. What can be said of the Tour Eiffel besides the first sentence of Roland Barthes' eponymous essay: "Maupassant often lunched at the restaurant in the tower, though he didn't care much for the food: *It's the only place in Paris, he used to say, where I don't have to see it.*"

The sky had grown bright by the time we landed in the 7th Arrondissement. We thought we could easily espy the tower, but Maupassant (as Barthes admitted) had exaggerated—there proved to be at least a mile's worth of places where one could not see it and so we shuffled on like the penitents in a new circle of tourist hell, where one carries both the indignity and the shame of being two of the few people on the planet not to have closed in, viewed, and captured one of its most recognizable monuments. When we finally did, we bowed and snapped away as incredible winds, the remnants of Atlantic Hurricane Gonzalo, swept over the large grassy plain to the south of the tower. I asked my wife if she wanted to get closer, even go directly underneath, where we'd find most of the action (buses, etc.), but it didn't interest her. After we shooed away young women in search of money for a bleeding-heart cause (money that would never reach poor souls) we walked eastward to Montparnasse. As before, however, the cemetery there had been closed; I would have to pay my respects to Eric Rohmer and Susan Sontag on another trip. We followed the glare of the sun to the Jardin du Luxembourg, where, just as we eased into slanted green chairs, the sky colored into a bruise and rain fell for fifteen minutes. Then the sun shone again for picture-taking on the curved cement arms rounding the gardens like the outer decorations of a shield.

Wandering back across the Left Bank, we walked the narrow blocks near the Sorbonne, past small expensive apparel shops where a pair of women's shoes cost more than our two high-speed train tickets from Amsterdam, and past other specialty stores including a number devoted to antiquarian books. Only after I followed my wife into these establishments did everything about my person seem ill-fitting. My fifty-dollar coat from Uniqlo, my discount Merrells from DSW, my $16 haircut from Luigi at Astor Place Hair. The male and female handlers at these stores had the skin of porcelain sculptures and from that skin I extrapolated their existences in nanoseconds. They enjoyed their café (one couldn't say "drink" of such a minute cup of liquid) with the distancing brio of the acculturated, they spoke of the trips they took each year to the Alps and to Spain, and they had sex late at night with the aftertaste and acids of fifty-dollar dishes coursing through their blood. Years before, in another arrondissement, I had walked into a small museum dressed in my 1999 outerwear, that is to say an ensemble fabricated by my station in life—I made minimum wage—and my place of residence, Eugene, a socio-economic bubble that held nothing against holes, screwy pastels, or crossknits in one's rags. Dressed in some unseemly outfit of earth tones, I passed two well-heeled men who worked at the institution. They spoke to each other garrously, but as I hove into view the eyes of the more sophisticated locked on my form and I saw his head move up and down as he pored over everything I was. This motion ended with a strong look of dissatisfaction that he pinioned to my soul across our eyebeams and I convulsed like a David Lynch shibboleth, as I was now ruled by his implanted disregard. Outside of my parents and a few lovers, that was the first time I had the mind of another person inside me, feasting on my ego after an easy kill. Years on, it remains a moment, or rather a confluence, that stays stapled to me like a lifetime achievement demerit slip. No matter what I do or where I go, the stain of that delicately cutting encounter lingers; the man's glare pointing at me like a convict flaunting a knife at the next heart he will harm. The incident is deep set, disappearing for a few years and then rearing up again as if it has only gained strength in its period of dormancy.

To embrace the Saint-Germain quarter of the city, we sought out Les Deux Magots, emblazoned in our guidebook thus: "Its name refers to the two *magots* (grotesque figurines) of Chinese dignitaries at the entrance. . . . Sit on the inimitable terrace. . . . Sip its famous shop-made hot chocolate, served in porcelain jugs." Stein, Joyce, Hemingway, and Sartre all went there when they were not so well-known, escaping a dim limelight only cast after success. To sit in the dining room, given our blue jeans and the shortage of euros or applicable credit in those jeans' pockets, would have required a caliber of effrontery we didn't possess. We took a table under the vinyl plastic shield, facing the nave of the Church of Saint-Germain-des-Prés. A stiff-faced waiter in his sixties, petite and fey with thin wire-rimmed glasses and a bow tie over his white serving coat (the regalia of any stereotypical barista at a fine establishment), mercifully listened to our order of a café and a cocoa—the most affordable items, six and nine euros respectively. The patrons were what one expects when paying astronomical prices for things McDonald's and Dunkin' Donuts sell for a song—there were certainly tourists about, and also Parisians, but everyone was there to look or to be looked at. Fine fittings, expensive outfits, the latest phones, the latest primary-colored handbags, eyes glazed by bullish calories, skin as soft as butter left out overnight. The elderly man next to us, who had padded in with multiple bags of papers and periodicals, decorated his table with a hand-sized journal and a shiny pen with an ink fuselage, though he did not indite, but fixed his eyes in an easterly direction, toward the church and those hundreds of people passing by in an early evening growing cold. An American mother and daughter came in and sat before us at the table by the window, though the mother could have been an older sister in a certain light—her beige leather boots still smelling of the box that had housed them on the Rue Dauphine the day before. Blonde from blonde, they were clearly chuffed at their outing and held a phone high to capture both of their faces, each one close upon the other in happiness at Les Deux Magots. What could these people be thinking about us? Though only a few feet away, did they even see us? If they did, what did they see us as? A married couple? Two people in love? Two people at odds? Two Americans at odds? Two Americans against all odds?

The popular cliché about the French, a cliché restated by my countrymen, is that they think Americans don't know how to live. We are savage and deficient in certain refined aspects pertaining to composure, compunction, and, certainly, to culture and its expression. As I primped for my wife's pic of me, tipping my miniature cup of café with my pinky out and cheeks sucked in, I came close to being the pitiful, ugly American who mimes the etiquette he is destined never to possess. At times, my wife and I act goofy together—there is no other word for the spirit of our connection. The best approximation in French is *joie de vivre*. This goofiness enables the easefulness that is our love. I told the audience at our wedding that this was the most important reason we were before them. Once I might have dreamt of sitting in Les Deux Magots, sipping coffee and smelling the cigarettes of a proper philosophically-enamored female, a.k.a. Susan Sontag, but I am happy to report the following: this is not my life. Wrongly, I once thought I needed someone to discuss Plato with in order to be happy. Uniformity is what I have been looking for all along.

A VISIT TO the Louvre is a typical thing to check off on a trip to Paris, making it something not so much to be enjoyed but endured for bragging rights. "And we went to the Louvre!" How perfect and how perfectly ineffectual a sentence. What happened? How did it feel? I had been there in 1999, at the height of my interest in art history. Fifteen years picks at and pulls the perceptions and unbuttons all kinds of rewards and regrets—the DNA of ever-shifting perceivability. The Vermeers once seen were seen, but not greatly savored. Nicholas Poussin's *The Rape of the*

Sabine Women only had potency because of the subject, not so much due to the draughtsmanship, the art behind the motion of all those bodies—in short, the form. What happened at the Louvre can't stay at the Louvre. It's a too-friable set of impressions. In some ways it's not unlike a visit to a great national park in the western states. It's that big, it's that large, lengthy, and exhaustive, and people-heavy, too, in front of the main attractions.

After walking the stone courtyard alongside militarized police assembled for a show of force, we came to see a friend's prediction of multiple hour-long lines being true as hundreds of souls queued by the glass pyramid. We had purchased tickets in advance, giving us immediate access, and so we soon coursed through the Sully and Denon wings, taking in sculptures with noon light flooding the windows. The Met has its Vermeers and its Egyptian temple, and the MOMA has its Picassos and its high stairways with a suspended helicopter near floor three, but they themselves aren't temples to art like the Louvre. In New York cars get too close, and horns and sirens mar the atmosphere, but, in Paris, the world's most visited museum is occluded from such disturbances. Sounds can't reach it because of its gargantuan stature, along with the fact that the Jardin des Tuileries, due west, is nearly as wide and as mammoth. All of this serves as the foundation for a transcendent experience of art.

We went to all that would be expected, the *Venus de Milo* and *Psyche Revived by Cupid's Kiss*, plus the busts of many a Roman to whom history had not been kind enough to pre-introduce us. At Michelangelo's two slave sculptures, created when no European had ventured north of the Rio Grande, we paused, and quickly became entranced. *The Dying Slave.* We crept around to other angles where differing casts of light lit the marble, trying to see how it breathed. Rapacious in our attentions, studying and studying, as with the Vermeers in Amsterdam and the Da Vincis to come, the stone placed us in the hard gem-like flame state that Walter Pater pronounced the essence of artistic experience. We were it and it was us for those moments. As we stood near *The Dying Slave*, life itself became more vivid, more gratifying, and sort of explicable. We fell in love with living. I took note of people passing this stone in the hall. Some recognized the very erect and carnal presentation of the sculpture, as if the slave stood in ecstasy about leaving life and abandoning all his travails, and so they thumbed many a pic. Others glossed over it like men passing perfume ads in a women's magazine.

At the Louvre, long before the time we spent there, Pater had set eyes on Leonardo's *La Giaconda* (the *Mona Lisa*) and said: "The presence that rose thus so strangely besides the waters, is expressive of what in the ways of a thousand years men had come to desire. . . . She is older than the rocks among which she sits; like the vampire, she has been dead many times, and learned the secrets of the grave . . ." I'm not sure how he'd react to the hysteria accompanying the painting today, but if I had seen him there I would have declared that if had he not written so persuasively and succinctly about her/it/Leonardo, there might be peace and no bulletproof glass, nor a five-foot moat between the canvas and the first row of spectators. The parade of people taking pictures of themselves in front of the painting shouldn't have surprised me.

Today, envy via ocular proof is at a premium. This proof makes the poor and middle-class temporarily rich, almost at the level of the obscenely wealthy. We can now easily manufacture our own permanence, often next to a person, an object, or a much valued vista, and cast it out to the world in mere seconds. Why does this commonplace behavior, so widespread and almost essential, trouble me? The thing itself in this case, the art, becomes a decoration, a large fly on the wall, the dressing surrounding the photographer's real subject—the self—whether in a foreground or background position. This ulterior subject can be none other than complicit in the version of our life as we frame it.

After a few hours immersed in art, we went to lunch less than a mile away at Bouillon Chartier, a spot my new father-in-law counseled us to visit. Though the fare was excellent, I found it more of a sustenance builder for returning to the Louvre. The working man's meal had existed here since 1896 and our waiter dutifully wrote out our order on the white disposable tablecloth. The Choucroute Alsacienne, a platter of meats including ribs, kielbasa, hot dogs, and boiled ham, touched up with garlic, Riesling, sauerkraut, bay leaves, and juniper berries, was placed before me and I kvetched. Twenty minutes of chewing into these potent meats ended with the white flag of fullness raised before even half the provisions could be consumed.

On Wednesdays, the former palace of kings stays open until ten o'clock at night. Able-bodied, we ringed our long arms around each other's waists and re-entered by skipping a smaller line, but still a line. We dropped our bags and coats at the same apparel check, and again escalated to the Denon wing's favored Salle des États. My wife wanted to see if the crowd at the *Mona Lisa* had broken, but though the museum had thinned out, the room still swooned. At the prospect of Brueghel, Vermeer, and Dürer, we drifted to the wealth of fifteenth-to-seventeenth century pieces, proceeding room by room, finding Dieric Bouts' *The Lamentation of Christ*, ca. 1460, a work of unperturbed beauty and a piece I cried out at, inwardly, due to its mention in William Gaddis' *The Recognitions*, a book I had just invested myself in for the second time.

Nearing seven o'clock, we reversed course nationalistically and went toward the grand museum's specialty: French paintings. Soon we came to an artist who had a large room of his own, perhaps the greatest French painter before the Impressionists: Nicolas Poussin. The last name trills, with the tongue lightly resting on the diphthong before a rush of *sss*'s takes it to another nasally termination, as beautiful to look at as to pronounce correctly. With a leering half-step we entered his main room (there are others; the Louvre has the world's largest collection of his work) and I saw his large canvases bedecked with light blues, yellows, and oranges placed amongst landscapes green with vegetation or beige and browned with road or architecture—all except the medium close-up self-portrait. Years earlier, my uncle had hooked me on Poussin, especially in regard to his place in the controversial book *Holy Blood, Holy Grail*, which alleges the existence of a secret society called the Priory of Sion, whose grandmasters supposedly included Leonardo da Vinci, Isaac Newton, and Victor Hugo. A key painting for them was Poussin's *Et in Arcadia Ego*, showing some shepherds looking at a tomb; the other version of this painting, made twenty years later, is in Britain. This work references the legend of Christ's life in the south of France, where, according to the book's thesis, he moved with Mary Magdalene and started a family. Jesus died in France, so the story went, and the tomb in the painting, etched with the Latin words *Et in Arcadia Ego* ("Even in Arcadia [paradise], there am I [death]"), was not only a reminder of death in paradise but also a portrait of Christ's resting place. A few feet away was *The Rape of the Sabine Women* (similarly, there are two versions of it) with its parade of pastel reds, oranges, yellows, blues, and golds, painted in 1637. In Poussin, the main noun is classicism, or a high regard for the ancient works of art found around the Mediterranean. This regard is embodied in most of his subjects and in the formation of the figures, many of which echo the sculptures of the ancients, and it is not surprising that Poussin spent much of his life in Rome.

We walked back and forth among these paintings, muttering this and that about the color, the drama, and the rhythm caught on the canvas, when I realized we were the only people in the room. A young woman in heels sauntered through and stopped for a few seconds in front of one of twenty paintings there, then she exited. To be alone in the Louvre for so long; if I called it ecstasy, if I thought it felt as if we owned those works—but such surmises would be so remote from my true feelings. We were witness to the artist's output—years and years of work, years of rising every day to make preparations or fresh attempts, to touch up the canvas, or to apply the final layer of varnish over the surface. Poussin's works, unlike those birthed by Gauguin in the humidity of Tahiti, have survived well. One could imagine the untempered self-portrait Poussin painted with palette and brush remaining in good keeping, even under a sheen of clear mountain water.

On reflection, and through the impressions I harbor, I'm able to pull back to the past, like an arrow from a bow, and see how the fact of work, its endpoint in a museum, and the edification one takes from art, altogether leave me more grateful for my life, and married life at that. Years before, when traveling and then living in Europe, I had visited museum after museum, and though the experiences were remarkable, I eventually tired of walking alone through those large halls in Bilbao, Grenoble, Karlsruhe, and the other usual suspects. Art, without discussion, could only go so far. My looks of longing gradually left the art, the Zurbaráns in Grenoble, the Gruenwalds in Karlsruhe, and attached themselves to the women I fancied, the espied couples sharing seeming happiness. More than anything, I've wanted to share my experiences with others, especially experiences of art and nature. I used to accomplish this by showing people movies, but while migrating I sought other avenues. If I had company in a museum, and since I did, one could engage with the work and then each other. Though we spoke of Poussin, I can't recall what we said. This one struck us, but another offered something very different. The more we spoke, the more I opened up, and though we'd been in the Louvre for nearly five hours I remembered only then that there was something I wanted to show her. The oversize French paintings are kept in their own mammoth room with Theodore Gericault's *The Raft of the Medusa* as the centerpiece. The enormous canvas, sixteen feet wide by twenty-three high, which we'd seen at Gericault's grave at Père Lachaise, looked as pristine as the day it had been painted. Had it been restored? Five years after our visit to Paris, it would be fully two hundred years old.

Weeks later, at home, while sitting on a couch purchased at a time when neither of us knew the other existed, a couch whose fibers used to be fire-engine red but had faded to a more bland hue, I thought of this phrase: "My heart is heavy." A helpless phrase uttered by who knows how many characters and people caught up in life. A cliché of a phrase, a naïve flick of a poetic wrist, but nevertheless apt. Why? Plato had made me cry. I had shed tears over the death scene in the *Phaedo*, where Socrates carries on about what he believes to be the prospect of the soul after death, its afterlife, and this in his last hours, before drinking the hemlock that will kill—his penalty for corrupting the youth of Athens.

See What I See

Ideas expressed artfully and meaningfully make my heart heavy, as the words that explicate them coruscate through my many memories of life. The moment of this pour over is imperceptible and I am grateful that there is no camera privileged enough to record it. While reading to myself, a key is turned in a very tender sector of my being—some memory or sensation fills me, or somebody does something I have done, or does the exact opposite—and the space between me and the text is broken. I've been intruded upon, which is to say I've learned or felt something I didn't expect.

Reading Plato and plumbing the depths of philosophy betters one's life in a way that is similar to how marriage improves communication and overall wellbeing. I do know many marriages end, but that's not my fault. If we keep listening to statistics the world will be an even more craven, robotic place. The heart can beat out of control and it can beat in temperate measures. Even someone who has never seen Paris knows love and knows how to be happy. Even we, who now carry countless shards of experience and have matured enough to know Paris doesn't belong to us, even we understand a truthful marriage is as strong as a sequoia and a honeymoon doesn't stand in for a lifetime. It might not even be the beginning of intimacy.

On Eating Combos

I WOULDN'T THINK I'd feel discounted by others over what I eat, though I've come to expect it from what I read. Just the other day, I responded—aptly, I thought—to my wife's charge of only wanting to read great art and not *Gone Girl* or Stephen King, no matter how popular, by pointing out her insistence at never wanting to consume a sandwich made by the Subway Fast Food Restaurant Company. On occasion, stranded in the city, I will partake of a foot-long tuna (not toasted) while she refuses to ingest the admittedly icky bread and plastic-tasting tomatoes and sweet peppers. Now what could ever be the difference here? One goes into the mind and the other the body, but they both touch spirit, which holds dominion over all organs.

My lifestyle choice, reader of great literature, isn't so outlandish. Sure, I started on Stephen King and other bestsellers, but as I've grown up I've been drawn to quite different sensibilities, becoming a "page-hugger" rather than a "page-turner." That is, I glorify each individual sentence for its words, and for the "world" or "soul" revealed in its architecture, something the late William H. Gass advanced. Along with this, I'll admit to the hypocrisy of ordering my mind over my body's intake of garbage, including the ignoble Combos. Most of us have our lubberly indulgences and ways of thinking. Mine affect the longevity of my body, but at least I'll be quoting Shakespeare left and right before I cash in my chips.

When a co-worker saw me with Combos Baked Snacks, made by Mars, Incorporated, for the third time in two weeks, she described how she'd seen Combos for sale at a highway rest stop and told her fiancé how she works with a man who likes to eat Combos for breakfast—and I do arrive a bit tardy to the office at eleven, after my early-morning driving duties. Everyone in the office laughed. Even I had to (on the inside) and replied with the punchline that I didn't want to be known as the man who likes to eat Combos for breakfast. (Did it matter that I had chosen the Pizzeria Pretzel flavor on two of those occasions? That's something I'd have to admit had more connection to the pizzazz of the Italian word "Pizzeria" and less the taste. Good job, marketers.) Then I kept the neurotic plates spinning with more one-liners, both for attention and to make others laugh in lieu of having my feelings hurt—a most complex Freudian complex. Yes, at some level, quite apart from my proud donning of the highbrow label in literary matters, I do care what people think of me in terms of food. Should I have parried, stating what only I could know? That I really planned on buying one of the five or six types of tofu, or seitan, or hummus and avocado (why are those two always bedfellows?) sandwiches that are sold, amazingly, at 7-Eleven, but the store I visited didn't carry them anymore.

Combos aren't really a guilty pleasure because there is little guilt— besides when more than one person judges my diet—and because they don't offer much pleasure either, as I don't seem to be afflicted with the unassailable cravings for junk food—salt, grease, or sugar—which I hear aired by many of those who were born after the Johnson administration. I don't need Combos like I require other vitamins, and although each bag is stamped with the pride point "Made with real cheese," the pride is of a quixotic sort because Combos taste nothing like real cheese. Instead, the smell of a freshly opened bag, no matter the varietal, carries a vague aroma of not-too-old vomit. It's a filling portion—when I multiply the serving sizes the front of the bag generously proffers, it's 780 calories, though I'm unimpressed either positively or negatively. When you have to eat, you eat—a motto I put in the second person to not be so closely identified with it when someone turns critical. But give me props—it's a small bag, so my green footprint is light. Food is food and I usually eat Combos because they can fill me up at least three-quarters-of-a-meal full for only $2.80. Also, I can eat them at a leisurely pace while doing something else, as I often consume them when driving or looking at the computer. They actually resemble few snack foods I've ever eaten. The cheesy middle eliminates pretzels and popcorn, while chips, whether tortilla or potato, are thin and undaunting, except for their awkward size and choking danger if not properly masticated. Yet, I wouldn't bill Combos as an exotic appetizer—how could I when the chemical aftertaste makes the thought of eating anything else comical?

The experience of eating Combos is not so different from that of Plato's mealiest cave-dwellers, who watch the shadows of the shadows of real things. It's an imitation food. For instance, the "pretzel" or "cracker" parts, depending on the concoction, could be made out of dried cardboard marinated in soy sauce for a day too long. The lark of the combination sends it into another realm—that is, the illusion that one is eating some form of bread and cheese, but more a form of bread and cheese preserved from 2008, when Mars, Incorporated bought out William Wrigley Jr., the world's largest gum company, for $23 billion, cash. I feel satiated for about five minutes after I finish eating a bag, but more often, I leave behind the last two of roughly thirty-five in a pre-emptive attempt to claim I did not eat the whole thing. After those minutes elapse—it's a different story. Combos largely affect my mood more than my stomach, which has been taught to put up with this travesty of a three-quarter meal around twice a month.

They are, in actuality, a quick-release narcotic and mood destabilizer, as I instantly begin to rebuke myself, hating the person who has slummed to eat something of no nutritional value, despite the company's boast that "COMBOS® Baked Snacks are a delicious and indulgent treat that can be enjoyed as part of a balanced diet and healthy lifestyle." Suddenly, I think my "food is food" stance paltry—reading Gillian Flynn, even if she wrote *Girl Gone With Combos*, wouldn't make me double over in pain, unless I put on a show—and I enviously recall people who are able to bring apples and bags of carrots or celery to work, and actually enjoy eating them. Soon I begin to see the world as rent and cruel because I feel my spirit sapped by the experience of having thirty-three Combos sitting in my stomach, sending into my bloodstream maltodextrin, sodium acid pyrophosphate, and food starch, which suspiciously carries a "modified" designation. Who said you are what you eat? I wouldn't be surprised if Combos caused temporary impotence, but I'm sure they cut down libido. How can you want to have sex when you feel like refuse?

But Combos are really worse than I'm letting on. They might be stand-ins for those cyanide pills people took in the French Resistance. I can easily imagine eating a few handfuls, then laying down in a ditch to die. But maybe it's good to have this type of life experience, to eat something so malnourishing and nauseating one could wish life would cease for a while. What other experience is like eating a bag of Combos? What other ugliness can be consumed wholesale and force one not to enjoy the sun, Bach, and sex? A nasty fight with a friend or spouse? Anything to do with politics? An evening with a living Burt Reynolds? I have made a pact with myself to avoid these obstructions. I don't have all the answers, but in the final tally between me and Combos, they're not bad enough for me to not eat more, though their taste keeps me verging on bipolar, allowing me to obdurately remain connected to the jetset.

On Being Looked At

I DON'T ALWAYS like to be looked at—an unfortunance not always serving me well in romantic relationships. But this is not worse than it sounds. I could carry a malady: burns, scars, dislocations, deformities—luckily I am nondescript if not tall. Surely the psychodynamics around this preference must have something to do with approaching three-hundred pounds at age nineteen. The therapists would say, and I agree, that we often retain the set of inhibitors that were given so much electricity when we were big that the charge doesn't altogether exit our bodies in the years housing a fitter frame. Still, time has passed, lives have changed, and one must begin the inquiry with one's location.

I don't admire people who talk about Brooklyn in any casually determinate way. Dammit, I live here. Yes, it's what it is if you abide, something quite else if you see it on TV or read about all the epithets directed at it online or in newsprint. There are different Brooklyns and I have no truck with the Williamsburg and Greenpoint youngins. I acknowledge and celebrate my status as not age-appropriate for those quadrants— places where Foxygen's funny little rock lyric "There's no need to be an asshole, you're not in Brooklyn anymore" was probably aimed after too many bewildering days and nights atop its streets holding many layers of unswept construction dust. Bed-Stuy had gotten well eaten up by developers fifteen years ago and I don't see it much today, though I know hot new restaurants open there every week. Coney Island, Sheepshead Bay, and Bay Ridge are distant lands with surf and turf, but I don't like straight beach and it doesn't like me. The neighborhoods branching out from the Brooklyn Bridge don't really nuzzle against each other like those in Manhattan, where Chinatown suddenly becomes Little Italy after you overstep a discarded pizza crust, but wait, two turns and now it is SoHo and there's Willem Dafoe—shorter in real life.

My neighborhood, Park Slope, is crack cocaine to fantasies of raising children by its more gentrified side of the park and inside its coveted schools, where people maintain an equipoise (with a modicum of granola), but will flail and flounder of their own brew with the curtains closed or under the pillow, changing the course of their blood by whatever chosen substance, just as persons in Duluth might. The people who shit on Park Slope do so because they can't order the contumely one feels in SoHo, where an outsider only exists to be envying the ungainly and overtan stars and moneymakers who live in the great towers of high security. You aren't necessarily excluded in Park Slope (though I recall dozens of Craigslist ads for roommates fifteen years ago where men were explicitly told not to apply); you're just not to be too vocal about what a charade everything is, while leaving room for stroller parking.

On its streets, I try to keep a low profile and tilt my head slightly forward to avoid making eye contact for fear of being misunderstood, though what the misunderstanding might be would fill their heads, never mine. When in motion, I hold to my half of the sidewalk, though on a few rare and fanciful occasions I have looked up to see someone with a homey kindness in their face (it's always a woman) and we both smile at each other in an ultra-platonic manner, happy to never get to know the other's inefficiencies. I'm not sure what they really discern that engenders a gift most often not given to the male sex; maybe I give off the correct safe signal. I should declare I can be comfortable in another person's presence—while also quietly caretaking against any of their disappointments surfacing—something on the bright side of my spectrum, up from the salty ogre-like manic moods I daily inhabit. The reason? I have lived in the hugging capital of our country (Eugene, Oregon) and, as attrition would have it, can easily clasp another soul, breastplate to breastplate, regardless of genitalia or degree of hatred. Though I know where I live now—what's kosher on one coast is not recommended on the other and the falsely sweet and labile men who offer "free" hugs in Union Square are looked at askance, even by Eugenians, who know you don't trumpet the worth of what you are offering, you just give it. Maybe the nicens women somehow see what I think, which, if I have to deconstruct the elliptic resonances I give off, are: a heartening aspect, a glaze of empathy, a mere mindfulness. So yes, a connection: we've both meditated, enjoyed forest silence at hot springs (nudity no bother), and maybe even have seen Krishna Das perform in our life, being one of the fifty or so New Yorkers who will ecstatic-dance to the sutras, while the other two hundred sit statically and post the pictures they take to the internet. Whatever it is, these silent moments are the nutrition making so much of breathing possible. But, of course, we don't all see the same thing—a phenomenon which might be counted as the purpose that art and religion endlessly try to serve, for despite our wildly differing periscopes (some looks are harmless but instill leagues of fear, and some casual glances carry a diabolical heat—what gets served has not always been fully cooked and what is received hardly ever captures the sender's intent), we need to get along with others to live a healthful, positive life.

Conversely, and much more wounding (and hence, more memorable), I have sustained such disdainful, scornful, dismaying, antipathetic, and surdful eyebeams, I thought I might be wearing a MAGA hat and an *I Believe Weinstein* shirt in a district voting ninety percent Democrat. Those were predominately eyefuls from the female sex, though a few men contributed some spidery bendings of their irises—maybe at the feminine (or what I'm told is feminine—by men) sunglasses I wear for no reason other than that I like their shade and shape. Yet, the two looks from women in the last months that bore in, like machete-metal through to my thrapple, came indoors.

I belong to a shared work space in a medium-sized industrial building near Park Slope. Cubicles are aligned in rows of three with a few branching off at right angles—no food, talking, or cellphone noise are allowed, ideally. People who don't mind a cavalcade behind them are probably among those seated along the narrow walkway from the back of the room to the front, where I sit in the first row—protecting their peace (and hoping for mine). The bathrooms are outside the work space, through a mostly soundproof door, but again, mindful (or monkish), I don't make the journey to the porcelain god unless absolutely necessary. On the occasion of recall, I backtracked to the door and just as I would have pushed, it was pulled open by a woman who I have seen at the space for over a year but have never talked to. Her fierce dark eyes stared into the pit of my orbs with what I could only call outsize rancor. So she could pass through first, I made way, and she did, full of a silent disgusted paroxysm (or so I guessed) for everything I represented. I hadn't done anything, but I existed—a fact the force made me more grateful for.

Some might say, *Don't read into things* and *Living in New York, dozens and dozens of people look at you every day—do you want to go crazy?* Some find it positively portentous—a man I explained the scene to commented, She likes you, dummy; a fifty-year-old should know this. I'm forty-five. Same thing. And some might dismiss the underpinnings of my pseudo-phrenology, finding flaws in my sussings out like they are the pap doled out by the same ten scientists, welcomingly cited by the right wing, who deny the earth is undergoing massive climate change. The above are all quick-fix responses, but I eschew such vanguard approaches—the examined life is the vulnerable one and while a part of me might like to think someone is attracted and so treats me like dung, I know real answers will go plenty deeper, beyond helter-skelter ego and heartmelt. The true answers might not have anything to do with this woman's biography, or mine—we might just as well be any two people of any gender, in any time. Proust cast more suspicions, in writing:

> The human face is indeed, like the face of the God of some Oriental theogony [a genealogical account of the gods], a whole cluster of faces, crowded together but on different surfaces so that one does not see them all at once. But to a great extent our astonishment springs from the other person's presenting to us also a face that is the same as before. It would require so immense an effort to reconstruct everything that has been imparted to us by things other than ourselves— were it only the taste of a fruit—that no sooner is the impression received than we begin imperceptibly to descend the slope of memory and, without noticing anything, in a very short time, we have come a long way from what we actually felt. So that every fresh encounter is a sort of rectification, which brings us back to what we really did see. We have no longer any recollection of this, to such an extent does what we call remembering a person consist really in forgetting him.

As Samuel Beckett said, the best way to forget about something is to keep thinking about it. And, by Proust's logic, I should not ignore these encounters, but possibly even seek them out—by accepting an invitation to the teeming and lesser recesses of ourselves, there is no telling the jewels they will cosponsor. The woman's look does effortlessly leap into and out of my biography like a wild animal running into an official scene, such as a pro-sports game or wedding ceremony, only to skedaddle, unwilling to enfranchise itself into the texture of spectacle. In Djuna Barnes's Nightwood—a gorgeously wrought text in the mandarin style—there is an indelible line of dialogue: "'I have been loved,' she said, 'by something strange, and it has forgotten me.'" That's a monument to heartache and one feels many of the sharp shocks and long love pangs that have gone on in one's life, but feels them inside-out—art as a great medicine. This was one of the many lines of writing that danced into view with that look's knuckle sandwich, along with Liv Ullmann's distraught face in Ingmar Bergman's The Passion of Anna, where she wants something from the man she feels for, but can't ask it of him, as well as a stricken view of my parents on the day they announced their separation to their children—their solemnity in accepting the worst. To be looked at is to be alive and it fuels reflection on how we came to be on whatever geographical point we abjure—it's also a colonic for all of our impressions that threaten to imprison us: If you thought that was *xyz*, try this.

The mind's orogeny is at stake, including how we make mountains out of molehills, how some people never forgive a bad first impression, and how the persons we think nothing special of turn out to be those we love forever. Though I probably will never exchange word one with this woman, I can imagine her fitting the form of each of those haptic branchings that get bleached in memory and forever muck our hours. As per Proust, I do see what might be trippingly harbored in my arsenal—just as in art we are given something not about us but intently remake it into a cog of our life—so that woman's face was for me and all about me, about my secret, my not wanting to disturb and, keeping all cards close to my neck. We weren't at a bar being loosened by drink, we were in the trenches, each person trying to be alone with their thoughts, attempting to make those fancies into something syntactically precise and rhythmic: Don't bother me—important stuff going on here!

The origin act of the glance can send our nascent geologies, which are lined with strike-slip faults, a panoply of rifts, thin-and thick-skinned deformations, and passive margins capable of sudden activity. To be looked at is an honorific act as well as a causal will-o'-the-wisp scratching of that irremediable itch, less often a prelude to further truculence—it's something more like the oxygen trees create. It is an infinite replication of our life's first moments when we opened our eyes to shapes and colors and so our awakening every morning is forever Act 1 Scene 1: Open your eyes—child with mother or child with mother and father. Those visions get imbricated over time with lapses, shifts, and unfoldings so when the kindness or cruelty of a stranger meets our mien out of the sea of possible protozoa, a full deck of looks have long been prepackaged to perennially repeat like the goose's yearly urge for south.

Today there is no doubt that we look at people less than at any other time in human history. The device holds something even more immediate, programmed to be predictable, and trained to deliver the correct dose of narcotic that our ego, however tetchy or jaundiced, will react to. One might think I would seek out such a device as pendant, but no—I want to be like most every other human who walked the earth before 1990, and I need to be more than aware of the streets in New York, as just last week, in less than twenty-four hours, three people were killed by cars in three separate incidents. Plus, I desire the dilemma of looking up or down when passing another and the destabilizing or mordant rush of that often split-second decision, rather like a joust with us as our own cowering, mainly unsnorting horses. I'm not alive on a device; I'm coping with the surfeit or lack of love and attention social media bewrays us into thinking are life's true riches, while driving us to the worst circle of them all—a solipsistic cell where we need adoration to function. Is it possible I fooled myself into thinking the quagmire of being looked at is losing some of its sacredness because so many people are not looking anyway? This is only my irrelevant valedictory sense straining to fuse with the quizzical manner most of my public faces are dismissed. If so, the joke is duly on me, because I'm lucky if I get a look at all, technology burning an effigy of eros every second it can.

The basket-weaver and print-shop operator turned cryptic writer of koans, Antonio Porchia, is good on the negative capability of living. "You are sad because they abandon you and you have not fallen." Waiting for tea to boil at the work space the other day, I stood by the kitchen window and looked at a forlorn tree planted into the cement, with barely any mates on the large industrial block. Its bark had multiple deep striations showing almost coal-colored against a prime blue January sky. When had I last done this, simply stared at nature? I was happy to be in some communion, the way two strangers might. Maybe this was why we don't fall, à la Porchia, more often—the plenitude, the steadfastness of something spiritually unknowable that accepts all looks, and even the chance that a human being might warm to us rather than calcify back to their safe, virtually desiccated places. I may not like to be looked at, but if it's a call between tracelessly losing my humanity and a chigger bite to my ego, I'll take the immediate wound every time.

Highlight

I'VE OFTEN HEARD people speak of a "cultural inheritance," meaning something nonmaterial, whether wisdom, generosity, or some other positive trait increasingly defrocked in the current zeitgeist, and passed down through acts both unconditional and impartial—"I demonstrate, you do what you will." Yet cultural inheritances can be more diluted, problematic as well—"His father was an asshole, too." And if you are from the Middle West, where soporific scenes dominate, a love of drinking is handed down more often than a love of books or an interest in great philosophical questions. There were books in our house when I was a child and I ogled them. Some mighty ones were at my eyeline in a bookcase my father constructed. Impotent were the words, but behind those glass doors . . . the spines, hard and soft with no formal arrangement—and then the covers. The thick *Brothers Karamazov*, small-fonted to save paper, but with the menace of a large, black, typically stout Russian torso like an Easter Island stone on the cover—no features, no dress, just blackness. But I came into literature later, and more fetishistically, when living on the West Coast.

College couldn't make me into a writer, let alone a close reader. I knew only the canon and I respected it in the way a civilian looks at a retired warship in harbor. Yet, soon after, I would finally begin to read the current fiction of repute, thanks to an irreducible, improbable friendship with someone a decade older. He'd grown up on the Upper East Side, regularly strolling the Met, MOMA, the Frick, and Lincoln Center, seeing the best jazz musicians, and filing through The Strand for the latest Updike. If the inheritance came from anybody, it came from him. Simply, he knew what was good to read.

The summer after college graduation, I embarked on a gardening internship at a community near the small town of Dexter, Oregon, in the foothills of the Cascades. On the first evening, following some seven hours of hard labor, I fell asleep right after dinner. Still, the earth was beautiful and being so close to it for the first time fostered a hardy affection. Working the same fields hour after hour, day following day, I came to know nature better. As we tended the soil and it formed, sometimes changing overnight, covetous feelings were sparked, like the earth was a baby, my own child. I was part of a team, working alongside ten other residents and interns—some innocuous, some challenging, and some merely spirited. One fellow stood out, diminutive and intense, but sad, with a straw hat askew over his blond, curly locks. I had met him some weeks before in Eugene. Blue-eyed and haughty in his concealment of some great blustery emotions, he struck me as a threatening presence. Judgment harkened and seeing him as too much a mirror of a prior, discarded self, I instantly disliked him. To live and work together, I would have to give him a second glance, but for the first days I circled around him, staying close to the younger, more approachable women full of skin and smiles.

On the Fourth of July, the community was invited to our distant and famous neighbor's property for a celebration. Ken Kesey's land had a bunch of young hippie chicks and enough special lemonade to send the hundred people there into unique spells for hours. Sharing the same general sense of unease in the face of this frolicking, the mystery man and I both left the gathering around the same time to walk the two miles back to the community. I stayed a safe distance behind so as to avoid the inevitable awkward hello, but my gait was almost twice his and he kept slowing down, though I was sure he didn't feel my presence, given I hung back on the straightaways. Too frustrating to keep stifling myself (I wanted to get back before it started to rain), I finally caught up to him with not much distance to go. We muttered a few things and I instantly recognized a reader. Even though we divulged little merriment about this shared interest, I immediately began to recast my hasty judgments. Soon, he became my closest friend.

He could have a thorny way of relating and many asked what the hell he was doing in a small community of people in search of inner light in the Pacific Northwest. He had broken with his prep-school and Dartmouth upbringing and had already lived in a truly cultish community in Florida, where, under the influence of his fetching partner, he gave away thousands of dollars and became involved in a legal tussle, eventually declaring bankruptcy to save face. After this and other stints in NYC and Seattle that came to similar tired and spent ends, a long depression cloaked him. Money and status—the hallmarks of his upbringing, what he paid attention to, what he read about, and what he admired in others—still obsessed him. Yet, he'd followed his own path in Oregon, driving a red Datsun truck, listening to bluegrass music, and searching for a nature girl, while still subscribing to *The New Yorker*. He also loved films, especially *Nashville, Hannah and Her Sisters,* and *Goodfellas.* We spent many a time in the garden quoting lines to each other and laughing. The people around us, many earth-firsters, sat mystified as we all picked hardened clumps of dirt off pungent garlic knobs, a vegetable taking up almost a fifth of my internship with the additional cleaning and braiding.

Two years on, and we both lived in Eugene, a happy hippie bubble kept afloat by its university. A Catholic Midwesterner and a Jewish New Yorker. Two people who looked like Abbott and Costello together, just with less weight on their bodies. Why did we continue to work so well? He had tasted what I yearned after. Ten years older, he had spent most of that decade in assorted relationships, while pressing to break into the photography world and briefly succeeding. The blank, blunt stare accompanying his no-nonsense attitude and strict beliefs in living and art also actuated a few parts of his own unique pain of love, career, and home gone sour. Joy did lurk. He could erupt into a long cackle, reddening his face until he hid his head. He had the gift of gab and could extemporize for many minutes on a number of subjects, his words interspersed with hiccoughs of laughter aimed more derisively at himself than at others. He could be severe—once at a community meeting he told another male resident he had a whiny way of currying favor—but he could also have a good time and he introduced me to a variety of art and psychedelics.

Strong opinions were manacled to the former. *Barry Lyndon* was the greatest—*The Shining* not so much. Monk over Coltrane. Into my hands he put books authored by four writers who would come to have as much influence over me as any: Paula Fox, Alice Munro, Cormac McCarthy, and J. M. Coetzee. Incredulous, he would deny my knowledge of a certain subject, up to the point of checking an encyclopedia or the internet, though still dismissing me when I turned out to be right. I didn't mind—it was part of our banter. The young always have more to prove. At times a boyish recalcitrance kindled our interactions. Making fun of this, grousing about that. Our thoughts, as satirically laced dark sides, were aligned, but out of step with the more politically correct and country-mannered people of Eugene, our "community"—a word we drew out in speech to accentuate its wide range of rearguard connotations. Sometimes the sappy seriousness of the self-help culture was too much to bear and we cruelly picked on obvious targets, criticizing their bloviated, sentimental manners—moments now many times more spiteful in memory. But this was only the fraught side of the friendship; those poisonous digressions to make one feel better about the psychic pain installed for ages. Movies and books propelled the rest.

It surely wasn't enough to suggest titles, there had to be discussion as well, and during the numerous potlucks and lazy days particularly in the winter of 2002, creeping into the infamy of the new year and the second Iraq invasion, we convened. In the sepia-toned existence that is Eugene's gray sky and dreary atmosphere, a daguerreotype predominating from Halloween to Memorial Day, we had little choice but to nestle in and avoid the damp chills in the Willamette Valley (called "The Valley of Sickness" by the area's last known Indians), often in a rich friend's large house a few hundred feet above sea level on the way to Spencer's Butte. While others trafficked in the *plat du jour*, processing (that is, working out one's issues face to face with the source, and sometimes with help from a "mediator"), we'd break off into a corner, or even sometimes in the midst of a cuddle-pile (the crowd we ran with did ignite and continue to broker a weekly cuddle club), because it didn't matter where the literary tête-à-têtes took place. It didn't bother us that pretty much no-one out of the dozens and dozens of people we knew from the college town (most were older and only a few attended the school) did not relate to or even read any of the works we considered—they were too engulfed in Barbara Kingsolver or the aforementioned processing. These talks on the fly were integral to our shared existence, for why else have friends? Our book-club-for-two did speak of story, of characters and their motivations, and also of structure, dialogue, foreshadowing—all things that make fiction imaginatively sweet. Less about language and syntax, unless considering some of McCarthy's abstruse vocabulary.

For May Day, we went to the annual Beltane celebration (an ancient Celtic holiday co-opted by contemporary Wiccans). We camped in the cold, twisting hills of the Coast Ranges, which don't warm until July, stretches of land where every few miles another travesty of industrialization, the clear-cutting of large swaths of forest, moved an economy that had no sales tax and somehow supported the Oregon Health Plan. Nearly everyone at Beltane made less than $20,000 a year or they had made a mint in the Bay or L.A. and retired in Eugene or Portland, buying a house for a song. I'm not a pagan. I thought of Hawthorne as we danced around the Maypole, chanting something vaguely Middle English. Sex with strange and new women sounded fine to me, but I also reserved time for reading. My friend had just put me on to McCarthy then, and after *Blood Meridian* and *Suttree*, I went on to begin *The Border Trilogy*. On Sunday morning I warmed up in front of the lodge's fireplace (the lodge served as the kitchen for the gathering), reading of John Grady Cole's final movements in *All the Pretty Horses*. Next to me a nearly verifiable wood nymph (like many of those in attendance) sewed pieces of corduroy onto a homemade journal's cardboard covers. My friend came in and I told him I'd just finished the book—it wasn't as strong as the first two McCarthy books I'd read, but it was strong. He began to speak of it in grave tones—enamored of the moral weight of the questions McCarthy posed, particularly of the hero's return to America and confessing his murder of a man to a judge, after-hours at the judge's home. John Grady had to clear himself or at least check his karma. Didn't regrets shape our lives, with murder just an outgrowth of many different ghosts in our closets? We were often speaking like this about fiction. We'd insert ourselves in the story, even if we didn't mean to; that is, we did with literature what it can rarely do for young people studying it in school—play life experience both against and within it. And what else but art, displaying characters like themselves, makes people question their own morality so vociferously, as it does not indemnify their life choices, but simply stands as a mythical portal? If life teaches life, art teaches hindsight.

I came from television, but he came from money and the anxiety about holding on to it. Money did something to the chemicals controlling his thoughts, which often revolved around understanding the greenbacks and their effects, and how they commanded and curtailed lives, empires, and epochs: from real estate prices on Second Avenue to the tuition fees at Columbia, and the record-breaking amount paid for a van Gogh on auction at Christie's. Money harpooned him like no other setup, except art; hence, his calling out how the father in *All the Pretty Horses* answers his son's disappointment when he refuses to play chess with the boy. When the father says you need patience to play chess, the son replies:

> You got patience to play poker.
> That's different.
> What's different about it.
> Money is what's different about it.

We rented a house together with our respective lovers on the Oregon coast one chilly March weekend. A couples' weekend—cooking, watching movies, walking on the strand, and fondling the mighty basalt boulders near Yachats which had been there at least as long as the oldest local's grandfather could remember. A time of timelessness—and reading. His lodestar, and mine for a while, Alice Munro, had just published a story, 'Passion,' in The New Yorker the week before. He had already read it and now wanted to share it, out loud, to us. It would take a while—eleven thousand words is probably sixty minutes through someone's mouth, maybe more. To do something like this, to hold three people's attention captive for an hour—it is almost unimaginable these days. There was no internet there. No cell coverage, either. We had space and time and started an hour before dusk. Even though I considered myself under a moon of Munro, it proved hard to listen. I couldn't still my mind, and for the first half of the story I heard only every fourth sentence or so. Nothing to do with the speaking voice or the story—in fact, the long setup to one life-altering experience (something mostly foregone in her final two collections) was a Munro specialty. She was adept at handling time, which is to say, memory, and how memory transforms the way we think of the events making up our lives, how the ego grants certain clauses and refrains, while omitting others. The sun continued falling, a rare warm light on the windy rugged coast. I kept resisting all the spoken words—a familiar feeling I could often sense when I'd tried to read others my work. During those dismaying minutes, I would have to pretend we were in an early Godard film, and I read aloud while beautiful French actors or actresses (stand-ins for my friends and lovers) listened attentively and offered some pithy rodomontade to rebuke what I thought peachy, instead of the gaggle of blank looks. There was a much different quality and experience to the reading I heard in our house, than one in a bookstore or public place, where the creator gives people an experience or an excuse to buy the book. My friend, I noticed halfway through, gave something of his soul to the reading, while striking a confident tone owing to his familiarity with the words; plus, he had a great investment in this tale.

Munro has three or four basic narratives to her stories, and this one, chance sex with a stranger, she'd tackled a handful of times before. The story easily transfers a reader inside it because of its familiarity, its everydayness. In the recognition there is a loosening—I don't know if my friend had had sex with someone he'd hardly known. Probably. I had. Maybe the women had, as well. Suddenly the experience was not the story on the page, but the story of our lives interred in our memories. The story itself marched on to its improbable Munrovian conclusion— the woman has sex with her fiancé's alcoholic brother, who the next day dies in a drunk-driving accident. The fiancé's brother somehow knows about the infidelity, and although he and the woman never see each other again, his father approaches her some days later and hands her a check for a thousand dollars. Given the ending transaction, my friend was understandably alert and he choked up and cried for a time before he read those final lines:

> Immediately she thought of sending it back or tearing it up, and sometimes even now she thinks that would have been a grand thing to do. But in the end, of course, she was not able to do it. In those days, it was enough money to insure her a start in life.

Culture—the Sistine ceiling, Gaudí's La Sagrada Familia in Barcelona, the falling bone becoming the descending spaceship in *2001*—opens the sense of beauty. We were quiet, but not morose; buoyed, rather, but with the decorum not to try and cross out the seeming sadness of the humorless occasion, which the incontrovertible emotional act sought to cement. The tertiary character's actions in the short story—giving money to a young woman who would have been his daughter-in-law, though what she did resulted in his own son losing out on a bride—made it a very curious and distant, maybe even lunatic gesture. Something taking place only in the imagination could be so powerful as to provoke but also absolve some of my friend's pain about the role of money in life, how gifts can once in a while trounce greed.

What was my response to the act? The giving of the money didn't hold the layers it did for him. When you're thirty you're still searching for evidence behind all the great realizations in your twenties. I probably read Munro to keep the flame alive of how I might one day get to a place where I might have a stable, successful relationship. I never thought I'd get married or ever become a father—so much for my auguring powers.

To cry in front of a group might be the most cathartic event many of us will participate in, considering few would want to be caught with teary eyes by a stranger standing a hundred feet away. I had wept when reading *Disgrace* out loud to my honey, clenching at the final pages detailing the killing of the last dog. But this was different. When you do something in front of a number of people, a switch is turned, the gain is far greater, more worlds collide. The general feeling of release wasn't uniquely heavy to him; we all felt taken and no longer marooned, intimate in an inimitable way. It resembled how the breeze blows during high school, maybe college days, when you are held by friends who all have to apply themselves to the same matrix and the same landing spot— like a Friday- or Saturday-night sleepover that could go on forever—that crystalized feeling of togetherness common to humanity no matter in which corner of the world.

So the inheritance grew to showing one's emotions. Years later, I interviewed Paula Fox. She told me she'd apologized to a delivery man after she had been in his way and he told her, Don't apologize, it's a sign of weakness, and quickly she corrected him, saying, No, it's a sign of strength. If anyone would have known, it was Fox; if I would have taken anyone's word, it was hers. Honor was in admitting when one had erred, something my friend also valued. The year prior he went into a fiery coupling with a lady who satisfied where she made most hungry and, as that relationship exploded into a mess of dependence and drama, he came to me early one morning at my girlfriend's house and confessed, "I'm a mean motherfucker," while draining his eyes. Later in the year, at a self-help seminar, I sat with him and another woman on a picnic bench while I busted a psychic rampart and unleashed the waters, grasping how I'd not felt unconditional love from my mother, how she always seemed to hold a trump card in the hand she dealt herself where our intimacy was concerned.

I never had a friendship with another man where we could cry with abandon, not worrying how what we did not only went against the grain, but made the grain embarrassed for our masculinity. As we found our place in the world, we saw each other's ugliness festooned by the delusions we'd been feeding our murky sides, long grown knotty and bulbous with metastasized roots. As we constantly sought peace, honor, and beauty, we continually shared, failed, and laughed. We loved each other with a blind impartiality, as the narrator in our favorite shared Kubrick film remarks about Barry Lyndon's love for his son.

Ours is a culture in love with highlights and I feel no bitterness in reporting this one occasion in a foreign house on the coast as probably our apex from which a very slow descent of years has followed. "Icarus wasn't failing as he fell," the poet Jack Gilbert once wrote, "just coming to the end of his triumph." Now, mostly, our revels are ended. We haven't lived in the same city for fifteen years, and the visits are less frequent, with the duration of one-on-one time shrinking when they do occur. But this means less and less, because the inheritance was two-pronged: information and entrée emblazoned by that Oregon afternoon. Only amnesia will take it out of my life. It is all the more vivid for being so quiet, the type of instance that when caught on camera is lessened by the gloss and caterwauling of the person shifting into pantomime, turning into one too cognizant of instant capture's sinister implications. It returns to me every few years or so. I sit like a stone and look at a bookcase or out the window, often in winter's wine-dark light, at the end of the dusk, and there it runs—simultaneously in the full duration of the entire reading and also the cherished moment's super slo-mo, drawn out to the pregnant silence of the audience. More than any other dramatic piece, Samuel Beckett's *Krapp's Last Tape*, in which a man, a failed writer, sits in a dark room listening to the diary-like tapes he has made at various points in his life, has to be the most apt microcosm of all our day-to-day existences—replaying certain memories at certain times, gorging on or being brought to bulimia by the stories we tell about ourselves.

"Everything perishes but tradition," according to Hugh Kenner. Tradition might be a better umbrella term for cultural inheritance, call it humanism or what you will. Tradition, the fair courts. That one simple act can end a host of suffering almost always supports our casual ontology—our agency being much more oblique than direct advice would want to make it. Jesus Christ himself knew parables spoke to people better than direct haranguing, bar-room advice, platitudes, clichés. And when I easily reach for one from the Bard—"Speak what we feel, not what we ought to say"—I am double-charmed and double-crossed. Words the flint, but often not the spark.

People grow apart but the past remains. Searching for lost time comes to occupy us more and more as our hair changes color, as autumn comes to a lifetime. Yet, in opposition to *Krapp*, I think this type of pastime can truly circumvent regret, the bastard child of memory. To live a bit in the past doesn't necessitate reordering the wires and telling off dad or the Daphne who haunts our dreams. That's why the icky edict "Stop living in the past" doesn't plunge in the knife up to its hasp. The silly recrudescence of "I carry a part of you with me always" is just a withering corncob for the more robust, Heraclitian wording:

> All men are deceived by the appearances of things, even Homer himself, who was the wisest man in Greece; for he was deceived by boys catching lice: they said to him, "What we have caught and what we have killed we have left behind, but what has escaped us we bring with us."

We don't feel something as lost until it has demonstrated a value to us. To "miss" shouldn't be synonymous with "regret." To "miss" is as natural as a course of water down a mountain. We always carry what escapes us; that's the essential in any survival kit, since we often take for granted what we have, treating it as another old pair of shoes we wear every day.

Finally, we are left with memory. But more often now, I am pulled away from that window or bookcase to memory's enemy. If the internet can be said to be live (and to be alive), we will risk death to write a rashness that will probably not be seen enough in the time we'd like. As tides to sandcastles, every few hours a new parade of opinions washes out those now grown old from the other hour, even before the coat of arms can be hung from the drawbridge—they vanish and a newer base begins to rise. The great internet of the mind has better access to raw experience, and memories of it, because it has had sex, swum with dolphins, stood on the side of the volcano, eaten fresh mozzarella in Florence, and, for all this, can experience the flickerings of sunset and not have to think, Once we lived in what we saw—light, color, contrast, and away went the day. The great internet of the mind doesn't have factual answers but lustres and rich colors, preserves in multitudinous pantries, nooks, and garrets. It contains me at every age and holds people I know and love in their many stages. So when someone asks me a question about living, I don't look at the frothy screen; I examine their face with mine and herd the experiences, attempting to vacate the contumely and spout something saturated in my truth, my mysterious chloroform.

I believe I'm writing against the propaganda trying to make people think "now more than ever" or "in dangerous times like these," because maybe our relationship to time, which is our relationship to family, friends, and enemies (with technology as prime broker), will destroy us quicker than climate change. It used to be that our ancestors thought deeply about certain hot words, values and traits, often along spiritual and religious bents. Ralph Waldo Emerson used a single-word title for most of his essays, naming them for these values, these large ideas. His essay "Fate" is a crown source for me more than for most people, who prefer the often anthologized early Emerson of "Self-Reliance" or "Experience" to the later thinker who is a little darker, a little more in love with the fall of man, yet still allows the lights of nirvana to beam through. For him, how we understand time and memory is inherent in how we consider fate, in how we take or leave it:

> A man will see his character emitted in the events that seem to meet, but which exude from and accompany him. Events expand with the character. As once he found himself among toys, so now he plays a part in colossal systems, and his growth is declared in his ambition, his companions, and his performance. He looks like a piece of luck, but is a piece of causation—the mosaic, angulated and ground to fit into the gap he fills.

It has to help to think I've had a hand in gathering the light or gloom to myself, my luck being rooted in the residue of my hopscotch designs. It's a swaggering delusion to think we are at the center of history just because we are alive. Today's disciples of this sprung neuroticism would reach back to an Emersonian word, "blasphemy," to brand such a trenchant view, when a much more American way of causality, that injunction to forever blame someone else when any accident or badness befalls us, swiftly takes Emerson's mosaic of causation and nukes it out of existence. Earlier on, Emerson wrote: "The day of days, the great day of the feast of life, is that in which the inward eye opens to the Unity in things, to the omnipresence of law—sees that what is must be, and ought to be, or is the best. This beatitude dips from on high down on us, and we see. It is not in us so much as we are in it." So what we get is something we fleetingly, even if consciously, asked for. Eugene always filled us with sappy sweetness, and its unofficial motto was: We create our own reality. Yes, I create the reality again and again by the lights of the past, no matter those fools living in the present. I know the possibilities—that true intimacy can bloom between people where no sexual weaponization exists—and that tenderness, unselfishness, and honesty tends a friendship, even if fatal to it. This does not heave "now more than ever" out of its counterfeit spotlight. Our world is rich in anniversaries, and to suddenly forget won't help us endure the present any better.

THE SILVER SCREEN

Oh for Antonioni

I'M SENSITIVE. I do have a nerve disorder in my right eye, but also I'm sensitive to language, to people offhandedly saying something because they couldn't staunch it. During a Q and A, Kent Jones and Noah Baumbach (two motion-picture writer-directors I admire) spoke of artists who were in direct and oblique competition given their proximity. Fellini and Antonioni came up, with the endpoint being an understanding that people, given a choice, should go with Fellini. In addition, as Orson Welles's *The Other Side of the Wind* hit Netflix, a puckish and foolish legend hellbent on being fact sprang up. Certainly Welles didn't like Antonioni—in a 1967 interview he equated his work with the experience of boredom—but too many critics parroted the belief that the movie-within-a-movie section—where a man and woman silently chase each other, closing in and apart before sex and during, the woman a toro to his matador—was based on Antonionian longueurs. Maybe Welles was more taken with Antonioni than he cared to admit, because that section of the film is the most alive and adventurous of the production (when living, Welles spent most of his editing time on these scenes, which were largely conceived of by Oja Kodar), even if the whole enterprise was left in the air and edited by a committee of acolytes. The continual ballyhoo about Welles, who struck Antonioni as a very masculine filmmaker, and the continual diminishing of Antonioni, which may have started with Pauline Kael's dismissals and Andrew Sarris's term "Antonioniennui," eventually took a toll. I have to admit there is something about Antonioni that is deeply embedded in my soul, and though the psychical manifestation of his art is a little riven by time, its granite face can still proudly display a freckling of mica by my own sun. It is a force that surely resists many people, and though I believe I've grown out of taking up a cause to rebuke those I would label impoverished, I extol only to eradicate my own glowering, to teach myself the lesson of how, as I get older, much of his work only gets better.

I came to Antonioni just as his star began to rise again in 1994–95, ten years after his stroke (which ended his speech except for a stray word or two), when he was given the lifetime-achievement Oscar, prompted by Martin Scorsese's campaigning. *Beyond the Clouds*, his first film since the stroke, had just been shot with Wim Wenders as co-director and would be released in the fall of 1995. It was a time of resurgent interest in cinema, with US film schools drawing many candidates after something vaguely independent emerged in the mid-to-late eighties and early nineties: Jim Jarmusch, the Coens, Spike Lee, and Steven Soderbergh, topped off by Quentin Tarantino. Whatever the faults of the Clinton presidency, at least the art of that period was interesting—more chances were being taken, even as violence came to be the dominant and delimiting idea, the strangling source material.

Like Henry James, Antonioni had always been attentive to emotional violence, almost especially the type that roosts deep under our integument, waiting for the wrong remark or appearance to sprout those insular cravings that would make one's friends cringe if given too much slack. His characters display an ardor, but it is lockjawed and more defined in that word's second, dubious sense of "vehement and fierce." During *L'Avventura*, while in Noto, a town full of Sicilian Baroque wonders of architecture, Sandro, the tetchy and pompous architect, can't help spilling ink on a young man's drawing because of his jealousy over the former's talent (he checks the representation against the real thing), his looks, and his youth, but more importantly, because Sandro's wish to see a church had been squelched just minutes before (and right before that, Claudia, the woman he is having an affair with, asked him to tell her that he loved her, which he didn't). When he returns to the hotel room after the encounter, he is disturbed and goes out on the porch and smokes, then chucks his cigarette onto the street before the camera violently whips back, so quickly there is a fast motion discernible as in sporting-event photography, and he is framed with the very grand architecture across the way that quietly shames his own remedial efforts. He closes the shutters of the hotel room and comes close to raping Claudia—proving the truism that we take out on others what people have done to us.

In the tetrology, Antonioni primarily tackled the "love-sickness"—a term amplified in his Cannes statement at *L'Avventura*'s premiere: "Eros is sick; man is uneasy, something is bothering him. And whenever something bothers him, man reacts, but he reacts badly, only on erotic impulse, and he is unhappy," though the English and American characters of his three late English-language films—*Blow-Up, Zabriskie Point*, and *The Passenger*—sport a more vainglorious and primitive, that is a more English and American, by-product of love-sickness than their Italian counterparts in the four films and *Identification of a Woman*. The British and Americans show an inability to be in their own skin, let alone to love—after the orgy in *Blow-Up*, Thomas goes right back to his photographs with no endearments after ejaculation, and in *The Passenger*, there is the strangling death drive of Locke. Geography makes the man and nowhere is this more evident than in *Blow-Up* and *Zabriskie Point*, where one could argue (ahead of *Chung Kuo, Cina*, his documentary on China) that Antonioni in fact documented the swinging sixties of London and the radicalization in the late sixties' US political protests. In the case of *Blow-Up*, he said, "A character like Thomas doesn't really exist in our country. . . . He has chosen the new mentality that took over in Great Britain with the 1960s' revolution in lifestyle, behavior, and morality . . . it is not by accident that he claims not to know any law other than that of anarchy," and in *Zabriskie Point*, just before shooting, he went to the infamously bloody 1968 Democratic National Convention, in Chicago, pushing him to rewrite the screenplay, which would feed into the greatest and most expressionistic emotional violence in his work—*Zabriskie Point*'s repeated explosions and demolitions of the house and various consumer objects in the imagination of the earth child, Daria.

The greatest piece of Antonioni's cinema is how he positions his actors in the space of the frame and in confluence with the earth and architecture, creating a certain force and communicating feelings that may elude most audiences—states that can't be pressed into existence by any other means. There is a poesis to his cinema; as Andrei Tarkovsky wrote of cinema's possibilities, "It possesses an inner power which concentrated within the image and comes across to the audience in the form of feelings, inducing tension in direct response to the author's narrative logic." William Arrowsmith, in the best Antonioni book, *Antonioni: The Poet of Images*, says of this narrative style, "It is astonishingly elliptical, but an ellipsis wholly characteristic of a director who fastidiously disdains traditional narrative realism, insistently demanding that the visuals, not the script, carry the essentials of the story. As in poetry, whose meaning often lies in the density of the unspoken thing . . ." Poetry also offers a good correlative to Antonioni's preoccupation with appearances—mirrors and reflections in glass are frequent and dazzling, as time shifts within the same shot, like in *The Passenger* when Locke switches passport photos near the dead man while their first meeting, caught on

Locke's tape recorder, plays. Locke looks up from his work to the veranda, and the camera meanders over, showing the continuance of that talk there, the two men standing together in the afternoon sun, creating a time-space gap that feeds into the void death has created.

But what is this "inner power . . . concentrated within the image" Tarkovsky speaks of? One might be compelled to call it his mise-en-scène, but in Antonioni's case there is some other element—the outgrowth of his philosophy and psychology and his readings of the great thinkers and writers are all over the frame. Fittingly, Roland Barthes in his speech "Dear Antonioni" says how ". . . the artist, unlike the thinker, does not evolve; he scans, like a very sensitive instrument, the successive novelty which his own history presents him with," and that Antonioni is a "utopian whose perception is seeking to pinpoint the new world." The composition of Antonioni's frame is his great legacy, and P. Adams Sitney writes how he is "particularly sensitive to the compositional power of vertical elements—the corners of buildings, door jambs, and so on—to isolate characters in the larger, horizontally extended form of the widescreen image." These frames (often uncanny when seen in their motion-picture movement) are like great Byzantine stone traceries, passing before our eyes every few minutes, giving us the feeling we are sitting not in the darkened motion-picture theater but in the staged light of an art museum as various canvases of Vermeer, Caravaggio, and Velázquez, and, of course, de Chirico the proto-surrealist, move past. Technically these images are photographs, but in the mind's eye they coagulate and sink into the viewer's own personal memory pools, no matter whether they are viewing on a record-thin computer screen or on the wide gargantuan silver one—they now live aboveboard, their iconography swarming and then possibly settling into the highlands of recall after brief periods in the low countries.

The other ballast to his art is the editing, the fracture made as one shot tests another—sometimes the cut is deeply ground into the stone of the film, sometimes it only takes a few grains of sandstone off, but the subduction and uplift, when one gets something seemingly incongruous to what has been given before, is glorious. Nathan Dorsky describes an edit in *La Notte* after a number of shots of the two main characters talking in the hospital with their sick friend. The friend's mother enters the room but sits on the periphery. The talk continues, but the next shot is from the mother's head as she watches. Dorsky notes, "It has no particular symbolic meaning but allows us to see the hospital room and the interrelated presence of the characters unexpectedly from the mother's perspective."

Being so armed with this bounty of Antonioni for twenty-five years, where has this magical panopticon gotten me? Antonioni commented fruitfully:

> Cinema is a mnemonic synthesis, which always presupposes in the memory of the viewer what is not present on the screen, or what happened before, as well as all of the possible developments of the present situation. That is why the best way to watch a film is to have it become a personal experience. At the moment in which we watch a film, we unconsciously evoke what is inside of us, our life, our joys and our pains, our thoughts—our "mental vision of the past and the present," as Susan Sontag would say.

All those stone traceries of despondency, but also of mystery and unresolvedness, are not wasted. They do not contribute to a low red-blood-cell count, marking me sallow, making me choose to live in cooling darkness with shades drawn while others enjoy the heat of life in the big city of archetypal and mocking splendor. The movable stone traceries are parables, with wisdom and ideation we will take much more easily because it is indirect, visual (unbound by dialogue), and seemingly impersonal, unless we make it so. The penultimate shot of *L'Eclisse* is also the last of its main character, Victoria, before ending in a seven-and-a-half-minute montage of objects and strangers. It comes after showing what Victoria does instead of continuing on the road to a lustful relationship. She leaves the man's office and walks the street briefly, bumps into someone, and then looks in a shop-window before turning around, her head tilting up to the large dense trees on the other side of the street above a brick wall. Then there is a low-angle shot of her so all the city is wiped out, except for its sound. No smile, but she's taken refuge in something more abundant. The poetry of film, but also the poetry of street smarts. Sitney writes:

> The proper viewing of a film requires the spectator to organize its disparate elements by intuiting the poetic linkages of its construction, guided by the fundamental metonymy of cinematic imagery. The tension raised by this activity releases feelings of pleasure in the recognition of the associated links.

Images like this are not for entertainment's sake, they are white-hot shards I can't shake. They keep me seeing the world unassumingly, but in the light of Antonioni's remarks, they are also a part of my history, a deeply private attic I more often than not don't share unless circumstance puts me in touch with some aesthete I recognize by the subtle flame wavering above her head. So potent is Antonioni that even though I haven't been in Africa, I have been in his version of Africa in *The Passenger*, and to a far greater extent than in David Lean's *Lawrence of Arabia*, who didn't make many films (with the exception of *Brief Encounter*) that plunge into one's dark and desert places, where muddied and pained emotions threaten our every day. Rather, Lean entertains and ennobles as the Edmund Hilary of cinema, an ethos that works for many persons but not for me and those I love, those I look up to. Triumph overcoming tragedy? For Antonioni, cinema itself is the arrival of and relishing in enigma.

On a visual level, my viewpoint has strongly taken on the Antonioni mise-en-scène. We see with an even greater depth of field than a film camera, though Antonioni often stretches his to its deep focus lengths. I move about the world with this scanning sense wholly cognizant of the Bresson nugget, "Life is mysterious, and we should see that on-screen. The effects of things must always be shown before their cause, like in real life. We're unaware of the causes of most of the events we witness. We see the effects and only later discover the cause." I explore the world in this invisible armor. I never go searching for beauty but can arrive at it—per Antonioni's way of creating, his method:

> My films are always works of research. I do not consider myself a director who has already mastered his profession, but one who is continuing his search and studying his contemporaries. I'm looking . . . for the traces of sentiment in men and of course in women, too, in a world where these traces have been buried to make way for sentiments of convenience and of appearance: a world where sentiments have been "public-relationized."

Little things. The overarching ache of the world and its political corruption is always lessened for me by witnessing those slight accommodations, those mere adjustments when someone thinks of themselves second, or when people skirt the flatlining public order though grand displays of joy, romance, or sadness—how else can we be human except by being what people don't expect? So Antonioni aptly reflects the careworn world—there aren't too many traces of sentiment, but here and there they pop out, often in the climaxes, as in *Blow-Up*, where Thomas begins to use his imagination to hear the pantomimed tennis rally or the aforementioned imaginative explosions in *Zabriskie Point*, something many people would not admit to wishing for. But often the finales are solemn, as the grasping one in *L'Avventura*, where Claudia comforts Sandro, even though he just cheated on her, and they stand and sit holding each other (a mountain on her side of the frame, a building on his) in perhaps the most willed stone tracery. Here Sitney believes, "the elegant composition contributes to the distancing effect which encourages us to ponder and analyze the affective gesture rather than empathize with it." This is probably why Antonioni was and is still blasted as cold, something Sontag easily refuted years before when she said, "But to call a work of art 'cold' means nothing more or less than to compare it (often unconsciously) to a work that is 'hot.' And not all art is—or could be—hot, any more than all persons have the same temperament." Films and art which tell people what to feel don't tend to have a long shelf life, like fair weather friends, they aren't the type of works that will speak to our multiplicity of moods and the stranger hours we keep; they are the quick fix, the entertainment after the repast or prior to coddled sleep, a pot of plastic flowers never given a chance to spoil because they hold no vital breath.

Yes, I took Antonioni into my life and he affected how I saw the world, but such a statement requires a well-hewed explication—there is nothing in Antonioni's nature that is toss-off, nor should there be for his acolytes. I was a virgin when I affixed to Bergman and Antonioni. The women who starred in many of their films—Liv Ullmann, Bibi Andersson, and Monica Vitti—would come to form my ideal squeeze. Unconsciously then, I pursued women molded from these cinematic representations; they would be austere, unbedecked with scent or makeup, terse, willowy, but not necessarily fair and hardly ever blond; they would be troubled, with enough despair to keep us mainly focused on their issues, so I could recede and, beholden to the paranoia of my own desires, destroy our intimacy, retaliating against eddies I set in motion because I couldn't know my own needs, only the morass of a self-preservationist pique. It's easy to stomach what I couldn't belly up to back then, but I had only just begun finger-cutting the stone that makes one relationship-functional. Still, I held no tool to grout the layer of inevitable dysfunction, the carapace that indulges the fantasy of falling in love, which is simply a requisite chimera needed on the resume before getting to know people who will have a much greater affect because of their ability to seem like nothing special. Because *La Notte* was next to impossible to come by in the nineties—everything fell squarely on Monica Vitti—and more for her roles in *L'Avventura* and *L'Eclisse*. Maria Schneider makes an interesting case for inclusion as well (and some of her blank looks in

The Passenger are incomparable, never have I seen another actor look so natural in their silence). But Vitti, who would often remain sullen until a youthful playfulness appears like steam from a once thought dormant volcano, is the driving force.

I was granted my perverse wish and hooked into the perfect foil, the ultimate Antonioni heroine, wrapping her birthday presents at the moment I found out he died. I knew I was deep in Antonioni country when she told me she would sometimes sit in a room and stare at a wall for hours. I watched her, as I viewed Vitti, and later Jeanne Moreau in *La Notte* (perhaps the most extreme of Antonioni's women, and certainly the most assured and dour). I recorded this woman raising her arms in joy, as Vitti does when dancing in *L'Aventura* and *L'Eclisse*, or making a funny face unexpectedly, as she also does in each film. She also slumped and slouched in despair as many a heroine, walking into nature to touch trees, soil, and stone with child-like innocence and docility, though a minute later her face might be scarred by circumstance or memory. I didn't recognize this transformation as part of the allure then. The whiplash emotions often tormenting Vitti or Moreau were too close to our holt, with my lady's emotional states passing us in frenzied ellipsis; and from one crest to pit, I didn't know whether to don pity or pride, whether to live vicariously or thank God it wasn't me, when on many levels it was. Did I love her or the unconscious Antonionian foibles inside her, the way she squirreled through the world? Any answer will poison the surface tension in the other possibility, though the art itself goes a long way. Critic Sam Rohdie writes, "The films pose a subject (only to compromise it), constitute objects (only to dissolve them), propose stories (only to lose them) but, equally, they turn those compromises and losses back towards another solidity: . . . a wandering away from narrative to the surface into which it was dissolved, but in such a way that the surface takes on fascination, becomes a 'subject' of its own." This diagnosis seems to be a perfect evocation of love in all its splendorous and dour crenellations, that is to say, its eternal vulnerability. And if "love's not love that's not vulnerable," I was surely ready to give my life to star in our own *L'Eclisse*.

Our twelve seasons are well-established in my memory loop, as is the city of our imprimatur and destruction, Buffalo—all contained in a quasi-Antonionian-grade B-movie, with the lonely unpeopled arcades and those barren dismal rotting buildings of that dying Rust Belt city I often had to convince myself to endure until I had been forgotten by what had loved me. Many times we cavorted and then snapped into diffidency up and down those lonesome streets, feeding and starving our own love-sickness—something cold-blooded but vital: "as the motion of a snake's body goes through all parts at once, and its violation acts at the same instant in coils that go contrary ways," per John Ruskin. The few locals who watched our charade displayed faces wrought perplexed in the extreme, as if they were shown Antonioni when they asked for Spielberg. And so I could play the controlling and constipated egotistical elder Italian man full of braggadocio, bringing up the words of Robert Musil, "The tenderer feelings of male passion are something like the snarling of a jaguar over fresh meat—he doesn't like to be disturbed." But to reference the other towering novelist of the early-twentieth-century, who isn't Irish—the typical Antonioni male, bent on satisfaction, is also working at cross-purposes, channeling the congeries he calls feelings, as Proust describes Swann:

> . . . he was like a man into whose life a woman he has glimpsed for only a moment as she passed by has introduced the image of a new sort of a beauty that increases the value of his own sensibility, without his even knowing if he will ever see this woman again whom he loves already and of whom he knows nothing, not even her name.

This blanketly happens to some male in every film from *Il Grido* to *Beyond the Clouds*. I knew my lines or the movement I needed to make my ego fit. Perhaps one shouldn't let art even barely dictate one's love life, because, with the precision of an expert forger, we, eventually, nearly duplicated that exquisitely shot twelve-minute breakup scene at the beginning of *L'Eclisse*—with every excruciating moment and phrasing of our mutual death being accompanied by many minutes of silence before someone had the temerity to utter a response.

This sequence regurgitates many of my break-ups—those silences, moving from one piece of furniture to the other, while appearing stunned, and seemingly seeing but not, exemplified by the boyfriend sitting frozen in the chair. It may be an homage to Francis Bacon's screaming Popes, but the emotion is all interior, land-locked and ironclad—the shattering of something inside that can't move while docking in a new world of great pain. If life imitates art, it inevitably imitates the white space and noise art avoids in order to be interlocking, not phlegmatic. There is no self-help in art—it doesn't give answers, but dramatizes the questions, as it prescribes them; I had an inkling of this ten years ago, but I couldn't pull myself free of our latter-day reenactment to find the right measure so as to not land us in a bedeviled conceit. And maybe I should have been thankful for how we could so aptly embody the love-sickness, tracing and coloring it with vivid unsentimental lustre. And maybe we should have just been grateful to be alive.

And so the years pass like a flutter of calendar pages in a Golden Age of Hollywood film and Antonioni's reputation is currently half in the ditch. Ingmar Bergman said Antonioni gave us two masterpieces, *La Notte* and *Blow-Up*—he didn't like Monica Vitti's acting. For me, the most compelling and eerie shots in *Blow-Up* come when Thomas walks into the park at night, and then the next day, to find the dead body. He creeps in at night and the camera tilts up to a glaring sign across the way that may be lettering but is indecipherable, as he passes out of the frame. In the morning, he returns to find no body and when he stands up after kneeling on the ground where it once resided, there again is the sign in the background, still lit and blurry, though a few seconds later, it goes out, after which he turns to look at it, the camera pulling it into focus.

But what has proceeded this? After finding the body at night, he goes to a Yardbirds concert and races to take the head stock of the guitar Jeff Beck smashes and throws into the crowd. Everyone wants it, but Thomas runs away with it. Yet, when he is safely on the street, he tosses it away like a piece of junk. More than a few times over the years I have pondered the import of this because what we value tells a great deal about how we lead our lives. Things, objects and emotions (approval), are so important to us, even if fleeting, though when we've secured them, they deflate like the priapism desire is. Then I dwelt on the odyssey of further events that night, how Thomas thinks he needs a friend to go see the body with him, saying, "We've got to get a shot of it," and the friend replies, "I'm not a photographer." "I am," Thomas answers, but he doesn't go that night and when he finally does, the next day, it's gone. I believe this is the greatest mystery film in the history of cinema because he keeps returning to the park and every time it changes, but not in a surreal way: no special effects, no David Lynch jittering camera or itchy-bewitching sound, no moldywarps coming out of the ground to rescue people—yes, Thomas does dissolve into the green grass at the end, but that is more an afterthought. Thomas has failed, but the crowd is there, carrying on, and soon, he is touched by their act and uses his imagination to give sound to the pantomimed tennis game. It is the easiest lesson to state, the hardest to live—"open your eyes and see what is before your face," instructs Jesus in the *Gospel of Thomas*. Go with vitality, live all you can—the admonishments as clichés are paltry, but in Antonioni the image is all.

Does Eric Rohmer
Have the All of Me?

I HAVE A FRIEND. While talking together once, I mostly wondered when I should tell him my news: that I had just seen *My Night at Maud's*. Should I have told him while he told me about his wife? No, not then. When he's telling me about his wife, it's his time, wife time. She had some problems with someone from work and they had problems with her, but she was in the right. She makes a lot of money, but she's stressed out. I listened, but I kept listening for the words that would signal an end to the sentences detailing his wife. Ah, I thought, here comes the end. No. That turned out to be only the beginning of another aspect of her issue. Should I have interrupted? His wife's name is Maud, too. Should I have said, "Speaking of your wife, I saw *My Night at Maud's* and do you know what it did to me?"? I started to say it, I said, "Speaking—" but he kept speaking, speaking and talking, and I stopped. What just happened? He looked at me when I started speaking, directly with the word "Speaking." He watched me and I thought he saw my mouth move, a visual signaling that I would take the reins. Actually, he had to have seen me. His eyes met mine and the eyes often move when the mouth opens; they round and dilate as the tongue and lips ready to free the sounds words make when they pass out of our core as communicating nitrogen. Yet, if he stopped talking he would lose something or at least give something up. He may have seen my eagerness and it was too much for him. My delight lessens his delectation about his personal events. But he's my friend, so how could there be too much of me? Then he spoke, not of his wife, but of someone else's—a woman who is sleeping with someone his wife knows. I confess I didn't care if his wife knew her or if he did. I cared, I care, about Eric Rohmer. I want to tell someone what I care about, but I am able only to tell myself.

As my friend continued, I nodded and said, "Mmm," at what seemed like appropriate intervals. Inside, I asked myself, *Why does this tall but dead Frenchman fascinate me so?* Maybe it's the women in his films, maybe the men. Maybe it's the women's names put forth in the English titles of his first series of films, the Moral Tales—*My Night at Maud's, Claire's Knee,* and *Chloe in the Afternoon* (possibly the best title, though the French original was *L'Amore L'Apres-midi,* a nod to Billy Wilder's *Love in the Afternoon* from 1957)—and later, in one of the films from his Comedies and Proverbs series, *Pauline at the Beach.* When one christens a piece of art with a woman's name, the art, if beautiful enough, can take on certain characteristics of a woman herself, quite unlike a boat or car christened in the same way. For instance, improbably, to my nasal passages, the films smell like women because of their characters and settings. Maud and Chloe—both the characters and the films—have a somewhat more indoorsy fragrance, where the crescent of odor in the small of a woman's back betters the tang the underwear veils, where what dominates is the slight perfume of their choice lightly rubbed into the linen of their bed. This is an enormous draw, but this strange reality of being so close to what is desired, though it is only a film, parallels the male protagonist's issues in each scenario, outlined in Rohmer's own words: "A man in love with one woman meets another. For a brief interlude, he flirts with the idea of a liaison. In the end, he decides against it and returns to the first." The men embrace the tempting women placed before them. They kiss them and share their deepest ideas, but there is no consummation and, instead, the men all take an ascetic turn, seeing a greater beauty in not yielding and thereby gaining greater power.

It is not just Rohmer's actors who warp my mind and bring me in touch with something beyond his films. Rohmer said his films were meteorological and in *La Collectioneuse, Claire's Knee, Pauline at the Beach,* and *A Summer's Tale* (from his final series, Tales of the Four Seasons) the sun touches the bare skin that is desired, bare skin so lapped with rays and lotion that it smells like the beach. As I watch women and men frolic or lay on the strand, the sounds of the sea and the sights of the water bring to mind something primal. If some people live vicariously through others, through their children or through friends and lovers, other people live through art. Yet, apart from the sun on skin, even when the bodies are covered in Rohmer's cold weather films like *My Night at Maud's, Full Moon in Paris,* and *A Winter's Tale,* I am turned on; I am in instant eros because of the faces and the renowned Rohmer-speak, philosophical dialogues often between men and women flirting—a way of relating more charged than most skin shots in Hollywood. But I can also be instantly chagrined even within the same film because those representational heavens will lead to hells I wouldn't ever want to be reminded of again. Thanks to Rohmer's dialogue and his camera, I can smell those fetching French women, women who give off scents I have sometimes experienced before—scents that tie into past relationships, distant pain.

As much as people would like to live in a film or in a book, a work of art can only be benchmarks or previews of the life to come, like the sparkle of stars, which are sighted at night, but disappear by day. And though my heart would like to live in a town called Neversink, it knows that Rohmer, especially early Rohmer, reflects the checkered experiences of life. The temperature of his career is similar to Shakespeare's as the more realist early and middle stage works give way to mostly lighter fare like Tales of the Four Seasons and *The Romance of Astrea and Celadon*, in which there is a mellowing magic, a greater compassion, and a celebration of life's bounty. More than anything else, Rohmer's *oeuvre* is about love, with his actors speaking of it in a sometimes philosophical, sometimes Bacchanalian celebration of its impenetrable ingredients.

A part of me believes Rohmer's initial readings in philosophy, history, literature and other arts (he was a literature teacher, a failed novelist, and all the Moral Tales were written as short stories first), and his large swath of everyday experiences (his first successful feature film didn't come out until he was almost fifty) subsumed his work to such an extent that he came to know men and women as well as the Bard. He could draw his "types" with such richness of consciousness that they are more than miracles; they are the people I had become, been, and been with throughout my life.

WHEN SEEING *Chloe in the Afternoon*, a window of time opened and I began to catch a *mélange* of the women who reminded me most of Chloe—a flighty, brusque, young female with a face somewhere between a Fra Angelico and a Modigliani. The actress who played her, Zouzou, was a model born in French Algeria, but drug use would curtail the rest of her career. She's the woman who shows up when she's in trouble and if one doesn't see her for a few weeks, one feels she's found another occupation or at least the unlucky man who's going to temporarily save her from her disorganized life. Her abnormal equipage of boot cut, uncumbersome jeans, and a fruffy royal red jacket with rips, speaks of her struggles, but so does her posture when she sits down in the law office of Frédéric, her old acquaintance: her legs splayed, she is desirous of a real home, of a greater purpose to her rudderless life. It seems out of character for her to be sitting at all—a character so uncomfortable in life can't be comfortable in a lawyer's posh chair.

The carnal side of Chloe, what is hidden but perfectly explicated by news of what is unseen—her affairs with other men who treat her badly the bartending work that sends her into more compromising positions— stands out as the aftermath of her lifestyle, and is embodied by her posture with a man who doesn't relate to her physical being so much as her soul. She doesn't truly "fit" on chairs most people sit in because her carnality can't be so easily emplaced in normal society. When she does finally take a job at a clothing store she is happy for a moment, but one thinks she is only there to please Frédéric, who helped her get the job and whom she continues to seduce even after meeting his family.

With the physical scope of his characters defined by his literariness, a phrenologist like Rohmer would have to choose the only actress right for the role (Zouzou—an eerily angry dryad) because that statuesque face and will-o'-the-wisp countenance convert her past, present, and future into the audience's purview. We are able to read her character through her silent, intimidating looks, which broker other understandings.

This carnal side of her character is something I experienced with a woman, a series of women. These women were made-to-order in some ways—sexually they were perfectly irresistible, but psychologically they clashed with my own unresolved issues. Their pasts were filled with their own unbridled disasters and traumas: having been psychologically abused, raped, abandoned by a father or father-figure, they all lived with an overwhelming need to garner a co-dependence that could suffocate and kill relationships like a poison placed at a crack in the wall. I had come to regard cuddling in bed or on a couch while spilling secrets (actions performed with my first lover) as the romantic necessity to true intimacy.

Because most of those who caught my fancy had unwieldy crosses to bear, I went on expecting most every human I fell for would eventually, and, hopefully, sooner rather than later, release the bitter secrets as promised by my previous evidence. Secrets and lies were the stutter step to greater closeness, and if someone I doted on denied their past to me, I had no choice but to become highly suspicious of their durability, their soulfulness, and trust.

For a few years I'd loved someone like Chloe, who contained components of Chloe rather than being her whole. She had a bronzed Mediterranean face and the same sparkling, bedecked wardrobe, but life continually beached her. In further concordance with the character, she spoke often, and often of herself, freely displaying her frustrations with a society that wasn't recognizing her for who she was—though if she knew the answer to that question, she wouldn't say. Depression, emboldened by her complaints, grew on her dreams like a threatening fungus. If I fit in anywhere, I had to assume the role of a coach who gave pep-talks and demanded intimacy in the form of sexual union in the hour after said remedies. It was one of those tremendously perverse and systematic dysfunctions where each person gets what they want, but their candies are forcibly fed, with a trickery debasing all the currency the squamous souls ache for.

After I rewatched *Chloe in the Afternoon*, other women came back to me not only through her characterization and the actress' portrayal, but also through the way the camera regarded her in terms of distance and lighting—frames precisely shot by cinematographer Nestor Almendros, but finally dictated by Eric Rohmer. And so, I not only watched Rohmer's Chloe and Rohmer and Zouzou's Chloe, but Rohmer and Almendros' Chloe, including Chloe's final pose as a nude reclining on a bed (anticipating sex) alluding to Western art's depiction of the goddess Venus from Giorgione through Manet. I viewed this while episodes of my life passed, as if I myself and the principals were dressed in the fashions of Paris *circa* 1971. Like Chloe, pain informed many of these shadow faces in all their colors and shadings, and the most spurious returned. A woman who came to me through the computer had a very similar, tightly-controlled narrow Mount Rushmore visage fitting her tall frame, and though her skin, height, and bounties of flesh were opposite to Chloe's in pigment, density, and other metrics; carbon copies of face and temperament were enough to convert all that extraneous architecture into the thing itself. She said similar things to Chloe—her face twisted as she wrung confessions of past indiscretions and hurts out of her memory bank, delivering them with emphatic and knowledgeable words that sharpened the cut into my world. How her father abandoned her family, how she had lived with a woman. As she spoke, my feelings for her grew like an ectoplasm that had finally encountered its most fecund environment. I could hold her secrets and help her get to a happier place and I could do this while undressing her provocative body and kissing all the parts I growled to consume. And when she arrived at the other place, that mystical vibrant breeding ground of pleasure, I would be there as well—a blessed union.

Rohmer's visions of flesh easily fit the molten creation that memory can cast, but so did his dialogue. I wasn't in love, as the protagonist of

Chloe asserts he is, but our relationship cast a dilemma like the one that plagued the film's couple. The theme of *Chloe*, desire from a distance, posits the sometimes true thesis that those one speaks to freely are those one doesn't live with. When Frédéric talks to Chloe, he is able to share things with her he can't share with his wife. Marriage closes him in, as he admits in the voice-over to the prologue. He has everything he wants; yet, when he sees the women of Paris, fantasias occur and he lands a rationalization for his desires with a deft blow: "When I hold my wife, I hold all women." This is a man made to have an affair. Chloe could also be seen as the man's therapist in their sessions, in their "afternoons," but he rightly leaves her naked body untouched in her bed at the end because of the promise marriage contains. This decision is made even more profound by the following scene at home, in which Frédéric announces to his wife, even after he initially says he has nothing special to say, "I feel guilty because I don't talk to you and . . . confide in you . . . while I talk endlessly with people I hardly know, who mean nothing to me," to which she cries and answers his question, "Are you crying?" with, "No, I'm not crying. I'm laughing, can't you tell?"—one of the most credulous miniatures of the seesaw any relationship rides.

My main imbroglio with the aforesaid woman concerned the nexus between communication and sex, what Frédéric and Chloe never have. All those pesky angels who put up their hands to stop people from coming together too soon were summarily dismissed and we had sex very close to immediately. In our case, communication and sex became adversarial—tussling even when one was permanently put to bed. Our time qualified as a great vaudevillian sketch, with relentless action, problems at every turn, and only a minor sense of reprieve after every cliff we avoided. If there had been a live audience to our relationship, they'd never leave because what they'd witness would keep changing and morphing, even within minutes of its previous about-face. Making up produced goodwill, but later in the day, some adverbial phrase, some stray locution would diffuse our near freedom and all we had again went haywire. Sex was our hustle. We wound around each other, coming together with intense bouts of lovemaking, then taking preposterous breaks for greatly argued upon amounts of time, breaks to medicate the dysfunction that only drummed up more anxiety because our lust could never wait for our minds to be reasonable. We couldn't pretend to be forward thinking enough to let time dictate our connection when what we so often sought was the mutual orgasm to release us from it. I came to play the part of commandant both fetishistically and masochistically—deciding things were possible between us when I was horny, before taking a dim view when her co-dependence reared like the elephant that would crush me because I couldn't see it like anything else, while conveniently denying my own. My therapist asked if I wanted to be taken hostage. That triggering word did wonders for my eventual letting go of the idea of us, but coming into the country of Chloe, I was again face-to-face with a force that had perplexed me for nearly a year and sometimes still did. By avoiding sex, Frédéric had obviously avoided the pitfalls. The road not taken sweetened what was, but in my case all I had was lost.

Chloe was only one of the infamous women of Rohmer, and when I moved on to Maud and Claire, both the same and a different era of my life alighted. Maud, visually reproduced in a high contrast black and white, is around Chloe's age, probably in her mid-thirties, but she has been married and divorced and she has a daughter around seven or eight years old. Since most of the events in *My Night at Maud's* take place on the same night (Christmas Eve), this girl is seen only once, when she creeps out of her bedroom and asks to see the miniature Christmas tree lit up: a brief cameo mirrored by the appearance of the narrator's son on the beach at the end. Everything else is very adult. Because so many of Rohmer's women are tied to their hair color and the clichés that go with them, Maud, with her raven black locks, could be called the dark lady of his Moral Tales. Powerfully compelling and bracingly intellectual in an unsnotty way, she speaks assuredly, and sometimes surlily, about how she sees her life and the follies of those around her. This is most notable in her judgments about Vidal, her one-time lover, who brings Jean-Louis Trintignant's unnamed protagonist to meet her and of whom she gloats, "He's not at all my type. I was stupid enough to sleep with him one night, just out of boredom. I'm very . . . hard to please, you know, where men are concerned. It's not just a physical thing ... ." It was in the look of Maud that I was warmed and warned—blue eyes in reality, but a shade of gray in Rohmer's, and, again, Almendros', 35mm film stock; a look of erectness and censure carried through a puzzling but smiling gaze viewing the world and her antagonists (men). She is just an image, a phantom, but a face that has shown itself to me before. She wants something from me. She sees all I have: my body, my eyes, and my thoughts; and she knows they are there for her to reduce to a sketch of a person I don't want to seem, as inevitably she will. Through her articulate speech and Trintignant's perturbed body language in response, she has seduced me. Plainly I now desire her. Her grand screen appearance signals me to let go of my satiety and rekindle my wild, unconscionable ways in relationships, like falling for someone else when I'm already grasping another's skin. As Trintignant's character can tell after being around her, I know

Maud will lead me down a path trodden all too frequently. She is the wrong woman. That is why there is no consummation.

Throughout the film, Maud fights to keep her sadness in check at not succeeding in seducing a smart, Catholic man; a wound that can't be staunched when they see each other five years later on the path leading to a French beach. Maud has a tan, she almost doesn't look like her pale self out of her wintery apartment, but her eyes are similar, though they have less ice in them and are more downcast with news that a second marriage isn't going well, as she admits: "I've . . . never had any luck with men." Soon afterwards comes the mysterious ending, in which the narrator discovers his wife and Maud had once shared the same lover and they knew each other but kept it secret from him. In response, the secrets of my life waved. The coded emotions that made crenellations in Maud's face, keeping a wide-eyed, flirty half-smirk hovering above her pain at never having the man she wants, would probably be similar to what lived in those women who only told me a half of what they thought, a quarter of what they felt. When I encountered Maud, I encountered a gap. She is the sought-after that breaks apart the inapproachable space I imagined between myself and the women I had tender feelings for. She is the suture.

No doubt I watched Rohmer's films because the women were mirrors, but the desire, the emotions, the anxiety of both sexes around finding one's "type," a word used in nearly every Rohmer film, mostly translated as "category," were, until meeting "the one," a lifelong preoccupation. In viewing them, I concocted a therapy of sorts. The more I watched and re-watched Rohmer, the more I relived and, oddly, lived. Could I see again, through Rohmer, why I had come to the decisions I'd made or what I had seen in the women who could so easily trigger a raw impulse emitting from my testes? Helplessly, I grew romantic tentacles toward those troubled souls of whom I thought—by meeting my good Catholic bones, my noble heart and uneclipsing eyes—I could absolve their past sins. How else had my dealings with women gone?

Some said they were waiting for me to read their minds. If so, they're probably still waiting. Some said they weren't right for me, that they would have told me what they wanted if they truly wanted me to give it to them. But Maud gets most angry when Trintignant starts to kiss her and then pulls away after their "night" of talk and sleeping in the same bed without incident. After she runs to the bathroom to shower, he grabs her by the door and she says, "No, I like people who know what they want." Some partners aren't good at sending signals, because they don't know what they want, and some traffic best in mixed signals. Some even send the wrong signals time after time while professing they don't. Because people can't always understand their feelings, they can't describe them—that is why the face is often that extra-planetary orb that stands in as the better designator of what halts the mind, what shoots it into ecstasy. Like Rohmer, like Dreyer, Ozu, Bresson, Bergman, and Cassavetes, I've had to invest a good amount of my time in phrenology to call the situation and discern where I might stand. That is why these directors speak most to me—and, it is no surprise, they are directors mainly concerned with love. The most crucial question tied to the calisthenics performed by the face, which is also the most simple, becomes, "Do I feel love?" Women who looked at me akin to the way Maud ogles Trintignant certainly liked something I represented—at least one variation of a beauty that spoke to them. Maybe it was height, or humor, or kind company—whatever it was, every characteristic flicker of my beauty was born from their quivering desire, their drenching realization that something of my substance moved them. Though I could not see my face, I imagined that while they watched, my muscles and flesh must have formed some codex to marshal the intrigues I sought from them. Did they think about the future, about what could be done together?

Most certainly. The tall woman asked me about children. Did I want them? Did I see myself as a father? My answers were vague, but in the positive. Such a slurring assent to such a mighty topic had to be disappointing. But I had spoken. She had words to go on and she reclined on a park bench, eyes to the sky, instead of trailing after the mother and stroller that had engendered her questions. What passed might have been a scene from Rohmer or even Ozu, but we weren't buoyant or bashful with the lines a writer/director ascribed to us—we were guarded because we hardly knew each other. We didn't sit in a Parisian park on a spring day or kneel on pastel-colored tatami mats in Tokyo. We were in Brooklyn, four hundred feet from the Soldiers and Sailors Memorial Arch (modeled after Paris' Arc de Triomphe) in Grand Army Plaza and getting sprinkled by mist from Bailey Fountain. This mythic scene, frozen high over our heads, presented the bronze sculptures of Wisdom (male) and Felicity (female) standing on the prow of a ship, while Neptune, his attendant Triton, and a boy holding a cornucopia clamoured at its base.

Our fountain had its own calling—unfortunately devoid of both wisdom and happiness, a two-faced Janus would control our ironwork. We were only a month into finding out if love could exist apart from lust, ingloriously plugged into the stage dubbed NRE by my former co-religionists in Oregon self-help classes. NRE: "new relationship energy"—probably the puffy point at which people are most deluded about what another means to them and what they mean to themselves. Life is brimming then, it is the happy second reel in a seven-reel film showing how joyful two people are after they have met. In NRE, problems are suddenly no more—one forgets there are other people in the world, one forgets to eat—salvation has come at last. We certainly knew facets of each other, height and weight, which direction the lips would go to meet other lips and the approximate heft preferred to move one's body for pleasure's sake—favorite color and favorite food, too. We knew we liked film and theater, we knew we liked to kiss one another—we loved each other's smell. We also knew of past flops, relationships that had nettled us. Still, we didn't know essentials, like what would ultimately produce happiness in the other person, how to treat them, and how much leeway they needed. We were making frenetic love, but we were making it based on the uniform concept that each of our bodies greatly appealed to the other, not that our philosophies had met their match.

We were caught in the first passage that the men in the Moral Tales get hung up on—the body. Something was being transmitted when I came into her and it wasn't a need for distance or a license to disrespect her—it was a plea. A plea trying to cement something, but finally only able to shout that what we were wasn't enough. For a while our intimacy could handle the fornication necessary to make the mind a slave to the body, but then, no more. With sex as our euthanasia, we easily branched out into misdemeanors of communication that enjoy primacy when love is not love because it changes with every new discovery of the soul's aspects inside the body. A few weeks after the talk of children, the plastic shield we'd constructed already had many cracks. Our unraveling took place on the cutting room floor side of the Moral Tales, the side avoided or unseen because the men had been smart enough not to choose the wrong woman. It became bad and then it went worse. We started to balk at each other's sadnesses, as those were the only despairing lights of our respective theaters that still functioned, upset that they could continue to dare to. I had just shaken off the stench of a three-year involvement that left me blitzed and she had coiled around the notion that "relationship" meant full impersonal devotion. She had been out of the game for a time and craved someone to be with her, to check up on her, to reassure her, to be there day and night, on-call. But on the basis of a month's knowing? Our bodies had met their other half and sex put us peacefully to sleep against each other, though we more resembled car crash victims. This area of relationship was plain—we were fully engrossed in addiction. I won't deem our time a failure, I won't dub it any more than it was, except to call it extremely unmatched.

SOON AFTER SEEING *Chloe*, I also saw *Claire's Knee*—the most "outdoor" of the Moral Tales, though *La Collectioneuse* is a close second. The film might be a picture postcard of summer vacationing in the Alps, though Rohmer sought to downplay the landscape by offering only brief glimpses of it, a practice making it even more alluring. A fresh breeze of a film, *Claire's Knee* captures the mostly pleasant June weather over Lake Annecy. Not surprisingly, the only time the wind kicks up and rain pushes people off the lake is when Jerome, the pompous man about to be married to a woman only seen in a photograph, metaphorically bites into his object—the young, flinty Claire (though she has rebuffed him, fully in love with her boyfriend Giles)—and pointedly touches her knee, possessing it in the way he foretold the desire to his friend, Aurora, a loveworn novelist who lives at Claire's mother's house. All the characters are very beautiful in distinct ways, even Jerome's wife and Claire's wide-eyed, precocious younger step-sister, Laura, who becomes infatuated with Jerome but soon wards off his advances after seducing him. Claire enters halfway into the picture. She is young, but her body is womanly, developed, and ripe. Compared to Laura, she is silent and the most notable demonstration of how her jolly, innocent, but devoted soul shines has to do with her body—how she plays volleyball, how she innocently laughs while awkwardly taking a stance, and then awkwardly hits the ball so she injures her thumb. Immediately afterwards, being tended to by Jerome and Aurora, she says she doesn't like volleyball; she only played because Giles does. Already she is wise enough to know that making other people happy is one of life's essentials.

How can I see my past better in this film? Jerome enjoys a charmed, easygoing existence in Sweden, where he can take a few months off from his lax job as a French diplomat. Obviously well-off, he is in town to sell a childhood house to become even more so. All these things I don't have a subscription for. Rohmer has been quick to say his male characters in these films are complacent, and the other characters attack their complacency, and, he added, "You should never think of me as the apologist for my male character, even (or especially) when he is being his own apologist." I cannot root for Jerome in his desires, but I do applaud his later effort to tell Claire that her boyfriend is lying to her and is involved with another woman (as he sees by accident one day), only because the often bare-chested Giles is in some ways an even more titled and sloppy man with his outright dishonesty and his disrespect, demonstrated by his blatantly driving Jerome's boat too close to a teen camp on the lake. Besides his vampiric lust for the knee, even Jerome, with his ridiculous pastel sun hats, cashmere sweaters, and a full bristling beard, has some grounding and doesn't lie about his desires. If the film is anyone's tragedy it's his, and he is so strenuously convinced he knows himself that when relating the story of touching the knee, he says, "What I took to be a gesture of desire, she took to be a gesture of consolation," and further gloating, "I don't think I could have experienced such perfect pleasure if it weren't for the good deed I was doing." Rohmer widens the circle around Jerome so that his life is reduced to nothing but apology, the most self-satisfied kind that can fool some viewers into thinking him a suave, knowledgeable man, when the absolute reverse might be most true.

I dwell on these characters, their acts and ignominy, because to come to *Claire's Knee* is to be in the company of a woman I lived with the longest until my marriage, and to dwell on that time reminds me of my greatest failings. Michelle had not Claire's knee, but Claire's cheekbones, and though her genes hailed from Southeast Asia and the Bay Area, I can easily imagine her pushing the language of Brittany though her photogenic lips, something she sometimes accomplished with skill. When I saw Claire in the film, I was able to see the late teenage life of the person I had gone to great lengths to know and love during her late twenties. And not only the cheekbones carried a resemblance; the *laissez-faire* spirit etched into the eyes also reigned. Because of the sun, Claire's eyes are catlike slits until the light is obstructed. Only when she sits in the small hut by the water while it rains, after the revelation of Giles' deceptions, does their full blackness finally gleam—a way of seeing mirrored by someone who eschewed sunglasses and whose hardy Asian jowls rose during her many squints. The aura of silence and the quiet mooning over something delectable or ineluctable in her life—they shared this also, as well as the slight frame of a runner's body. The film carried this ghost, but a ghost created by my life experience, so only I could see it. Without me, there was no ghost. Without *Claire's Knee*, no ghost would be called to port. Did I have to go to Lake Annecy four years before my birth to read my fate?

Though *Claire's Knee* takes place over a compressed period of time, Claire is only briefly deterred by Jerome's barging into her life—her trust of Giles flickers for a day or so until she speaks to him after Jerome has left the area for good. Aurora walks along her balcony and sees them below her, stepping toward a small bench in the shade of a tree by the lake as Giles puts his arm around her in conciliation. Giles contests the story of his infidelity, and lies to cover himself, and Claire says, "It doesn't matter." They sit on the bench. Then the French "FIN" appears just below the bench like a quiet dispatch or admonition saying, *to go* beyond this would imperil the viewer.

In *Claire's Knee*, a spate of wonderments makes itself visible, but in the end, all the meddling, all the concern that Jerome and Aurora have about the younger generation lying to each other and then setting a rectifying course, comes to nothing. Those characters have what all the others want, though it is unvoiced: youth.

The Jerome and Aurora of our relationship was this woman's mother, who, the first time I met her at the doorstep to her large Bay Area house, acidly asked, "So, you are the one who wants to take our daughter away from us?" That would have been away on a weeklong camping trip, not forever—still, because of her daughter's engrossing medical profession they did not see much of her. Already tarnished, I could only smile and offer my truth. I cared deeply for her daughter and I wanted to spend time with her, and though we'd only met four months before, we needed to be together because the force of falling in love is the strongest human madness outside of the urge to murder. Michelle's family, represented by her Southeast Asian mother as a bullying kingpin of sorts, was rarely a priority for her. She endured the woman as one has to put up with harsh winter weather. Michelle's sister had already disowned their mother, but whether face-to-face or phone-to-phone, Michelle had an inestimable knack for letting this elder woman, enamored of soap operas and her rental properties in various cities of the state, press on about what her daughter's future should be, why I was an unfit partner (my career—social worker on the outside/writer on the inside; my income—little more than minimum wage didn't amount to much), and why she should be doing about a dozen other things she wasn't although she worked close to eighty hours a week as a first-year surgery resident. I stood as witness to these thirty- to fifty-minute phone calls during which Michelle often held the speaking end of her cell in the air and sometimes the entire phone away for minutes at a time while a stately drone of oblivious verbiage carried on—the tinny electronica of her mother's voice shrinking its authority into a ridiculous type of exhortation. Who in the world could respect this cold-hearted canary's call? No doubt there had been years of this prior to my arrival. Nothing would be good enough for the tiger mother—not love, not money, not position. Fault could always be found and exploited, blown up to unrealistic proportions. At first, I viewed such meddling as cute and even caring. I never heard the exact words, but the hypervigilance reflecting off Michelle's sullied face was unmistakable. When I asked what her mother had said, she spoke dismissively. But it was her mother. That she still spoke to her at all lent some credence to the woman's not-so-diminished role in her life. At first Michelle might have regarded it as mere duty to listen, but after three years of constant haranguing, coupled with the pathos of our second and third years together, the grousing added up to something.

The ending of *Claire's Knee* is booby-trapped with dynamite for my wellbeing because I see what I could not ever possibly have accomplished—overcoming Michelle's mother's declarations by sitting on a bench with my love and reassuringly petting her legs, telling her how I would come to something, that my life was not a series of artistic frustrations and underpaying employment. I had done that, though not on a bench by Lake Annecy; rather, in the isolation of our cold apartment in Buffalo. Successfully importuning, I had abated a few untoward moments in our connection, moments when we might have fallen from each other sooner like two kestrels done faux-fighting in the sky. Through the bird's-eye view Rohmer affords the audience at the end of *Claire's Knee*—that is, Aurora's point-of-view—I could again see myself, this time as Giles, even though nothing of his fragrance could I smell as close to mine for the entirety of the film. But this conciliation, this comforting, this seeing through, wrapping up, and entreaty was exactly what I didn't need to see, for so well I fit the behavior behind it. Also, wouldn't I have to say I had attained the ballpark age of Jerome and that his supercilious manners weren't so far off from how I had begun to see the world in a fifth decade? Showing people on the same train but on a collision course with the imminent ends of their relationships, including their relationships with themselves—this was Rohmer's purpose. At the end of the day, slippery incompatibilities could overcome all joy, all good times, and so, it would be with this Moral Tale that Rohmer summoned me to speak up instead of cowering before my truth.

My dirty secret was how I had behaved with Michelle and how maybe I did resemble both Jerome and Giles, as well as parts of Trintignant and Frédéric. I should add, the translation of "moral" in the "Moral Tales" is a false one, as Rohmer offers:

> In French there is a word *moraliste* that I don't think has any equivalent in English. It doesn't really have much connection with the word "moral." A *moraliste* is someone who is interested in the description of what goes on inside man. . . . [The characters] try to justify everything in their behavior and that fits the word "moral" in its narrowest sense. But "moral" can also mean they are people who like to bring their motives, the reasons for their actions, into the open.

Open for the audience. The relative innocence of Claire, the spidery sense of Maud, and the despair of Chloe—all were red herrings. Shouldn't I have been looking at the men? As Rohmer's words attest, his men are more problematic than his women. Because they are being dissected, there is more spleen to see.

Our struggle? Like many a couple in trouble, we weren't communicating about what was most important, and what was most important revolved around the main issue of cinema: space. It wasn't our space in the house or the inches or feet between us in the bed, more the psychological and spiritual space of relationship, as elucidated by the penalizing Rainer Maria Rilke in his *Letters to a Young Poet*: "The point of marriage is not to create a quick commonality by tearing down all boundaries; on the contrary, a good marriage is one in which each partner appoints the other to be the guardian of his solitude, and thus they show each other the greatest possible trust." A boundary is set, enabling each partner to become their own person, so co-dependence is kept at bay. We could freely say we loved each other, but could we be as demonstrative? Because of her schedule we didn't see each other much and I preferred this, given the time I needed to write. When we were together, oftentimes a wonderful happiness flowered, but eight months into a way of living impelled by her mother's imputations, Michelle felt she needed to spend her nights studying for an important medical exam and our connecting had to be mortgaged. By the next day, she'd forgotten about her promise to study every night, but guilt had already been born in me. Soon I left for a month, staying with friends on the west coast so she could concentrate and not feel I kept her from achieving high marks. But this was negligent overkill, and though distance made us fonder, it also introduced a dark worm into our associations. If it is natural to be together, restraining that desire might be the most unnatural of all urges. Then the untruths. She had started to sneak about doing what compelled and quelled her (drinking) on the *qui vive*. Why? I asked for honesty. Other events followed. Because of her access to various medicines and medical aids and devices, she could treat certain maladies she didn't want anyone else to see (she didn't trust doctors with her own body) including me, leading to more cover-ups and finally the great schism.

How does one tell the person he or she loves that no matter the love, on a fundamental level, they trust them too little to further cohabitate? How does one admit to oneself that they are attached to a liar of sorts? I began to shape my anger at the situation into a lumpen ball, and eventually I had a murky, medieval flail on hand. Of course, I did make overtures and say things, many things, but I lied when I said nothing mattered except our love. My revenge? Withholding the physical, taking away touch. I couldn't caress her, I couldn't cherish her. As I dismissed my own pain, so I discredited her role in my life. The shrinkage of my endearments shouldn't have resembled that of Jerome, or did it? He emotionally blackmails Claire with the information on Giles just before he finally touches her knee. In my withholding of intimacy I sought to break Michelle down, to puncture her sense of self, even though she couldn't help her dishonesty—it's how she survived childhood, it's how she survived adulthood. Hadn't I seen her holding the phone away from her ear, fooling her mother into thinking she took in the drivel her mother adored doling out? Rarely listening, but pretending to. Just as Jerome feels spurned by Claire for most of the film, I felt cheated by my love's untruthfulness and my comeuppance poured out in infantile behaviors, in scintillas of passive-aggressive babbling. After I treated her with an abandoning, cold edge, she might cry—the tears as painfully wrought from inside her skull as Claire's, when she cries just before Jerome touches her. Michelle didn't cry often, but her releases hardened my resolve to teach her more lessons in efforts to soften her. Emotion, no matter how painful, was intimacy. But my bullying always left an obscene and sour scar. I couldn't judge the quality of mercy. I would hug and pet her in the aftermath, coddle her and coo reassurances, and then take her, lift her high, put her on the bed and make a brittle, desperate type of love that would end in the same vanquishing manner all our sessions terminated in. We forgot who we were and maybe who we were with because the storm had carried us beyond the normal reaches of the emotional seas. Revenge or hunger? Hunger or desperation? An apologist would say she wanted it, too. But what about a *moraliste*? How would they weigh such a transgressive dénouement? Sex often had the final say: *If you two are good enough to fit so well together, you'll be good enough to get through life, too.* Spoken like a true asp.

We had no interlocutor, no Aurora, no supporting character or *ficelle*—as Henry James called those "aid[s] to lucidity," the characters who are the reader's friends, who intercede and clarify. That absence had to be a contributing factor to our failure. Living while dying in a dying Rust Belt city, bereft of any real support, how can there be success? We may have had a few friends newly made, but they weren't deep friends, they didn't have our histories at their fingertips to sample against our current gradient and pitch of entanglement. I'm fairly sure relationships work not only because of the two people in the middle of them, but on account of those souls who surround them, and Rohmer's films forward this theory because there is always an intercessor or a friend who hears out the issues and often pronounces a strikingly stark opinion, as Aurora continually spars with Jerome. In Rohmer's films, the community directs the action, whereas in Bergman's films the doomed relationship often implodes precisely because his men and women are cut off from the world and other people.

Our ending was as despondently abrogated as one of Rohmer's Moral Tales, with little finality to it. I left Buffalo, something I'd yearned to do as soon as I'd arrived, and would have done were it not for Michelle, but my possessions remained there and for two months we stayed in a limbo of not wanting to be the one who said with strength that what we had could be no more and never again.

For nearly a year I suffered through fits of self-abnegation at the loss, at what my ego claimed mattered so much. Initially, it told me I was very wrong to be away from her, then I was to blame for being away from her, then she was to blame for me being away from her. Away from her. Away from her. The sounds of the words came to have their own declamatory reverberations. I suffered so many romantic notions in that time, I swear I wiped my eyes with tissues painted by the Rossettis and other Pre-Raphaelites. The mindfucks I'd successfully carried out on myself were more than vainglorious; they were contracted to occur with the regularity of a nine-to-five occupation since I marooned myself in the ultimate metropolis without a job or a place to live, assuring the friends whose couches and airbeds I slept on that I was fine, even as my mind eerily combusted and I whisked away any life-threatening alarm with new exploratories of other women's fundaments.

My life tried to expand upon Rohmer's work of art, but I became vice-gripped. For a retrospective moment, I wanted *Claire's Knee* to tell me where I had gone wrong. When Giles and Claire sit on the bench by the lake and the word "FIN" appears, the air goes out of the art, and, in those seconds, my straight-jacketing feelings of loss did arise briefly. But whether it takes hours, days, or years, love does prove itself not to be time's fool. The greatest chimera each of us has to confront is our sense of ourself. The overriding "aliveness" of a work of art, how it keeps speaking after time has gone by, is the only thing it owes, for, as Walter Pater said, "art comes to you proposing frankly to give nothing but the highest quality to your moments as they pass, and simply for those moments' sake." Though it is frozen in time, art makes different appeals to our different ages. Without it, how could I make better sense of what informs my choices? The happiest and best kind of ending I could wish for was that of *Claire's Knee* and, after all, the end of the relationship.

In answering what would have happened if *Claire's Knee* lived into the future, it is easy to see that once a man lies, the deceptions will continue, and though Jerome is initially proved wrong, his intrepid wisdom will win out. Giles and Claire will go on, but eventually his lies will bring a fatal knife to their love.

I used to think Kubrick or Antonioni had the best endings to their films because of their grand, bombastic images or final sign-offs, with "Fuck" in *Eyes Wide Shut* being the best of all. Rohmer has his own marvels that speak softly, but are more philosophically biting. In Rohmer's own words:

> [The endings] are not what one is expecting to happen, they are to some extent against the person concerned. What happens is against the wishes of the character, it's a kind of disillusionment, a conflict— not exactly a failure on his part but a disillusionment. The character has made a mistake, he realizes he has created an illusion for himself. He had created a kind of world for himself, with himself at the center, and it all seemed perfectly logical that he should be the ruler or the god of this world. Everything seemed very simple and all my characters are a bit obsessed with logic. They have a system and principles, and they build up a world that can be explained by this system. And then the conclusion of the film demolishes their system and their illusions collapse. It's not exactly happy, but that's what the films are all about.

There is stasis yet space to think at the end of a Rohmer film. In the final minutes of *Claire's Knee*, the audience is given this luxury away from Jerome in order to judge him, as he nearly begs Aurora to do and not to find fault with his "perfect" pleasure. "Not exactly happy" might be the best definition of one's emotional state through life. But the best consolation to this ending is the same one that is bound to occur when one walks out of a movie theater, recombining nearly all the energies one must navigate to get through things. Again, Rilke: "You must change your life." Rohmer doesn't create the illusion that I must change my life; the frames of his films fulfill it. Haven't happy endings always been misapplied to the cinema? There is no ending to the art. Film is too effervescent to have pop-psychology direct its credos, but is also often too beholden to money not to. Some directors gain independence from these constraints. They are the artists who give me so much.

BY SOME COINCIDENCE, a few months after my Rohmermania exploded, I went searching through some old boxes when I found a copy of Samuel Beckett's story 'The Calmative.' In my impecunious days I

had copied it onto the back of scrap papers at a startup company I used
to work for. The flipside of one included a partial list of movies I'd seen
and books I'd read in 1995. There was *Claire's Knee*, on June 10. For one
miniscule moment I did remember it.

It had a reputation, it had a VHS cover that made me drool—Claire's
knee poised on the ladder by a leering Jerome, a still photograph that is
not duplicated in the frames of the film. I hadn't had a girlfriend at the
time, I'd never had sex, nor even passionately kissed. As does many an
American, I reasoned that French films were more erotic than their Hollywood counterparts, more sensually and sexually knowing, and by consequence would show more but be much more nuanced and refined in
doing so. I remembered the skin, the sun, the lake. The talking I couldn't
recall. It's interesting, but not so strange, how Rohmer gave props to our
country: "In the beginning," he once said, "the public that sustained my
career the most was not the French but the Americans." Why? Maybe
because speech from the serpent to the macho shithead radio talk show
host is seductive, and because what the average lonely American craves,
but is unable to receive except through this medium and TV, is someone
to talk to them.

I stared at the forgotten scrap of paper for a while—all the plays,
short stories, and screenplays read and the films seen in preparation for
a life I knew little of. At twenty I never thought to question existence, but
at forty-five I can never not ask why so many things are as they are, why
I might feel dastardly or beyond compare, or why people continue not to
choose a world of lies and pain and kill themselves. Like in the fiction
of Henry James, few people die in Rohmer's films, but their beliefs do,
which is perhaps even more painful, because with the death of belief
goes the soul, no matter if one is unaware of the loss.

I see both the little world Rohmer refined and our bigger one while
I now share this fascination with someone who promises to be the final
woman in my life. What I remember has a hefty hand in this present. It
can't be any other way. Rohmer's *oeuvre* is an exclusive territory that aids
and abets a memory full of anxieties—a process that puts me in mind of
the final lines of Shakespeare's Sonnet 31:

> Thou art the grave where buried love doth live,
> Hung with the trophies of my lovers gone,
> Who all their parts of me to thee did give;
> That due of many now is thine alone.
>> Their images I loved I view in thee,
>> And thou, all they, hast all the all of me.

Bergman's Spell

I'VE TOLD THIS BRIEF STORY of how I was first bewitched by cinema's potion so many times I've become brazen to it. At eighteen years, in February 1993, I found Ingmar Bergman's *Cries and Whispers* (dubbed) at the video store. Because I'd heard Woody Allen speak of the Swede in hushed tones, I decided I should try a film. Ninety minutes later, I sat stunned and spellbound, not sure what to do or think, but surely sure I must be onto something. Cinematic rapture still has a physical aspect for me, the minute torque of the sedentary body holding stoic while coping with the images before it. I can always tell how good a film is if my armpits smell afterward. The body doesn't lie. Ingmar Bergman is an easy crush—one writer I know didn't want to admit he loved Kurosawa above all others, because it was too predictable. Some filmmakers may have come to be more important to me in other ways—like Cassavetes, who had the brio to say, "I can do anything and I only need a camera and film to do it," a rallying cry for anyone—but I should write it unabashedly: Ingmar, you are my most favorite.

It's astonishing to think how Bergman and his films were so widely influential between the late fifties and the mid-to-late seventies. After 1983's *Fanny and Alexander*, his self-proclaimed swan song, he directed two other features, *After the Rehearsal* and *Saraband*, and his late screenplays were made into acclaimed films by his son Daniel, Billy August, and Liv Ullmann. Only Hitchcock and possibly Orson Welles have more books written about them. *Cries and Whispers* was nominated for a Best Picture Oscar and the New York Film Critics Circle named it best picture of 1972 over *The Godfather*. Bergman was a touchstone for Andrei Tarkovsky and Stanley Kubrick, the latter of whom wrote a letter to him in which he made this confession: "Your vision of life has moved me deeply, much more deeply than I have ever been moved by any films."

In childhood Bergman was fascinated by moving pictures. At age nine he acquired a magic lantern (his autobiography is titled *The Magic Lantern*), a projector made in the seventeenth century which uses two glass slides to produce images in motion. He played with it endlessly, creating many theatrical effects, including enlarging the slides so the images are magnified. Early in *Fanny and Alexander*, Alexander uses one similarly.

The religious aspects of his films (his father was a Lutheran minister) have been played up for years, but his overall fascination lies more in an outgrowth of religion: the spectral side of life most luminously represented by ghosts, demons, and dreams. Mishmashing these things with death, psychosis, and the war between men and women results in the essential root system of almost any Bergman film. "It's the same film we make every time," he once said. "The only difference is we are older." Though admittedly afraid of death, he wasn't afraid to have people speak to each other in the most cruel ways imaginable. In *Cries and Whispers*, one sister asks another, "Do you realize how I hate you?" But don't discount his comedy, as evidenced by the extended "farting" scene in *Fanny and Alexander*, as well as the bed collapsing during sex in the same film, before the free and easy first hour gives way to the doom, rebellion, and mysticism of the next few.

Godard sang the praises of *Summer with Monika*, calling its Paris reissue in the late fifties "the cinematographic event of the year." A film of youth made by youth, it is about the first blush of eros, the long days of a short love affair, and how people disappear from our lives. Its most remarked upon scene, the wordless track into a close-up on Harriet Andersson's face, is an early example of Bergman's propensity, especially when filming female faces, to reveal a character's soul wordlessly, through all its colorations and emotional entanglements—notably relying on the obverse of an audience's perspective at the theatre, where Bergman enjoyed a storied career, directing over 170 plays. His cinematograph, a technological outgrowth of his magic lantern, probes and bores into his characters like few others in the cinema. Gunnar Fischer, who favored more medium shots and characters walking into close-up (as in Death's first appearance in *The Seventh Seal*), photographed Bergman's films up to *The Virgin Spring*, when Sven Nykvist took over. The style of the Nykvist/Bergman partnership was refined from deep-space composition in *Through a Glass Darkly* and a frame stuffed with faces in *Persona*, to the zooming close-ups and more free-range aesthetic of *Cries and Whispers* and *Fanny and Alexander*, where the camera often moves with the characters, intimately bringing the viewer into their spaces, as when Alexander walks into a voluminous room in the family house at the start of the film.

Why the close-up? That is cinema's plainest advantage, as film can bring one closer to a live face than any other artform can. People's minds and faces propel Bergman's work, never landscape, architecture, or machines. Fittingly, Bergman is the psychologist of the cinema, and—perhaps because his dreamlike films, with a hankering to excavate our many glorious neuroses, came at the same time as growing numbers swarmed to psychoanalysis in the flowering sixties and fad-happy seventies—he enjoyed a notoriety and success unsurpassed by any arthouse director. Psychological breakdowns and people going into psychiatric hospitals dominate his films, especially the latter ones, when often a relative of the main character is locked up or kept at home as a shut-in. In *Fanny and Alexander* there is the enigmatic Ismael, confined to a cage. He takes Alexander under his wing while Alexander is hiding out at Ismael's uncle's house from his evil stepfather. A magi of sorts, Ismael shows him that his fantasy of his stepfather's death can come true.

Being the psychologist, equally in Freudian (unconscious urges) and Jungian (mythopoetic) manners, there is a greater emphasis on the numinous and uncanny, which fill Bergman's *oeuvre* from the character of Death in *The Seventh Seal* and the revisiting of many characters long dead in *Wild Strawberries*, to a woman waiting for God to appear in the attic of an island house (and doing so as a spider) in *Through a Glass Darkly*, to *Persona's* and *Cries and Whispers'* fugal dream states—and then to a blending of reality and fantasy in *Fanny*, ushered in by Alexander's propensity to indulge in the latter. In a wonderful book from 1990, *Images: My Life in Film*, Bergman wrote: "Today I feel that in *Persona*—and later in *Cries and Whispers*—I had gone as far as I could go. And that in these two instances when working in total freedom, I touched wordless secrets that only the cinema can discover."

Persona, in which a nurse watches over an actress who has had a breakdown and gone into voluntary silence, retains its inexplicable status. It can be read many ways: as a commentary on the workaday innocent layperson versus the bloodsucking artist, as an essay on psychosis or doppelgangers, or as a treatise on seeing, in which a long conversation, centered on the the actress' unseen and despised son, appears twice, once from each woman's perspective. It remains enigmatic and biting because of its minimalistic settings: a psychiatric hospital and an island house, each populated only by a few actors. There aren't a lot of contemporary foibles to date it, though the outside world is obliquely present: the TV news shows a Vietnamese monk immolating himself, along with a photograph of arrests in the Warsaw Ghetto, including a close-up of a boy with hands raised and Nazi guns aimed at him. Both overwhelm the actress, Elizabet, the latter being a clear reminder of her son.

Made at roughly the same time as other cinematic landmarks—*2001, Faces, Two or Three Things I Know About Her*, and *Blow-Up*—the film's images speak simultaneously to the conscious and the unconscious, with its slim eighty minutes filled to bursting, including a prologue and epilogue showing an unidentified boy in a hospital setting (a few critics think he represents Elizabet's son). *Persona* is as much about actual motion picture film and what we see it on (what is projected) as it is about the story of the two women, interpolated into the overall like a long dream in a short night of sleep. It begins with a movie projector along with a seemingly random set of images. Then, halfway through the film, the nurse (Alma) exacts violent revenge on Elizabet. She reads a letter written from Elizabet to her husband, in which Elizabet speaks poorly of Alma, even after Alma's many self-revealing confessions. In response to her discovery, Alma leaves out a piece of glass that Elizabet will step on while barefoot—an act that literally breaks down the film, pushing it across a threshold into its more hallucinatory second half. Just before the end, there is the meta-flash of the actual shooting of *Persona* (with Nykvist in the cinematographer's chair) as Alma leaves the seaside house. Why? Something too encoded to explain. It is being meta without the thought of what the meta implies, certainly when shot more than fifty years ago. The ending of the film—in fact, one of many endings—depicts celluloid running off a spool, and a carbon rod pulling out of an old-time projector, so the light dies, leaving only darkness. Throughout, the grain of the black and white film speaks—it is especially visible on non-film formats in the early morning fog scene after Alma's orgy/abortion confession, which is when the blurring of identities begins. Most of *Persona* came to Bergman while he was in the hospital, under treatment for exhaustion. Of the basking in physical film, he has said this:

> When I was a boy, there was a toy store where you could buy used film. . . . I put . . . forty yards into a strong soda solution . . . the emulsion dissolved . . . images disappeared . . . the strips of film became pictureless. . . . With colored india inks I could now draw new pictures . . . [and so] the strip of film that rushes through the projector and explodes . . . I had carried around with me for a long time.

What does it all mean, all this Bergmanian celluloid from thirty, forty, nearly seventy years ago? Maybe it is a reminder of how a spiritual life, no matter the configuration, used to be taken much more seriously. The main conversation of those days didn't revolve around a sub-human puppet president whose comings and goings were detailed by a plethora of emboldened cultural critics, many self-appointed and bereft of basic spelling and grammar skills. In April 1966, *Time* magazine ran a cover story titled 'Is God Dead?' a few years after Bergman completed his loose trilogy (though he rejected the term) on God's silence. Beyond that, the same question echoes through the heavy, headstrong works of August Strindberg, the Swedish playwright who might have been the most important artistic influence on Bergman's precisely hewn screenplays, and, of course, the philosophy of the redoubtable Nietzsche, who originated the phrase and had an epistolary relationship with Strindberg. Today, the ego, as demonstrated by social media and our text-happy world, has won out. How is a spiritual life possible in a techno-Gomorrah such as we inhabit? Its impossibility may be the reason why Terrence Malick's recent films, which earnestly investigate notions of joy, love, and hate, albeit through very different narrative means, are, outside of the cinephile's pantheon, largely rebuked and belittled as out of touch with the zesty snark of the age. But if joy is retrograde, what of Bergman's *sine qua non?* Call it harrowing, or Aristotelian melancholia, defined by Julia Kristeva as "not a philosopher's disease but his very nature, his ethos . . . With Aristotle, melancholia, counterbalanced by genius, is coextensive with man's anxiety." Why are we here and what are we doing with our time? When something truly awesome occurs, how do we react? Are we too apathetic and sanitized from death to appreciate the marvel of the sick sister Agnes, in *Cries and Whispers*, coming back to life after she dies?

I hear the outcry from the collective pop chorus: *I don't want to watch something too depressing.* Melancholia is easily dispelled by drugs or violence, or fucking people or fucking with them. Bergman is not a tonic for our neo-pagan age. His confrontations and dream states endure, but not because they can shred the shilling notions we apply to our moment's disquietude. One of the most ubiquitous taglines is usually something like "the assault on truth," but, of course, Bergman was always calling out the delusions of his characters—Alexander, though treated unfairly by his stepfather, still has to mend his ways, as his stepfather's ghost bittersweetly reminds him that he will always haunt him. In *Cries and Whispers*, one of the sisters has a flashback to a scene in the loveless marriage she still inhabits. After a strained dinner, she retires to get ready for bed and, alone, calls what the couple has "a monumental tissue of lies." Then she mutilates her vagina with a broken piece of glass (a glass broken during dinner), before her husband joins her for bedtime. She reveals her bloodied thighs to him and smears the blood over her lips. It's an image that speaks directly to the renewed cruelty of our dehumanizing age, because we seem to still take violence at its word. Lying, which many people view as a harmless vice, is one thing, but violence speaks to what is primal in us, what is impossible to shed.

Rossellini's Bergman

How did Italian cinema manage to become so big when from Rossellini to Visconti and from Antonioni to Fellini, no one recorded sound
with images? A simple answer: the language of Ovid and Virgil, Dante
and Leopardi, spoke through the images.

— Jean-Luc Godard, Histoire(s) du cinéma

IS THERE ANOTHER paragon of the cinema whose works have van-
ished so ubiquitously from the spotlight? After the early success of *Rome,
Open City* (*Roma, città aperta*) in 1945, Roberto Rossellini has slowly
descended into neglect from his heyday as one of the main progenitors
of neo-realism. Vilified for an affair, a child, and a marriage to Ingrid
Bergman (their films together are mostly ignored), his cinematic art
soon made a dramatic about-face when he set about creating the austere
history films that dominated the last ten years of his career—films much
less viewed in the United States than his earlier work. These extremes
of fortune are ultimately only a reflection of public morality or trends in
popular tastes, but they also indicate responses to the artist's philosophical beliefs, as encoded in his films and set forth in voluminous interviews
and essays. These are packed full of grand words holding pregnant and
dismissible connotations, like "humility" and "freedom"—terms he kept
breaking down throughout his life, like a child suddenly running his
hands through his toy blocks, destroying one thing to build another.

A well-to-do, erudite ladies' man, Rossellini, who had four wives and
six children (one son, Romano, died at age nine, which had a profound
effect on his father's themes), was a sphinx capable of great change.
Few directors gave as many interviews or wrote so much extra-literary
material to films that themselves came to be bellicose, didactic, and

more enamored of scientific theories than drama. Yet, all the films he
made—those of the neo-realist period, those more documentary, such
as 1959's *India: Matri Bhumi*, and the later history films—were parables
that reflected his own conflicted thoughts on the world and the purpose
of humanity. These ideas were first cemented by Italy's defeat in the
Second World War and the events of the post-war reconstruction, but
they were later informed by how science has affected our place on our
planet. Indeed, one of Rossellini's last projects was a documentary about
overpopulation produced by UNESCO.

 Germany Year Zero (*Germania anno zero*), the last of Rossellini's
War Trilogy, was made in 1948. It ends with a young German boy's suicide prompted by a world rife with corruption and deception. The war
itself is over, but humanity still faces a host of problems brought about
by mass death and displacement, with an estimated seventy million fa-
talities. Rossellini went on making films about people at their wit's ends,
before his relentless creative life (he made ten films in eight, mainly war-
soaked, years) was profoundly altered by arguably the most popular Hollywood actress at the time: Ingrid Bergman. She had sent him an admir-
ing letter expressing her hope to make a film with him some day, and it
was by a small miracle that he received it at all. There may be hyperbole
to this claim, but when one sees the first three films they made together
between 1949 and 1953, *Stromboli* (*Stromboli terra di Dio*), *Europa '51*
(*Europe '51*), and *Journey to Italy* (*Viaggio in Italia*)—there would be
three more, but none as immense—one may well believe that the in-
tervention of Bergman into Rossellini's filmmaking career was indeed a
divine one. With Bergman as star, the films should have been seen by
many people—especially as they were the famous Italian director's first
English-language works. RKO Studios financed and distributed the first,
using the scandal over the couple's on-set affair as fodder to enhance the
box-office takings by billing *Stromboli* as a smoldering passionfest under
the active volcano of the title. Following denunciations by the Vatican
and the United States Senate, the scandal overshadowed the work and
their films mostly failed with critics and audiences alike. Then, another
miracle followed—as all three works inspired the directors of the French
Nouvelle Vague, exerting upon them an influence Rossellini attributed
to his simple methods:

> [I]f I did make any contribution to what they have done, it was through
> stressing again and again that, above all, they should not regard cin-
> ema as something mystical. The cinema is a means of expression like
> any other. You should approach it as simply as you pick up a pen to

write with.

For years the three films have only been available through scratchy prints mostly located in Europe. They were missing certain scenes Rossellini was forced to cut, or contained scenes dubbed without Ingrid Bergman's voice—an essential sound element to the definitive editions, though they were all mostly post-synched. The Criterion Collection's box-set edition includes *Stromboli* and *Europe '51* in both their English and Italian versions. *Europe '51* alone came in four versions that Criterion reviewed before settling on an English-language edition nine minutes shorter than the Italian. Amongst the wealth of extras on the box-set, an interview with film historian Elena Dagrada provides detailed insights into the cuts censors imposed on the film.

Bergman wanted to continue to make films on the order of *Open City* and *Paisan* (*Paisà*) and each of her first three films with Rossellini were similarly produced with a very minimal shooting script—the booklet to the box-set includes a reprint of the original proposition Rossellini sent her, which only details the general story of *Stromboli*. Since Rossellini had relied on his then-lover, the renowned actress Anna Magnani, in the two short films that made up *L'amore* in 1947 and 1948, the experience of filming a woman he loved wasn't foreign to him, and, in fact, Bergman carried their son, Robertino, during the filming of *Stromboli* and then their twin daughters, Isabella and Isotta, through that of *Europe '51*. Like the first part of *L'amore*, each of his three subsequent films with Bergman is excruciating and never light-hearted, with a rigorous progression of scene and dialogue that displays the wiles of a major playwright, though, in some cases, Rossellini and his collaborators supposedly wrote dialogue the night before shooting. The struggle of love, a compromised action in the post-war world, is their subject, as demonstrated in *Stromboli* when Karin leaves a displaced persons' camp for another kind of imprisonment with the man she marries. In a 1954 *Cahiers du cinéma* interview, reprinted in the box-set booklet, Rossellini said:

> What I find most surprising, extraordinary, and moving in men is precisely that great actions and great events take place in the same way and with exactly the same resonance as normal everyday occurrences. I try to transcribe both with the same humility—there is a source of dramatic interest in that.

The ensembles of Rossellini's War Trilogy gave way to a figurehead, but more so a single face, and even though the films were made over the course of four years, they capture Bergman's visage and body changing as she ages from *Stromboli's* long-haired, sexual, plump-faced woman, into the broader role of Irene in *Europe '51* where, now short-haired and with a more bourgeois wardrobe, she shifts from a selfish woman to a selfless one, and finally to a more embittered woman hiding behind sunglasses in *Journey to Italy*, seeking out the treasures of antiquity and nature that will eventually redeem her and her childless marriage.

Knowingly or not, Rossellini also comments on the fact of Bergman's stardom, her beauty, and her place as an envoy of the Hollywood dream factory. Although she was a Swede, Bergman was of Hollywood breeding and, in some ways, she was symbolic of the liberators (the Allied forces), primarily the many Americans in Italy, as detailed in *Paisan*. All three of her characters have their class, their refinements, and their vanity to buffer them against more plebeian forces. Far taller and more fair-skinned, the 5'9" Bergman can't help but stand out on screen. The people she comes into contact with are the poor who work and live in squalor on the island, in Rome, or in Naples, and are happier than the rich foreigners who occupy Italy (in the two later films the couples are American and British). They look up to her beauty, her differences, and her indifference, which causes her breakdowns in the first and third films, and her conversion in *Europe '51*.

Joy is hard-won in Rossellini: there is more smiling and laughing in *The Flowers of St. Francis*—made between *Stromboli* and *Europe '51*—than both the War Trilogy and the three Bergman films combined, and for most of the nearly five hours of these later films, Bergman's characters are angry, anxious, and annoyed. In *Europe '51* her character turns away from her family and a life of worldly things after her young son dies. Perhaps Rossellini's thesis is that a privileged woman can only learn how to be human by encountering those lower than her, who lead simpler and more stable lives. One of the more direct indictments of these privileged characters comes from a townswoman in *Stromboli*; after Karin attempts to show others how she has decorated her home, the woman admonishes her for lacking in modesty.

Because of her looks and manners, Karin is an outsider in the small village her possessive Italian husband brings her to, and she insists to the village priest, of all people: "You are the only man here who can understand me." At the end, while newly pregnant, she tries to escape over the top of the recently erupted volcano. Yet, she can't cross this literal and figurative hell of smoke and fumes. She falls to her knees and says, "I'll finish it, but I haven't the courage; I'm afraid!" As she cries into the night, Rossellini briefly shows the stars overhead, and Karin falls asleep on the volcano. The next morning—accompanied on the soundtrack by Rossellini's brother Renzo's atmospheric, near-Wagnerian music—there is a provocative shot of Karin waking with the background horizon mirroring her own curves. It is a crystalline, thoroughly carnal vision of rebirth, a romantic image the obverse of nearly everything Rossellini had ever filmed to that point, signalling some change in Karin's mindset. Karin still fights herself as she walks back toward the village, but because of her night exposed to nature, she knows it is she who must change her views on class and sexism, not the villagers. She brought herself into her situation, and though she stops short when she sees the village again, saying, "They are horrible," and crying out God's name ten times after she sinks her head—she utters it with a broken desperation that could qualify as embarrassing in today's cynical climate—she will undoubtedly return.

In *Europe '51*, the setting changes to Rome, where the protagonist, Irene, is married to a wealthy American. She is a socialite, more concerned with parties than catering to the needs of her anxious twelve-year-old son, Nicholas, and in response to his calls for attention she tells him, in a tart splash, "You've got to stop being so spoiled, acting like little mama's boy." Nicholas soon falls down a stairwell and Irene veers back and forth between guilt and recrimination for his suffering. Incredibly, he does die (and this is only the first twenty-five minutes of the film), leaving Irene in a psychological coma. Spurred by the politically-charged words of her cousin Andrea, she only finds value in helping those less fortunate than she is, including the parents of a boy who can't afford an operation to save him, a poor woman with a large brood, and a prostitute. This character reverses in a different way—in the face of loss, she retreats only from her own myopic world, finding something foolish about the strictures of society that contributed to her son's death, including her own neuroses about keeping up appearances. Rossellini's impetus for creating this character came from the life of St. Francis of Assisi—the subject of *The Flowers of St. Francis*—and the idea of the saint returning to earth in the guise of an ordinary woman. Found to be a danger by the authorities after she helps a young radical flee, Irene is locked away in a sanatorium, where she decides to stay.

Cinematically, *Europe '51* is a moodier film than the other two—a much more "interior one," as the critic James Quandt says in his visual essay on the trilogy. This statement is qualified by the visual distortions Rossellini includes, such as the Wellesian image of the anonymous faces of neighbors in the circular stairwell right after Nicholas falls. The sanatorium scenes especially typify these distortions, with unsettling point-of-view shots displaying both Irene's view of her fellow patients and their perspectives of her when they first meet. Later, there is a striking close-up of Bergman coming to the aid of a woman who has tried to hang herself, as Irene then echoes the lullaby she improvised and sang to her son right before his death, saying to her: "You are not alone. Don't worry. I'm with you. I'm with you. I'll stay with you."

Irene's face doesn't correspond to the face of Karin—that woman is mostly still torn by her ego. Because of her loss, Irene progresses into a transformative figure, a "saint" in a post-war world, exemplified by the most Christian line of the trilogy, voiced very pointedly to a priest sent to comfort her: "When you're bound to nothing, you're bound to everybody." Irene's face is tauter than Karin's, less juvenile, with a more thorough knowledge of life's pain, and her voice is even-tempered and wise. Her cheekbones are prominent in the more modulated, old Hollywood lighting scheme—a change from the abundance of natural light on Stromboli. The creases in her elegant neck are rungs on the ladder to a face that has assumed a different power than stardom—the face of a woman who has flouted Hollywood's tawdry ethics and grasped her husband's philosophies, his losses, and his belief in something deeper for the world that he once outlined as:

> I think man must enter the struggle, with a great deal of compassion for everybody—oneself, others—and a great deal of love, but also with utmost resolution. I am not speaking of an armed struggle. I am speaking of a struggle of ideas. One must have the courage to set oneself up as an example. I know it can be very embarrassing, and it requires a great effort. It is easier to forget everything . . .

That net cast for something deeper extended even further, just a year later, with *Viaggio in Italia*, a title also given diverse translations, but now firmly monikered as *Journey to Italy*. Apart from the watershed *Open City*, this film has become Rossellini's most-admired, leading filmmaker and critic Jacques Rivette to say of Rossellini that he "is no longer filming just his ideas . . . but the most everyday details of his life." Unlike in the other two films, Bergman here plays against an actor (George Sanders, the epitome of a morose Englishman) who can stand up to her technically, with a greater pomposity and wanton cruelty, creating a marriage of mutual resentments. The Joyces—Katherine and Alex—are alone with each other for one of the few times in their late-life marriage and, like all the couples in these films, they are incompatible. Although their reconciliation at the end might be taken as proof they will go on to a new understanding, Rossellini took a more circumspect view:

> The couple take refuge in each other in the same way that people cover themselves when they're seen naked, grabbing a towel, drawing closer to the person with them, and covering themselves any old how. This is the meaning the finale was meant to have.

Because of its short running time and the large number of events that make up the film (each episode continually separates the couple), the drama is incisive and fleet. Before one can get a handle on another zinger by Katherine or Alex, Rossellini pushes them into the next frame, where they are often physically moving, whether by ascending or descending stairs, or driving in their car. In one of these scenes, Katherine motors around Naples, muttering at Alex who has left to go to Capri. She is stopped by a funeral procession that gives her pause, then she looks at the locals, who are far from her station in life, but so near to its solution. The Joyces move about constantly: going to the market, selling wares, seeing the sights or having an expensive dinner. Katherine sees pregnant women, who have no time to take a few weeks off and live the high life while trying to sell a villa with a view of one of the world's most beautiful peninsulas, as the Joyces are doing. This encounter heightens her emotions as much as the one with the sculpture in the museum, the tour of the Cumaean Sibyl, the smoke on the little Vesuvio, and the Pompeii excavations the couple visits near the end. Meanwhile, Katherine's husband explores the women of the country but comes away rebuffed or revolted.

The "journey" to the Italy of 1953 leaves this wealthy English couple headed for a certain divorce just two minutes before the end, but in that cinematic eternity, their car is blocked by a religious procession in which Neapolitans ask for a miracle from San Gennaro, making the Joyces leave its confines to be amongst all classes of people, not just those in fancy restaurants and bars. The anxiety of separation, ironically created by a force other than themselves (the crowd running toward the priests), is what brings them together. It's often been called a miracle ending, but what has come before—the saturation with Italy's civilization, from its land to its art and people—has made their ending up together as inevitable as the San Gennaro miracle revealed. The final shot of the film is not of the couple but of an anonymous member of a marching band in the background with faces of the townspeople walking by in front. In this case, the culture triumphs over individualism.

Bergman, though the lead actor, is never exactly "the star" in the prescribed Hollywood way—the star would never be made so vulnerable, so broken, so crazy, or so ignoble. Rossellini took the conventions of the melodrama and pushed them to more biting and cruel ends, just as Tennessee Williams did around the same time with *A Streetcar Named Desire*, filmed by Elia Kazan in the same year as *Europe '51*. Since Rossellini worked by different methods, with his cinematography shedding the traditions of neo-realism and coming into a sweeter embrace of the frame and gliding camera movement, his arrival at this type of enterprise is well beyond a chamber piece or even Kazan's stalwart vision. His dialogue flows from the images (perhaps owing to settling on the visual spirit and then penciling in dialogue late in the process), rather than the image emptying so the dialogue and the actors can fill the frame. His cinematography is born from compassion as well, presenting people without judgment, without a sedulous or overarching sensibility that tells one what side to take. All of the characters are greatly flawed—the neo-realist in him was only concerned with people whom he could portray truthfully, even in their deceptions. As Rivette remarked:

> [H]e tried to get to the *powers* of this look: which may not be the most subtle, which is Renoir, or the most acute, which is Hitchcock, but is the most active; and the point is not that it is concerned with some transfiguration of appearances . . . but with their capture: a hunt for each and every moment, at each *perilous* moment a corporeal quest (and therefore a spiritual one; a quest for the spirit by the body), an incessant movement of seizure and pursuit which bestows on the images some indefinable quality at once of triumph and agitation: the very note, indeed, of conquest.

The images aren't so grand and architecturally pristine as those in Carl Dreyer or Orson Welles, but are often more innocent and not as prone to nudging—the tracking shots peacefully follow the characters, granting the viewer the space to come to his or her own conclusions about the on-screen angst. Is there a greater example of the "indefinable quality at once of triumph and agitation" Rivette spoke of than the penultimate shot of *Journey to Italy*, when the couple walks away from Pompeii after both Katherine and Alex renew their calls for divorce? Even though moments earlier Alex had comforted Katherine when seeing the casts of volcanically buried bodies at their moment of death, they bicker once more during the circuitous walk through the ruins (again, movement) until they come to an open space lined with ancient columns. "Life is so short," Katherine says, and Alex curtly replies, "That's why one should make the most of it." The camera starts to track with them as they speak these words and then stops to frame them in a space lined with the ancient architecture as they silently walk away, background music swelling.

Perhaps here, as well as in many other places, the simplest sentiments fit the simplest pictures. History, and in this case the surviving antiquities, can engulf people and make them look at things in a way nothing else would. Can the space they take up truly contest the large and largely unvoiced emotions that circle so wide in our lives? With unrestricted images like these, Rossellini amplified his assent.

All Naked, All the Time

WHAT IS EMOTIONALLY NAKED ART and why do I think this is the only way to describe the films of John Cassavetes, particularly *A Woman Under the Influence*, and Gertrude Stein's *Three Lives*, particularly 'Melanctha'? Maybe emotionally naked art is art purified of any attempt to be meaningful while somehow obliging a certain political and moral agenda. Does one have to be emotionally naked to enjoy it? No, that's too drip-dry a proposition. So why go running to these two renegades, mavericks of their mediums? The artistic achievements of Cassavetes and Stein are important because they used their respective arts in ways that breathed new life into staid narrative forms. Their compelling and painful works examine, both cinematically and syntactically, many urges and drives which other artists gloss over when seeking to fashion tight, balanced stories.

Years ago, a friend told me to read *Three Lives*. I wobbled through a few pages and went back to something I could more easily handle. Stein's style seemed hokey—with the repetitions and seemingly unadorned language (going against the grain of many "rules of the road" for writing which say to vary words and not to repeat oneself), I couldn't appreciate the syncopation in her sentences. On a second go-around, her words subducted as if I were the Juan de Fuca to her as North America's mighty tectonic plate.

'Melanctha' follows a young black woman from her beginnings to her end, as she struggles to relate to her family, friends, and men. Early in the novella, Stein describes her main character in plain, unsymbolic language:

Melanctha was always losing what she had in wanting all the things she saw. Melanctha was always being left when she was not leaving others. . . . Melanctha Herbert always loved too hard and much too often.

These are the quandaries of existence as understood by Zen Buddhists. Set forth in each sentence like a fire blanket is an "always." This extreme word attaches itself to the novella's undesirable but always desiring character, who grows up with see-sawing emotions—feelings that carry on into her dealings with men.

In looking at 'Melanctha,' one also has to look at her lover, Jeff Campbell. Although the titular character carries the narrative, she doesn't do so by much. Of the roughly one hundred pages of 'Melanctha', the middle seventy are given to the dance between Melanctha and Jeff Campbell, the "serious, earnest, good young joyous doctor," as a maelstrom of tidings begins for both characters. When Melanctha goes and "wanders" after other men toward the end of their relationship, Jeff is hurt:

> And Jeff Campbell now felt less than he had ever, any right to claim to know what Melanctha thought it right that she should do in any of her ways of living. . . . Jeff learned every day now, more and more, how much it was that he could really suffer. Sometimes it hurt so in him, when he was alone, it would force some slow tears from him. But every day, now that Jeff Campbell knew more how it could hurt him, he lost his feeling of deep awe that he once always had had for Melanctha's feeling. Suffering was not so much after all, thought Jeff Campbell, if even he could feel it so it hurt him. It hurt him bad, just the way he knew he once had hurt Melanctha, and yet he too could have it and not make any kind of a loud holler with it.

"Hurt," "feeling," "suffering," "alone," "lost," "bad": the language of despair, full of suppositions that lend corrosiveness and instability to feelings once blooming with promise. There is a sing-song quality to Stein's prose. Things are proposed, their pinnacles and pluses outlined, but soon they are viciously and rigorously negated, so that pain is more painful. When Stein says the hurt is "in him" she takes us closer to the epicenter of sorrow. Because it is already "in," it is much more immediate and all-consuming. Also the "hurt" forces tears from him; he doesn't simply cry them. A mighty phalanx of despondency has taken hold and when Stein characterizes the "hurt" (a different hurt, the kind Jeff has passed on to Melanctha) as something he can have, too, it is transfigured into another, grosser djinn that assaults and confounds. Jeff Campbell finally forks himself with his knife, as the narrator reveals he "could not make any kind of a loud holler with it"—the "loud holler" being a term of Americana that grounds any loftiness in the plagued passage.

A Woman Under the Influence concerns a husband and wife and their three children. Nick (Peter Falk) is a construction worker. His wife Mabel (Gena Rowlands) is a stay-at-home mother, increasingly on the verge of a breakdown. My mother first showed this film to me in the early nineties. She loved Gena Rowlands and knew of Cassavetes from *Rosemary's Baby*. We watched the film together, stunned at the entire production, especially the everlasting, excruciating final hour, which unfolds nearly in real time. I can remember seeing it again in college in 1996 after a woman destabilized my senses. I wept wildly, overcome by the twenty-two-year-old mirror Cassavetes provided. I've been lucky enough to see it projected. I've seen it close to ten times, with each viewing sending me to rigorously examine my life choices.

Cassavetes understood human nature much better than his critics, who constantly maligned him, with Pauline Kael, one of his greatest detractors, saying of *A Woman*: "The scenes are often unshaped, and so rudderless that meanings don't emerge. . . . [Rowlands'] prodigious performance is worth half a dozen tours de force—it's exhausting." One can't hide who one is in one's art. It comes out whether one knows it or not. Ozu's calm is exemplified in his unmoving camera and 50mm lens always at tatami mat level. William Gass' anger spikes his sinuous sentences and Rilke's compulsion to look is always on display in his prose and verse. Cassavetes claimed many times that he was interested only in love. How many times do people tell each other they're in love in *A Woman Under the Influence*? How many times do they kiss each other? Hug? Stroke? Dozens. It's unrivaled in American film and why? Because it is hard to look at love; at least, straight on. American films often make their scenes too cloying and sentimental (Oscar bait like *Million Dollar Baby*), or they are too cruel (without being conscious of it) and incredibly affectionless (Tarantino and his ilk). These products have no real interest in duplicating the long durations of events and sloppy speech which are the stuff of real life (the basis of Kael's critique)—qualities Cassavetes confidently wrote into the script. One of the greatest conundrums of late-twentieth-century narrative film is how it came about that Kubrick's films, in which dialogue was often delivered the day of the shoot—with the re-shooting of scenes months later being more expected than not—were on some level more improvised than Cassavetes'. Obviously, time and money played a part. Cassavetes, who mortgaged his home to finance *A Woman*, had friends to help him out (Falk, of

Columbo fame, put in half a million, but also had to get back to the set of his hit TV show), while Kubrick had major studio financing and insisted on long commitments from actors. Cassavetes had to be prepared going in. In the last minutes of *A Woman*, after Mabel returns from an asylum and her husband suffers his own breakdown at her homecoming (he hits her and threatens to kill his children), the two come to some peace, maybe very temporary, and put their three kids to bed, comforting and kissing them. Most other films glaze over such details with quick cuts, smiles, and music. In Cassavetes, there is no sound except breathing, and the immense silences of people's gazes and touching—minimal words. The scene lasts almost five minutes, depicting the complete process of sending the children off for the night. Similarly, early in the film, Cassavetes spends four minutes showing Mabel waiting to pick them up. At the end of that scene comes another nugget—a mother and her young children having a significant conversation with no cliché about it. "I hope you kids never grow up, never," she says first, before she presses on: "Hey listen, can I ask you kids a question about me? Can I? When you see me, you know, do you feel . . . 'Oh, I know her; that's mom'? Or do you ever think, I mean do you ever think of me as a . . . as a . . . dopey or mean or . . . a . . ." "No," her eldest son replies, "you're smart, you're pretty. You're nervous, too." This shorthand might tell one more about our psychology than a week with Freud. Mabel shows her weakness and insecurity, but also her self-awareness. Throughout the film, the children act like children (if they are "acting" at all). Much has been written about Cassavetes' films having a documentary feel. Blurry handheld camera moves, uber-naturalistic dialogue, and non-professional acting are some of their typical traits, but much of this has been bandied about to insult his artifice. Because he bowed to no studio and practically financed his films himself, and sometimes distributed them, Cassavetes was able to create an environment that embraced open emotion. As he dissected the human heart ("That's all I'm interested in . . . love"), he found people to be both emotionally ugly and beautiful. He looked at his characters compassionately and celebrated them for being human and not conforming their pasts to the intricacies of a plot—there is no baggage to hold because it's all on view. During the making of *Husbands*, he said a profound thing to actress Jenny Runacre, who played his character's love interest: "It's when you're really saying something that people can hurt you. When you're not saying anything, no-one can hurt you." A maxim worthy of Emerson or Dickinson.

Cassavetes made films about himself, his wife (Rowlands), his family (his mother and Rowlands' mother play the mothers of Nick and Mabel), and his friends. He abused alcohol and most all his films show characters similarly imbibing. Everything he was culminated in *A Woman Under the Influence*, with the five films following it being aftershocks of this triumph. Cassavetes' characters aged throughout his *oeuvre*, so that by the time of his final masterpiece *Love Streams*, in which the main characters are a brother and sister who live with each other after their own marriages have failed, romantic love becomes something else, as it does when we age, showing how people attempt to love themselves when they are alone and nearing the end.

Stein loved sentences. Cézanne and Flaubert influenced everything she did, and just prior to writing *Three Lives*, she translated Flaubert's *Trois Contes* (*Three Tales*) into English. The first tale, 'A Simple Heart,' is, like 'Melanctha,' about a servant girl looking for love. As for Cézanne, Stein said that he "conceived the idea that in composition one thing was as important as another thing. Each part is as important as the whole . . ." Similarly, each sentence of 'Melanctha' is required to make the whole whole. Stein owned a portrait of Mme. Cézanne, painted by her husband, and she stared at it regularly while working on *Three Lives*. Stein became Stein by *looking*. Did looking create the emotionally naked result? Like many others (Cézanne, Rodin, Rilke, etc.), I would argue that intense looking promotes more intense feeling, more intense love, more intense compassion. "Stein was interested in compassion *as an artist*," Lyn Hejinian says in her essay on *Three Lives*, "which is to say *formally*; this is at the root of Stein's desire (and ability) to 'include everything.' It is a clinical, not an encyclopedic, impulse; there is nothing that can be considered unworthy of attention. . . . Inclusiveness in this context means a willingness to look at anything that life might entail. . . . [T]he detachment which it requires is what permits the shift from manipulative to structural uses of compassion . . ."

By "including everything," Stein gets closer to what is most joyous and painful about being human. The more fully conscious a work, the more repellent it will be to a certain cadre of critics and audiences—this fits both Stein, and her long march toward canonization, as well as Cassavetes. Although I am writing about her and his most canonical works (and their most popular), Stein's acceptance into the literary canon is still a grudging one, as William H. Gass notes in his own essay on *Three Lives*. "Stein's reputation has grown rather steadily through recent decades," he writes, "[but] it is a reputation in constant peril. One kick takes the stool out from under the otherwise unattractive weight of the lady. Nor would her downfall spoil anyone's afternoon."

"Anything that life might entail" is included in 'Melanctha,' according to Hejinian, especially the details of how people speak to one another. Stein's dialogue is a stunning jabberwocky of poetry, exemplified here by Rose Johnson, Melanctha's friend, talking to Melanctha early in the book, in words that will be echoed later on after their friendship dissolves:

> I don't see Melanctha why you should talk like you would kill yourself just because you're blue. I'd never kill myself Melanctha just 'cause I was blue. I'd maybe kill somebody else Melanctha 'cause I was blue, but I'd never kill myself. If I ever killed myself Melanctha it'd be by accident, and if I ever killed myself by accident Melanctha, I'd be awful sorry.

Five "Melancthas". Six "kills". When someone uses your name so many times you are endeared to them (unless they are patronizing you). These four sentences have the harmonics of a Bach fugue, with the "kill yourself" motif played in the first sentence and played back in different ways and repetitions: "kill myself," "kill somebody else," "kill myself"—ending with two more "killed myselfs", topped off with that scorcher of a word: "sorry." The sentences expertly demarcate the line between those who might not care to survive and the survivors. Rose Johnson speaks from the deep space inside herself that we often don't let other people see unless we trust them or love them in a childlike manner, not fearing hurt.

This example of Rose Johnson's speech is akin to the *mise-en-scène* that accompanies the famous spaghetti eating scene in *A Woman*, which contains close-up after close-up of regular guys, most of whom never appear in the film again. It presents individuals and it doesn't judge or condescend to them, especially when Mabel's pale white hands are splayed around Billy Tidrow's round, black, beautiful, smiling face and she says, "I love this face. I love that face. Nick, this is what I call a really handsome face." The actor is non-professional, the action is startling, accomplished so matter-of-factly, and for a few minutes one could cower at seeing race not being an issue. This beautiful, arcane image—even if rarely a true one—makes the audience see what it sees, as it sees it.

229

Pain Pays the Income of
Each Precious Thing

For an intellectual product of any value to exert an immediate influence which shall also be deep and lasting, it must rest on an inner
harmony, yes, an affinity, between the personal destiny of its author
and that of his contemporaries in general.
— Thomas Mann, *Death in Venice*

BARRY LYNDON. I can't believe there was a time when I didn't know
that name. *Barry Lyndon* means an artwork both grand and glum. Sadness inconsolable. A cello bends out a lurid sound, staining the air before a piano droopingly follows in the third movement of Vivaldi's *Cello
Concerto in E Minor*. This piece, which dominates the second part of
the film, steers the hallowed half of my head to bask in the film's heavy
melancholia. Why should I so often remember it? What do I have to
do with this film? I only received it with a steady swallow owing to its
three-hour running time, Stanley Kubrick's longest. What makes *Barry
Lyndon* my own story? Have I lived to subsume it or have I subsumed it
to live?

As the Criterion Collection saw fit to release a new restoration (the
first of Kubrick's five Warner Bros. films to be given such treatment),
isn't it time to ask if style and content are more inextricably wound together in *Barry Lyndon* than in any other Kubrickian enterprise? What
is *Barry Lyndon* if not the incredible research and work behind it by Kubrick—as well as by art directors, camera operators, costume designers,
technicians, musicians, historians, assistants, and actors? The yield? It
would be photographed (superfast lenses Kubrick obtained from NASA

captured the candlelit scenes) in a certain way (three hundred days of shooting) and what would be photographed would be the correct images: at the best time of day, in the best locations, with the best costumes on the best people, with the best words flying out of their mouths, and the best expressions painted on their faces—albeit through a chaos of sorts, as Kubrick reworked the script nearly every day and, according to an interview with production designer Ken Adam, shut down production for six weeks in order to reassess the entire project. That was an unconscionable development in major film production, and something Kubrick did again, to a certain extent, on his final three films—*The Shining, Full Metal Jacket*, and *Eyes Wide Shut*—making them only better.

Which people are represented by the Earl of Wendover, the man Barry leans on for help in obtaining a title? "My friends are the best people," he says. "Oh, I don't mean that they are most virtuous, or indeed the least virtuous, or the cleverest, or the stupidest, or the richest, or the best born, but the best. In a word—people about whom there is no question."

One brief scene frequently comes to me unbidden, more than any other. Barry sits in a boat with his son, fishing. Sunned by the light of the British Isles, they lifelessly hold their rods, as a dog sits frozen in the bow, for the entire thirty seconds of the unbroken shot. It is one of the patented reverse-zooms that make up *Barry Lyndon*, though it begins in the act of roaming, not starting on a fixed point, pulling back to show them in their enclave. Nothing moves except the camera and the small stream that Barry and his son barely float on as the Vivaldi plays over their ennui in the aftermath of Lord Bullingdon leaving Castle Hackton following Barry's brutal public beating of him—upstart behavior leaving Barry cast out of the high circles he once courted. We are witnessing one of the countless quiet moments that make up life—a solemn *durée* where people realize nothing, but are simply disconsolate while watching life pass by. These thirty seconds over the course of the film's three hours create a finite microcosm of *Barry Lyndon* as a whole. The downcast mood holds itself. The scene exemplifies Barry's sense of being perplexed, pinioned, and aghast at life, yet not intending to blacken the vision which created it. It wordlessly broadcasts despair in creating a monument to it.

How complex is the film, released on December 18, 1975, the last Kubrick to have a winter release? It ended a year already crammed with Chantal Akerman's *Jeanne Dielman, 23, quai du Commerce, 1080 Bruxelles*, Robert Altman's *Nashville*, Michelangelo Antonioni's *The Passenger*, Sidney Lumet's *Dog Day Afternoon*, Arthur Penn's *Night Moves*, Steven Spielberg's *Jaws*, and Andrei Tarkovsky's *The Mirror*. Why my continual hankering after *Barry Lyndon*? This epic downer of celluloid casts its perspicacious glow and I easily roll over to be bathed in it. Still, it has quiet doses of Kubrick's dark, droll humor, as person after person is deceived, insulted, purloined, and made to seem quite backward, even if they hold high societal positions.

Kubrick adapted a pre-Victorian novel for the screen, penned by the author of *Vanity Fair*—by far the more popular skewering of English society. In William Makepeace Thackeray's source material, Barry narrates his own story under the title *The Memoirs of Barry Lyndon Esquire* (first issued as *The Luck of Barry Lyndon*). Kubrick sifted and rearranged plot points and introduced an omniscient narrator who oversees and judges the actions of the scoundrel, putting the viewer at a seeming advantage in getting information about Barry—albeit at the whims of the narrator (or Kubrick himself), as will be shown. This obliquity fuels Kubrick's approach, playing against the audience's prejudices, challenging us to identify with Barry, as with his other renowned, vainglorious protagonists: Alex, Jack, and Dr. Bill.

The debits and credits of so much of man's inhumanity to man are portrayed with astounding opulence, but *Barry Lyndon* is a bunker-buster bomb for all ages, races, and genders. It won't even allow its eventual victor to hide from its rigorous and unforgiving eye. Lord Bullingdon is whipped by Barry and beaten, but Bullingdon is a bit of an asshole, as well, beating his own half-brother Brian (the only other child to be released from his mother's womb, but of Barry's Irish seed) because he can't stand how his mother has been taken in by the "common opportunist," as young Bullingdon calls him, and how their family fortune (and his) has been squandered. Everyone, except possibly Reverend Runt, is looking out for number one.

If my hankering knows its waist size, then it knows the object of the hanker is tragedy and the drama of a family created and destroyed with no key of sentimentality struck, not even when Barry's young child Brian, head wrapped like a shell-shocked soldier from the First World War, lies on his deathbed in front of his powerless parents, who have steadily become removed from each other's lives, and asks them, in a mushy, wholly girlish voice, to hold his hands and promise "never to quarrel so, but to love each other so that we may meet again in heaven. Lord Bullingdon said quarrelsome people will never go." No, not even then.

Some years ago in Oregon, my friend and I "showed" *Barry Lyndon* to our relatively new girlfriends—a double date to test dexterity. Recently, after another "showing," I was asked if I liked sad movies. I answered unequivocally—yes. I know I experience life as, for the most part, a sad exercise, a dolorous bath with a great number of seemingly happy but humorless people who will only lean on another so as to avoid a manic episode. To pretend we exist otherwise would amount to a patty-cake played when one is forty and not drunk or in love. Of course, there are joyful moments—watching waves, traveling, love, families that get along (in the end)—but just as often there is a tart jibe from a caramelized envy or a half-hidden hurt in one of our familiars, necessitating more sarcasm, but possibly creating pleasureless entropy. *I'm just kidding*, someone will say, and though I'll often laugh it off, I have dwelled some minutes on those harmless recriminations. They hurt. We hurt. People are in pain and no amount of brainwashing will have me handing in grand celebrations of sadness in exchange for the crooked farce of the television sitcom or social media's happy masks. There is joy in sadness, comedy in confusion, we live all sides of life—if there's too little drama in our art, we say it's not real enough, and if too much, we say it depresses us. But as William H. Gass avers, "If tragedies weren't tragic, no-one would go to them."

The only time I saw *Barry Lyndon* projected (not in the newer, digitally-modified print) was at New York's Museum of Modern Art in 2006. In the first few seconds following the end credits, an elderly woman bedecked in too much scent announced how the feature we had just seen was not her favorite Merchant Ivory picture. I didn't realize then, but can now decry with more authority, how people may look for hours at images and generate such conversely different views on what they have seen, spouting a tired testament to their intimates that will either be aped or avoided on the walk to the restaurant afterwards. To some, many movies look the same. The angles are similar, the light is nothing special, and when one anticipates a cut to see what a character is looking at, it is magically provided. The timing of Kubrick's editing isn't so disjunctive, at least here—what surprises and confounds is more what he chooses to display in the shots he cuts to. Why that shot then? Why the exact opposite view of Jack and Charles Grady in the red bathroom from one end to the other, breaking the unwritten 360-degree rule? Why the fascinating shot as Barry lies convalescing at an inn, after having the lower half of his left leg amputated following the final duel? Graham, the chief financial advisor at Castle Hackton, comes to visit Barry and his grim mother, who sits by his side. Graham is winded from his walk up the stairs when he enters the room, but Kubrick films this entry in a distinctive break from the style that has held the film for nearly three hours. Suddenly, there's a subjective shot from Barry's point-of-view, as he watches Graham pop into the room and sit down. It lasts only nineteen seconds, but it's enough to disturb. The viewer responds internally, all thoughts in a flash: I don't know what is happening, and, I may not know why, but it's exciting. Maybe it's the transfer of power, or essence, away from Barry.

I can also understand the outspoken woman's remark with a modicum of compassion, a grain of gold that has inchingly grown inside me in recent years, tallying more encounters with the cold and cruel as well as the joyful and ingratiating of our species. People talk in code, and if the listeners are affected, sometimes only those closest to their storm will be able to decipher the degree of forsaken emotion penetrating the inside of their neo-numbed hearts. Some people delight in equivocation and will not admit pain in the groin to be that, but rather something happening to someone else. Some are already emotionally neutered and know not how to accept the art presented to them, but instead keep their hurricanes situated in their own well-fed and well-groomed cages—strengthening by squats and curls of bland, unaffectionate sentences about most everything but themselves. *Barry Lyndon* is not my favorite Merchant Ivory film, either.

While being a very serious and sad work of art, *Barry Lyndon* retains some substructure of a comedy of errors. The great heresy that describes life, seemingly survival of the fittest, is presented as a multiplayer game of lies, theft, and cover-up. It starts in the film's second scene, revealing Barry's infatuation with his cousin Nora, who hides a ribbon on her person for him to find. Barry seems to know the ribbon is in his cousin's bosom, but will not search there and says he can't find it. She calls him a liar after she shows him where it is and then he trembles "at the joy of finding the ribbon." Then to the deceiving of Captain Quinn by Nora, as well as the duel, where Barry's bullets don't kill, though Quinn is reported dead. Then the deception by the thieving father and son, as Barry is robbed of his horse and money after trying to escape the Quinn business. Soon, he joins the British army, serves in the Seven Years' War, and deserts by stealing papers and pretending to be a British officer, sleeping with a lonely German war bride on his travels. After Prussian Captain Potzdorf calls him out, he serves in the Prussian army and begins the imposture of serving as a spy for Potzdorf and the Minister of Police. In turn, he lies to them about their spying into the Chevalier's life because he feels compassion for his fellow Irishman. The Chevalier devises a plan and Barry dresses up to impersonate him, to get them both out of Prussia. There follows the deceit and cheating that he and the Chevalier employ at the card tables in Europe. All of this is before the one-hour and thirty-minute mark, whereupon Barry espies Lady Lyndon and the rest of his life is fated.

Similar to *Eyes Wide Shut* in its incredible odyssey of encounters in its first half (which contrasts with the slow burn of the second), *Barry Lyndon* could have been played all for laughs, but in both films Kubrick enlists mostly melodrama in his case against humanity. Still, one can't help but chuckle at Barry's bilious statement about the paintings he might buy with his new wife's money, when he has no artistic appreciation about him: "I love the painter's use of the color blue." Or when Sir Charles Lyndon, the sick, soon-to-be-deceased husband of Lady Lyndon, caterwauls, "Come, come sir, I'm a man who would rather be known as a cuckold than a fool," while trying to stand up to Barry in front of the former's card-playing friends. These card tables are the same that pave the road for Barry to assume the title of Barry Lyndon, and the same kinds his wife seeks refuge in when they meet and, again, later, when her husband plunges into other women, with her money.

In *Barry Lyndon*, the comic repeatedly touches up against the cruel, so much so that we know we are in a world as real and unforgiving as the one outside the spectacle of the screen—a chilly place where on the way to the parking lot after the show, a young man will rush to give you the glove you've dropped, but an old man in an idling car will lay on the horn and *What the fuck?* you out of the parking space that you and the do-gooder are blocking by standing face-to-face, happy.

Barry Lyndon is another version of the Kubrickian pathos by which the world is webbed by desire for money, flesh, war, war-games, and other conquering excursions, including ultraviolence. With all the conniving dominating Barry's early life, is it a surprise he expands his chest like a pigeon to gain the affections of Lady Lyndon? Just before he meets her, the narrator, Michael Harridan, proudly confides that

> [f]ive years in the army and some considerable experience of the world had by now dispelled any of those romantic notions regarding love with which Barry commenced life, and he began to have it in mind, as so many gentlemen before him, to marry a woman of fortune and condition,

and there follows the storied wordless seduction at the card table consummated outside after Lady Lyndon announces she will have a breath of air in order for Barry to follow and fetch. As Kubrick himself stated in an interview with Michel Ciment,

> They gaze longingly into each other's eyes and kiss. Still not a word

is spoken. It's very romantic, but at the same time, I think it suggests the empty attraction they have for each other that is to disappear as quickly as it arose. It sets the stage for everything that is to follow in their relationship.

Aptly, in the middle of their first kiss, Kubrick cuts to them being rowed about in a miniature pleasure boat, a scene over which the narrator ironically says: "To make a long story short, six hours after they met, her ladyship was in love, and once Barry got into her company he found innumerable occasions to improve his intimacy and was scarcely out of her ladyship's sight." This shot, bridged by Schubert's indelible *Piano Trio No. 2*, bleeds over to a shot of the two of them walking through the extravagant grounds at Spa in Belgium. Their courtship consists of the enjoyment and view of the most operative word in *Barry Lyndon*—property: "I'm a man of property," Quinn blusters at the beginning of the film, igniting poor Barry's fire to possess the same. After these scenes, the happiness of Barry and Lady Lyndon only consists of the few minutes during the wedding ceremony where Reverend Runt glares at Barry while saying that marriage "is not in any way to be enterprised nor taken in hand unadvisedly, lightly or wantonly, to satisfy men's carnal lusts and appetites like brute beasts that have no understanding." Incredibly, in the next scene, the marriage enters its nadir, as the Vivaldi piece plays for the first time. While riding in the coach, Barry blows a long stream of smoke into his wife's face after she asks him not to light up. She coughs, but Barry kisses her quickly and tantalizingly, toying with someone he now has under his dominion. It is clear that he will not respect her anymore, for he now has what Quinn had so many years ago to steal away his first love—property.

Money. Property. Prestige. Conquest. How else could Redmond Barry survive? Barry is probably Kubrick's most complicated human subject. Barry cries, Barry kisses. He is fatuous in one scene and tender in the next. What made Kubrick fall for this character? Who did Kubrick see in this huckster? In one of the only books on Kubrick by someone who knew him personally over an extended period of time, Michael Herr, co-screenwriter on *Full Metal Jacket*, says:

> I don't want to give the impression that I didn't get extremely irritated, that I never thought he was a cheap prick, or that his lack of trust wasn't sometimes obstructive and less than wholesome, that his demands and requirements weren't just too much. . . . [D]on't think just because you've known a few control freaks in your time that you can

imagine what Stanley Kubrick was like.

From "I like the artist's use of the color blue," while trying to impress as someone aesthetically inclined when buying property that will garner him a title, to "You're not going to die," a directive to his soon-to-be-dead son, Kubrick colors Barry into a man who hardly develops morally until it's too late. He only ages to survive—as many of Kubrick's protagonists do.

Three distinct stages of man are on view in *Barry Lyndon*, from the shine of youth, to swindling adulthood, to the failure of old age—from life as gain, to life as loss. For each, Barry provides a face. Perceive how Ryan O'Neal appears in the first frames as a fresh, spry youngster, before his heart is broken by his cousin. Jilted by her wedding announcement, he looks on across the dining table, his anguished face suffused with the soft Irish sunlight. The close-up of O'Neal from a side angle is as reverent as it is magical. On par with the greatest portraiture, the understory of low light on his boyish features focuses our gaze at something simultaneously beautiful and sad. His blue eyes are blank—pain has frozen his features in an unclean rictus. How long did it take O'Neal to summon this? How many takes were requested to tap into such wellsprings of hurt?

Flash then to just before the intermission. At Spa, Barry's more angular adult face, the second, is powdered white, with his white wig knotted back and his lips repulsed from showing their obvious triumph by hiding in his mouth. After Barry learns cues from the Chevalier, he grows more cunning. His sly smile toward sickly Lord Lyndon infuriates his lordship. Barry says, "I hope you're not thinking of leaving us so soon, Sir Charles?" but the latter guffaws about how he will not die so soon for his wife to get remarried, presumably to Barry. In closing, Barry says, "Sir, let those laugh that win," and with Barry's luck, Sir Charles soon dies. The candlelight in this gallery warms and blurs the photography—in the eighteenth century, all wealthy people have a pallor about them. The rich have spoils, and the leisure to sit in their rooms, gambling useless money, despoiling themselves and spoiling away in the process. Barry is already so sure of his attaining a "position," he simpers with pity, looking down on Sir Charles as if the old man were an ant.

And finally, the third face, after his son's death, is embittered Barry. With no makeup, he painfully, meekly gapes at his step-son in the salon and during the last duel, knowing he must avail himself in response to Bullingdon's call for satisfaction. With his hair naturally grayed, his aged face impastoed with anguish, and deliberately sealed forever, Barry's cunning and vigor are never to return, for he has had all the little he loved in life taken away. Like Jack at the end of *The Shining*, Barry's ability to utilize language breaks down and he only says one word, "yes," three times during the duel. This is the extent of his speech following the deathbed scene until he repeats the doctor's line, "Lose the leg?"—a silence lasting some twenty minutes of screen time.

Kubrick's main theme is to track the descent of man. His later works (as well as earlier in *Lolita*) use the borrowed literary method of following one character and mapping his journey through the madness of living: from Alex in *A Clockwork Orange*, to Barry Lyndon, to Jack in *The Shining*, Joker in *Full Metal Jacket*, and Bill in *Eyes Wide Shut*. Yet in spite of how much of Barry is presented, he remains elusive. Because Barry hides from himself (understandably, as he can be barely said to know himself), Kubrick trots out the narrator, who reveals things before they happen, waxing over any narrative tension, so the audience is ever ahead of Barry, perhaps making it easier to view him compassionately because, compared to the Irishman, we are in the position of God. Still, even the narrator becomes insignificant. For twenty minutes, from the moment after Lady Lyndon's suicide attempt until the shot of one-legged Barry leaving the inn following the duel, the narrator is silent; the drama of the impending duel reigns.

How are we to take such a man who destroys most everything he sees, yet dotes on his son, loving him with what the narrator calls a "blind impartiality"? Is this selfishness in extremis? People speak of living for their children—they do, they must. If Barry's only happiness was his child, who can argue that his concern for Brian was the most selfless act of his life? But didn't he also carry his injured uncle off the battlefield, as well as Captain Potzdorf, rescuing him from certain death? Barry is advanced for his heroism, but his hunger for all other kinds of advancement pervades the film and his marriage to Lady Lyndon is one long, lonely means to an end (the death of his son) that he wouldn't have wanted or thought possible. Hence, tragic. Incredibly, Barry lands the fiercest malcontent's greatest dream—he marries into a position where people will serve only him, and his friendless existence will seem full because of his money and property, even though, in truth, it is more empty than before. The two women in his life might have been his most intimate equals, but he quashes his wife and his mother is an awful role model, only negatively charging him, speaking with a Lady Macbeth-like power-thirst during a quaggy interchange about his future:

You have not a penny of your own. Upon her death the entire estate would go to young Bullingdon, who bears you little affection. You could be penniless tomorrow and darling Brian at the mercy of his stepbrother. . . . [T]here is only one way for you and your son to have real security. You must obtain a title. I shall not rest until I see you Lord Lyndon. You have important friends. They can tell you how these things are done. For money, well-timed and properly applied, can accomplish anything.

It is perhaps too simplistic to say Barry relates to Brian best because he is a child himself, but it is false to assay any more convenient reason.

The death of Brian. Of the many deaths in Kubrick's cinema, this death is the most important, excepting maybe the destruction of the world in *Dr. Strangelove*. The deaths of others—Jack, HAL, Quilty—are called for, but this one goes against natural law. It's the one not prepared for and, incredibly, it is not the deathbed scene where I steam up so much as its curious precursor, where the narrator reveals to the audience ten minutes before it happens what is going to occur. Whatever joy we see Barry sharing with his son, while they page through a picture book or practice fencing, is truncated by the doomed words accompanying the shot showing Brian weakly swinging a croquet mallet as he is watched by Barry, his mother, Lady Lyndon, and the Reverend (with three dogs interspersed between them; the one in the middle, behind Brian, frolics), all in a balanced arrangement. A prideful film glazes their eyes, sightlines joined in a large upside-down pyramidal composition. This shot is again a reverse zoom, starting on the mallet and pulling back to show Brian, then his family and the dogs (a reverse lineage, a three ages of man—the parents are just behind him and his grandmother is in the background), while the narrator delivers the keynote on mortality. Here are the most precious words on Barry's tragedy (mostly transposed from Thackeray), for however much a crude deceiver he is, how can the audience begrudge him his coming torment?

> Barry had his faults, but no man could say of him that he was not a good and tender father. He loved his son with a blind impartiality, he denied him nothing. It is impossible to convey what high hopes he had for the boy and how he indulged in a thousand fond anticipations as to his future success and figure in the world. But fate had determined that he should leave none of his race behind him and that he should finish his life poor, lonely, and childless.

Does God take away Brian? As the miniature coffin is wheeled off by the same small white carriage the same two sheep pulled on his birthday, the Reverend offers a recitation, echoing his marriage remarks in sternness: "We brought nothing into this world and it is certain we can carry nothing out. The Lord gave and the Lord hath taken away. Blessed is the name of the Lord." God exists in *Barry Lyndon* because England is a Protestant nation. What of fate? What of karma? Barry cheated his way to his position. It's in keeping with the theme and action of the film that he should lose out as well. What is the history of Europe and the world outright? Enormous spills of blood over power, land, and money. Bloodsport, revenge. When Brian is killed by an insatiable need to enjoy his birthday present (a horse) and breaks his promise to Barry about going to the farm to see it (risking a "good whipping" from Barry), he continues the great chain of deceitful reverberations in the film. While Barry's many indiscretions mostly advance him in society, he climbs upward only enough to lose everything, including a leg. Brian's deception leads to his death and, by extension, Barry's—freeze-framed out of any more life at the end. In Kubrick, what characters desire the most gets them into trouble.

Why else would Kubrick relish the myth of Icarus in his only publicly recorded speech after 1968, the acceptance of the 1997 Directors Guild of America Lifetime Achievement Award?

How can I speak to the pain of losing a child when, thankfully, I haven't? Many would say "imagination," a fiction-maker's bane. And a few others, in the philosophical vein, would counsel how imagined pain can be worse than real pain. Most people who watch *Barry Lyndon* have not lost children and they still feel—they gulp and sniffle at what could be. They see their mother and father before them as many might in dreams. Parents they do or did have, even if no children. Everyone exists at that triangle formed by the parents and child at the deathbed. People either place themselves as one of the parents or as the child, or possibly in both positions at once. No matter what Barry has done or is, the audience ignites on behalf of Brian and vicariously for Barry, as Kubrick surely knew they would. This complicates the picture, asking us to delve into the dark of our hearts to try and explain this tragedy to ourselves. What makes identification with a film's essence is the ability to place oneself in character, and by extension, in the very frames—those figments and figures that could be life. To live a work of art—the salty surrender to a form more knowing and final, so these Bruegels, Bachs, and Becketts take our lusts and leech them dry—is to be informed enough to sense our time will come.

I feel pain beyond my means, my pity, and my years because Kubrick

sought to create the kind of art that makes possible the deepest iden-
tifications in the human soul. I can speak to the pain of losing a child
because Kubrick's artifice wills it. "Pain pays the income of each precious thing," says the Bard. I have seen myself and everyone else and
their deaths by this sequence in *Barry Lyndon*—one consecrated vision
flowing and flown.

Because the strains of an unhappy family spread through *Barry Lyndon* in a more stately treatment than the pompous "Fuck you, mom!" of
most modern art, I was most excited to show the picture to my parents. I
needed to connect with them, seeking their understanding of who I was
at eighteen years—a person invaded by and as indebted to Kubrick as a
drowsy, desperate lover. *Barry Lyndon* was the first of Kubrick's two films
with children playing a pivotal role, to be followed by *The Shining*. The
former seduced me to try and present it to my parents for connection's
sake. Divorced, my parents would, separately, meet Kubrick for final approval.

My father fell asleep watching *Barry Lyndon*. My mother fell asleep
watching *Barry Lyndon*. I fell asleep with my mother as we watched
Barry Lyndon, leaving a family friend to fend for herself through Barry's
early army experiences. As Abbas Kiarostami has said, "I don't like to
arouse the viewer emotionally or give him advice. . . . I prefer films that
put the audience to sleep," so I see no ill in letting oneself have Kubrick
put one to bed. Out of the rambunctious, violent, or threateningly violent final five Kubrick films, *Barry Lyndon* is the most easeful, encouraging snoozing more than any other. My mother and father recovered
after their early naps and did watch the rest—all the videoed celluloid
down to the last wordless scene and the all-word epilogue. I don't believe
I could actively place my contumely with the world at age eighteen by
citing a specific grievance or scenario of destruction wished for, but I
believe what I autobiographically asked both my parents, via Kubrick,
was: What if I were created by a marriage, as Brian was, between two
people whose connection seemed a tad unwholesome? And what if that
son died? Would it change your lives if I were to die? How would they
change? Was I wayward enough to believe that if they cried for Brian,
they would cry for me? I was, but did I know how recriminations can
make a piss taken in old age sting? Or how as the body breaks down and
hopes and desires become scores that will never be settled, certain obliv-
ion gets clearer? I believe I was aware enough to grok Kubrick wasn't
fucking around—that real life, however candy-colored or shit-scented,
did at some base, though dreamlike level, resemble the world of Kubrick.
That's why some of my elders with little aesthetic appreciation about

them spoke of his work in hushed tones, and why people still continually watch the films, repeat the lines, and pay tribute in myriad other forms of imitation and affection. Kubrick speaks across the spectrum. The film gave my parents pause, at least enough to satisfy my longing that they demonstrate feeling at the sight of tragedy, and maybe, by extension, at the sight of love. Love of which object? Art, creator of art, or emissary of art? Kubrick had the mass appeal I needed to entreat the two most important people in my life, whose divorce triggered an impulse to blame myself for its vagaries. If we could connect through *Barry Lyndon*, I thought we could share whatever else life had in store for us.

We did quietly connect over *Barry Lyndon*, but my greatest malfunction was thinking this would improve our relationships. We interacted in a zone of pushing and pulling emotional baggage, the driving force in Kubrick's universe. The mirror disturbed, and gave us a basis for unearthing, but love can leak out far from stimulus. If it comes from the heart, it's a maudlin intimacy. If it comes from the mind, it's a cold, rational gel. The charge and its after-expression is in the background of the painting or the frame, in the white space of the page. Art can only go so far, it can inspire, but it isn't the change itself—the human being has to take the art and make the next step alone.

And what of that epilogue? What does it speak to? All that was Rococo at the time of *Barry Lyndon's* setting (from the 1750s to 1789) does, finally, not come through, and for good reason. Schubert's music is from the nineteenth century, Vivaldi's from the sixteenth. The film might show us eighteenth century Europe, but the emotions and behaviors belong to all centuries, and specifically the world of the early- to mid-1970s. Why all the deceit? As Kubrick prepared the screenplay and film, the story of Watergate broke. Was this calumny transposed so easily onto another place and time which simply contained all the excesses and sour-faced problems of another without the benefits of the industrial revolution? As some historians argue that books of history are more about the time they were written than the time they describe, so it seems any artistic piece about another age is destined to be marooned in the era in which it was conceived. In Thackeray's novel, what would become Kubrick's epilogue appears early on, as a commentary by Barry himself about the early troubles of his mother and father:

IT WAS IN THE REIGN OF GEORGE III
THAT THE AFORESAID PERSONAGES LIVED AND QUARRELLED:
GOOD OR BAD, HANDSOME OR UGLY, RICH OR POOR
THEY ARE ALL EQUAL NOW

In examining this there is one curious word that has echoes: "quar-relled." On his deathbed, Brian asks that his parents never "quarrel," but Kubrick admits that the audience has just been watching a film showing people who "lived and quarrelled." Not "lived and laughed" or "lived and cried," but "quarrelled." Obvious, as it is, to say that everyone, no mat-ter their station in life, will one day be equal, Kubrick decided it bore repeating. And "in the reign of George III"? Most everyone lives under some government or rule—is this Kubrick's statement on humanity? His abacus for prefiguring carnage coming and past? The epilogue speaks in egalitarian tones to me, but it shares in the spirit of many of Kubrick's endings—we're all fucked but we're all in this together—especially *The Killing*, *Paths of Glory*, *Dr. Strangelove*, *Full Metal Jacket*, and *Eyes Wide Shut*. His endings are cosmic, as if he were a seer stationed in outer space, peering in on what makes us human and why we try and so often fail to be satisfied. If I attempt to account for the appearance of the Star-Child at the end of *2001*, and my head tingles from reincarnation jitters, it is only because the apparent awe of that finale is too inspiring. Okay, rebirth—but what is the next step? Are we going to do it right this time? How?

Kubrick is the great leveler. Bill, Jack, Barry, Alex, HAL, the govern-ment officials and generals, Humbert, Quilty, and Johnny Clay from *The Killing*—they all pay in different ways for their lies, their violence, their lack of conscience, and their unconsciousness. But in no other film is Kubrick's leveling so explicitly voiced than in *Barry Lyndon*, because it concerns a society dependent on etiquette as reinforced by the circumlo-cutions and eschewals of language—language is as key to one's survival in Barry's world as avoiding bullets is today. To deliver the message in his films, Kubrick utilizes pregnant dialogue intrinsic to his characters and their faults—be they psychotic lovers or generals, a conniving computer, a band of rogues, a failed writer from Boulder, an oblivious doctor in love with himself, the half-hearted figure of Barry Lyndon, or Barry's stupen-dously innocent son Brian. They are all fated to the same end.

Mr. Fincher and Monsieur Dreyer

The enjoyment of a work of art, the acceptance of an irresistible illusion, constituting, to my sense, our highest experience of "luxury,"
the luxury is not greatest, by my consequent measure, when the work
asks for as little attention as possible. It is greatest, it is delightfully,
divinely great, when we feel the surface, like the thick ice of the skat-
er's pond, bear without cracking the strongest pressure we throw on
it. The sound of the crack one may recognise, but never surely to call
it a luxury.
                    — Henry James, Preface to *The Wings of the Dove* (1909)

[The critic's] choice of best salami is a picture backed by studio build-
up, agreement amongst his colleagues, a layout in *Life* mag (which
makes it officially reasonable for an American award), and a list of
ingredients that anyone's unsophisticated aunt in Oakland can spot
as comprising a distinguished film. This prize picture, which has
philosophical undertones, pan-fried domestic sights, risqué crevices,
sporty actors and actresses, circuslike gymnastics, a bit of tragedy like
the main fall at Niagara, has every reason to be successful. It has been
made for that purpose. Thus, this year's winner is a perfect film made
up solely of holes and evasions, covered by all types of padding and
plush.
                    — Manny Farber, 'Underground Films' (1957)

IN 2012, on back-to-back evenings, I watched two films, one critically
lauded—*The Social Network*—and one with a more mixed reception—
Drive. Both were publicized as great hopes of commercial cinema. Both
were fêted with awards (many more for David Fincher's "Facebook film")

and a decent haul of money. After each, I felt equally empty, as I do after multiple hours of taking in a spectator sport on the tube. But my shriveling had precedence. Since these viewings I have gladly, yet embarrassingly, distinguished how Hollywood films mark me and make me sick with envy, fatigued as one is following a full afternoon of shopping. The more heinous odor of these films began to waft in during the mid-1990s, at the dawn of my twenties, and, today, my soul will go into remission after the consumption of an enterprise more pointed at selling tickets than asking the fundamental questions that haunt humans: *Why are we here? What is love? What can I learn?*

To put simply what has taken me years to articulate: these films produce a revulsion of my own life. The more I watch these works aimed at appealing to the mainstream and taking in the most cash, the more I feel steamrolled and emotionally abused by visions arresting for their slickness, yet saturated with a glamour that is anathema to art. Call it chic, call it camp, but it's something else—clearly capitalistic and exquisitely duplicitous. The experience of films like *Drive*, *The Social Network*, *Michael Clayton*, *Gone Girl*, or anything like-minded is that of a sensorium working on the pleasure-seeking areas of the brain, while any dialogue with the viewer concerning the reasons for existence is pushed aside for the running time of the film.

While a book is often little more than the size of one's hand, motion pictures when projected are truly gargantuan. The few old movie houses that have survived sometimes have screens with dimensions of 76 x 98 feet, while today, in the interests of real estate and multiplexes, some screens have shrunk to 10 x 10 feet, like the ones at the IFC Center in New York. When I was a child I marveled at movie theaters, stunned at the size of the images, but as I've aged that feeling of awe has subsided— almost exactly inversely commensurate to my physical growth. What is huge often doesn't hold, and, because the sound surrounds and punches loudly at the ears, there is no escape from the many-decibeled tyranny except to leave.

While I don't think the people who make these films, primarily the directors David Fincher and Nicolas Winding Refn, are "worse" artists than, say, Ingmar Bergman or Stanley Kubrick, they certainly are not similar, and they have different aims and less ambiguous conclusions. To be as manipulative as many Hollywood films are requires difficult work—a cunning and unholy persuasion on the part of the director. One must be plugged into what the masses want and what they will desire next after getting it. Having seen these kinds of films again and again, I am able to recognize their tell: the lifestyle of glamour. The British painter, writer, and critic John Berger delineated this process as well as possible in 1972's *Ways of Seeing* (reading his word "publicity" as the equivalent of many Hollywood films):

> Publicity is never a celebration of a pleasure-in-itself. Publicity is always about the future buyer. It offers him an image of himself made glamourous by the product or opportunity it is trying to sell. The image then makes him envious of himself as he might be. Yet what makes this self-which-he-might-be enviable? The envy of other. Publicity is about social relations, not objects. Its promise is not of pleasure, but of happiness: happiness as judged from the outside by others. The happiness of being envied is glamour.

Many Hollywood films don't do too much except advertise envy. What is so admirable about them is how much art is missing, how much questioning is not there. Stunning it is, how what are celebrated as the best, most innovative films are essentially publicity for the corporate control of the masses. As art they are as distinct as sand from other sand. They express glamour through reckless images that encase society types to sell a story. These are films made by the rich, financed by billion-dollar conglomerates, and advertised between nationally syndicated TV shows at a clip of several hundred thousand dollars for a thirty- or fifteen-second slot. When I observe the weedwhacker montage in *The Social Network*—making a point about the quickness of life, speech, internet traffic, and monetary transactions—I see a filmmaker trying to impress his audience as a man would flaunt a flashy car to attract attention.

The principals behind *The Social Network* are all men well attuned to critical and commercial acclaim. Aaron Sorkin, the screenwriter, has won Emmys for writing (his hit TV show was *The West Wing*) and ended up taking home the Best Screenplay Oscar for the film. David Fincher, the director, has made ten films with combined budgets of two-thirds of a billion dollars, including many commercial hits like *Alien 3*, *Seven*, and *The Curious Case of Benjamin Button*, as well as a single monetary flounder, *Zodiac*, ironically his best work—tense and vibrant in its dramatization of characters and information. While *Seven* and *Zodiac* were the most "realistic" pictures Fincher made before *The Social Network*, he has backtracked into gloss, cooking up pictures to be seared more and more as Oscar bait, including two adaptions of bestselling novels. His most recent film, *Gone Girl*, portrays a flawed couple through a slow-drip of information that leads one to take the conniving wife as a sociopath, who the weakened husband accepts back into his life for the sake of their coming child. The jerks of the plot lead one to expect the reshot *Fatal Attraction* ending, in which the crazy woman is extinguished, but Fincher relents and the result is something less believable—or rather, even more unbelievable—they stay together because the woman has inseminated herself with the man's sperm and he feels responsible for the child.

Examining Fincher's predilections, which tap into the roots of an America created by the product consciousness of TV and the consumerist culture of Hollywood, one sees he is mostly interested in mystery stories with an element of meta, glorying in high-tech violence (in *Gone Girl*, we are treated to the wife slicing open an old boyfriend's neck, spilling blood all over) while couching the films as noxious tonics for surviving in a super-rich world. If Fincher has a message, besides glorifying the lives of the super-rich in *The Game*, *Panic Room*, *The Social Network*, and *Gone Girl*, it will often lack morals and push a nihilistic superiority that most times identifies more with the bad guys and lets them win (as in *Seven*, *Fight Club*, *Zodiac*, *The Social Network*, and *Gone Girl*).

The Social Network was an enterprise considerably smaller than usual for Fincher—a humble effort, without lavish sets and explosions, whose only instance of expressionist pastiche (the dominant mode of Fincher's *mise-en-scène*) constituted a mood-breaker halfway through, a five-minute slow-motion ad for competitive rowing that destroys what pacing a proper chamber piece like the first forty-five minutes had promised in tone. It is not surprising that this director started out making music videos and has now filmed over fifty of them, yet he has not abandoned their bump-and-rush style in presenting his images. Reaction shots of characters who need a reaction in order to sate the audience's call for linearity are dutifully served up, and establishing shots give way to what has been already established.

Glamour in and for *The Social Network* was generated without publicity. The number of people active on Facebook when the film premiered in October 2010 was 550 million; as of spring 2020, the figure has risen to over two-and-a-half billion. With little fiction about it (of course, there was some added by Sorkin) the film relied on its subjects—Facebook and Mark Zuckerberg—for publicity, and enjoyed the bonus of having its main character named as *Time* magazine's Person of the Year halfway through the film's commercial release. Most people who went to see the film knew about the star and his story, yet it barely made back a week of Zuckerberg's income. It did make money—almost $100 million in the United States—but not enough to catapult it into the territory of a megahit. That people didn't love it (or see it enough) was a fact bemoaned by many major critics, who I find most culpable in the push for this sloppy film.

The laudatory soundbites from the critical precincts posted in CAPS on the DVD cover are as follows:

"A BRILLIANT FILM" — Frank Rich NY TIMES

"****AN AMERICAN LANDMARK"
— Peter Travers ROLLING STONE

"REVOLUTIONARY. ABSOLUTELY EMBLEMATIC OF ITS TIME AND PLACE" — David Denby THE NEW YORKER

"SENSATIONAL. A ONCE-IN-A-GENERATION MOVIE"
— Steven Holden NY TIMES

"MAMMOTH AND EXHILARATING" — Richard Corliss TIME

This shower of adulation is so much, so over the top, one would think God had made a movie. With their unabashed, unrestrained praise (are these the words of critics or of manic Little League parents?) the blurbs are eerily concomitant to the type of filmmaking they praise. The language of the hype machine is unmistakable: "Brilliant," "Mammoth," "Sensational." Triumphantly, in the hardscrabble of sell, "An American Landmark" is used to appeal to the patriotic in times of war. Most problematic is "Revolutionary"—an epithet delivered by one of our most respected critics, David Denby, from inside arguably the most august periodical in the country. Unfortunately, such a tag only swaps the film's subject for its credentials—Denby's other comment that the film is "entirely emblematic of its time" is, given that the United States is now largely a population of device-aholics, entirely true. Undoubtedly, what Zuckerberg did in creating a social network was revolutionary to some degree, but there is not a digital frame of *The Social Network* that could be called "revolutionary." An intricately plotted film that uses cross-cutting and fast dialogue has been made countless times, with many celebrated Hollywood products, including *His Girl Friday*, *Network*, and *The Big Lebowski*. *The Social Network* just isn't in their league.

Nevertheless, Fincher's film became only the second ever to be named Best Picture by the four most prestigious critical organizations in America: the New York Film Critics Circle, the Los Angeles Film Critics Association, the National Board of Review, and the National Society of Film Critics. Why did they latch onto it?

The Social Network eviscerates the entrepreneurial spirit (as well as thievery) of Mark Zuckerberg as it cross-cuts between how he created Facebook and the subsequent lawsuits and lawyers who question him after the company achieves success—a principle of narrative structuring that takes hold of the work until the credits roll. The film is a drama with tension arising not from cinematography, editing, or the performance of the actors: here, the script is on display and it dictates how it is to be filmed. The result is a series of conversations with the requisite over-the-shoulder shots dominating the film. Dialogue drives the narrative and the camera is often on the speaker, similar to the way a play's audience will focus on the character who is speaking. Everyone knows how the Facebook wars turn out. Zuckerberg is one of the richest people in the world. The question then becomes: will his friend and partner win anything after taking him to court? But even this source of possible suspense vaporizes after an internet search; the Eduardo Saverin character, who Zuckerberg apparently stabbed in the back (a fount of dramatization not fully exploited or explained in *The Social Network*, except for the caveat that Zuckerberg is seduced by the Sean Parker character into cutting Saverin out of the company), currently has a net worth of over thirteen billion dollars. Why should anyone in this day feel bad because a billionaire couldn't have been a few billion dollars richer?

The film begins and ends with two different women calling Zuckerberg "an asshole" in two different ways—symmetry. The story is cogent, the players have their roles, but there is no tragedy to the tale. People don't suffer. Again, all the clients involved in the litigation, including the gigantic Winklevoss twins, make out handsomely. When the Sean Parker character comes aboard and refashions and revitalizes Facebook about two-thirds of the way through, Zuckerberg starts to disappear from the story. Just when an in-depth examination of the Zuckerberg character and his process of cutting out his most trusted partner is most warranted, the film falls silent. The dramatic character of Zuckerberg lacks soul, taking form only through witty retorts and bullying tactics for anyone who gets in his way; the lark that he builds Facebook to get back at the love interest who spurned him in the beginning is one only worthy of the Hollywood culture that made the film, it has no basis in fact. While I normally enjoy Jesse Eisenberg's performances, his characterization is static and allows him to play only the feared but oblivious "asshole" throughout—he consistently displays only bluster, delivers crystal-clear line readings, and relies for pathos on triumphant elucidations of rack-and-pin putdowns drawn from his more forceful role in *The Squid and the Whale*. Because the script is the main artistic component of the film, and because the protagonist lacks a comprehensive and intelligent characterization, the film itself cannot be said to meet the basic criteria for a compelling drama.

The final shoving of shit in the faces of the poor and lower-middle class comes when we realize that the filmmakers have purchased the rights to one of the most expensive songs—the Beatles' 'Baby You're a Rich Man'—as Fincher fades in the first bars during the closing close-up of Zuckerberg and then blasts it loud and proud as the end credits meet the screen. What's meant to be ironic and to bring the film "full circle" is how the Zuckerberg character is awaiting a response to his friend request from the original girlfriend he insulted at the beginning of the film. He is now extraordinarily rich but he still needs love, or the "like," instant as always, of someone who has spurned him and spurred him on to create Facebook. The gift-wrapped conclusion crusts over because of its shallow, warped vision of dramaturgy and urge to tie the tie tight—both declivities akin to TV shows. Still, films are not beholden to networks, standards and practices, or affiliates. The MPAA does exist but its purpose is only to prevent most full-frontal nudity and anything that looks too much like grinding coitus. Where is the tension in the ending? Does the audience care about this Mark Zuckerberg's feelings or his accomplishments? That he's only vaguely interested in women as symbols of his own status is a small strand in his story made apparent in the film's first scene. Given a blowjob by a college woman, he is gratified and stunned—but the performer of that blowjob is not to be seen again. Of course, some people will still ignore him, but they don't have his money. The notion that money doesn't buy all is paltry, especially for a film with a budget the size of this one's. It is a theme Sorkin and Fincher can grasp at and appropriate, but this and other appropriations smack of business world takeovers—they are absent of drama, and the film language used to explore such a pie-in-your-face theme is vapid.

A film like *The Social Network* doesn't require much from its audience and one doesn't have to identify with Mark Zuckerberg ultimately because there is so much money involved. At one point Zuckerberg says of his net worth, "I could buy Mt. Auburn Street, take the Phoenix Club, and turn it into my ping-pong room," which is perhaps an all-purpose mantra for those stunted enough to want to lord something over someone.

THE SPECTER OF VIOLENCE has become the main cinematic question posed more than any other in the fifty years since *Bonnie and Clyde*. Not form, not editing, not digitalization. It is violence that has obsessed critics and audiences of cinema. And so, after the blood-soaked nineties, along came *Drive* dressed in a pomp satin jacket to remind those who grew up in the eighties (a good part of the consumer audience in 2011) what they were like and how cool they were, and to see by extension how cool the film itself was: hence, *Drive* is more a fashion statement than a work of cinematic art. Though it may be argued by some major critics that *Drive* has something to say about violence, it can't say anything because it is far too interested in titillation and disturbance, and most execrably, like *Pulp Fiction* before it, it assumes a wayward morality.

The film concerns a criminal known only as the Driver (Ryan Gosling), who is made to look good by being put up against members of the mafia in Los Angeles. He decides to help his female neighbor's partner, the father of her child; he falls for the neighbor when her partner is in prison for robbery and he also takes a shine to the boy. The mafia protected the husband while he was behind bars, and now that he has been released they want a boatload of money for their nicety. They force the man to perform a heist and the Driver agrees to take part (as the driver), but the plan goes awry and the ex-con is killed. The Driver takes the money for himself, which sparks a war in which the Driver's friend is killed and six members of the mob, including two bosses, also die—all by the Driver's hand. At the end of the film, before the Driver murders Bernie (Albert Brooks), Bernie knifes him in the stomach. The wound may kill the Driver, but the film does not answer the question of his death one way or another. It simply ends with him doing what he does best: driving.

The Danish director of *Drive*, Nicolas Winding Refn, demonstrates his knowledge of the cinema's maestros of violence, as he films death after death in orgies of quick editing replete with slow-motion shots and whip pans, and once, by wisely pulling back into a long shot when the masked Gosling goes into the Pacific to drown an already bloodied Nino (the other boss). This is one of the few moments of restraint in a film that shows the Driver taking a curtain rod and impaling it in a bad guy's chest, so the jet of blood created by a Hollywood special effects team is launched from his heart, as well as showing Gosling repeatedly stomping on another mafioso's head so the noggin resembles a squashed melon oozing brain and pus in a matter of seconds. The point of being explicit in depicting these gruesome and fairly supernatural deaths is to induce repellence in the audience—it is spectacle. In this L.A. of killing after killing, every day is as good a day to die as the next, and the audience is casually asked to identify with the Driver, a killer who supports people who lie, cheat, rob, and batter. He is played by an actor who is a friend to men and a sex symbol to women, and who does have a record of incredible performances in *Half-Nelson* and *Blue Valentine*. Are we supposed to be happy that Gosling is killing all these people? His purpose is to stay alive, but our purpose is to enjoy art. There are the garish colors of the iconic city, replete with its smoggy sky and a night diffused by the lights of the land, and Refn uses these like the great technician he is—but his vision of humanity, and, most despairingly, romance, is knock-kneed, and about as elastic as a teenage boy's bedtime fantasies. For a Dane, his sense of pathos is stereotypically American, which may be because he counts *The Texas Chainsaw Massacre* and Martin Scorsese high among his influences. The female character, Irene, played by Carey Mulligan, is all Hollywood screenwriter—in this case Hossein Amini. She loves bad men and has a child by one, and while the father is in prison she feels lonely and allows herself to be seduced by another. The Driver isn't a person anyone should yield to, and he doesn't embody a philosophy anyone should subscribe to, and because the actress lacks the language of a Lady Macbeth or the architectonics of a Meryl Streep, the character ends up on screen as nothing more than a cardboard cutout treated like waste by writer, director, partner, and seducer.

Unfortunately, like myriad other Hollywood films, and embodying the spirit of Noam Chomsky's dictum about television (the show is the filler, the commercials are the content), *The Social Network* and *Drive* are publicity for a lifestyle that reinforces consumerism, materialism, envy, survival of the fittest, and ennui. My feelings of emptiness derive from these films' adenoidal insistence on presenting the lifestyles most in vogue through characters who are, whatever their morals, more sexually and monetarily successful than most. Most Hollywood films portray heightened moments, only the most important scenes in a life. Surface excitement is their marrow. Violence, sex, and success are held in the highest esteem. Our capitalistic society burns away our souls under the cover of good business sense, with these ingredients being incorporated into any programming of note. As long as one or some combination of those three is being achieved, the audience is placated—and this is dangerous. It is dangerous because we live in an oligarchy where most dissent has been forced out by devices that save us time to fill with doing three things at once to save more, as well as noxious, consumerist culture TV and movies—all of which rarely foster thought, or questioning, or helps us to live our lives, outside of escaping them.

I'm empty because the art produced by this mindset gives very little that is meaningful or inspiring. I can't sing after such an experience because I was not meant to join in. I am not supposed to share with these artists—that would be *verboten* to the economics of appealing to the least common denominator. If something is mysterious, as Robert

Bresson says art should be, it does not invite most of the viewership to engage with it deeply, to implicate themselves in it. So much of Hollywood films is built on addiction and the return customer—the drug in itself is worthless.

In her day, Virginia Woolf did not keep her perturbations about books private. When faced with the fusspot Arnold Bennett and his claim that the novel was in crisis due to the failures of Georgian writers (modernists) with respect to the art of "character-making," which he found crucial for successful novel-writing, she wrote in response a seminal essay, 'Mr. Bennett and Mrs. Brown.' In the following, read "books" for "films" as Woolf concentrated on the novels of those Edwardians (traditionalists) who were considered to be "successful" character makers:

> Yet what odd books they are! Sometimes I wonder if we are right to call them books at all. For they leave one with so strange a feeling of incompleteness and dissatisfaction. In order to complete them it seems necessary to do something—to join a society, or, more desperately, to write a cheque. That done, the restlessness is laid, the book finished; it can be put upon the shelf, and need never be read again. But with the work of other novelists it is different. *Tristram Shandy* or *Pride and Prejudice* is complete in itself; it is self-contained; it leaves one with no desire to do anything, except indeed to read the book again, and to understand it better. The difference perhaps is that both Sterne and Jane Austen were interested in things in themselves; in character in itself; in the book in itself. Therefore everything was inside the book, nothing outside. But the Edwardians were never interested in character in itself; or in the book in itself. They were interested in something outside. Their books, then, were incomplete as books, and required that the reader should finish them, actively and practically, for himself.

So there it is. Ninety-something years before I asked the question—Virginia Woolf, sitting in shell-shocked England, answered it. "Put the book on the shelf . . . never [to] be read again." Some films, like some books, aren't made to be seen into and some are made to see us. If films are produced for diverse people, but everyone is allowed to see them, there are going to be different audiences (running from consumers to geeks) and many differing reactions. Fincher and Refn are celebrated as *auteurs*, not studio hacks, but if their appeal is wide enough for full financing, their philosophies are artificial.

Robert Bresson never enjoyed the audience of his contemporaries, but almost forty years after his final film, his work garners ever more plaudits and followers. Bresson was extremely articulate, able to expound upon the process of filmmaking at will, as evidenced in a 1966 French interview about *Au hasard Balthazar*:

> The difficulty is that all art is both abstract and suggestive at the same time. You can't show everything. If you do, it's no longer art. Art lies in suggestion. The great difficulty for filmmakers is precisely not to show things. Ideally, nothing should be shown, but that's impossible. So things must be shown from one sole angle that evokes all other angles without showing them. We must let the viewer gradually imagine, hope to imagine, and keep them in a constant state of anticipation. . . . Life is mysterious, and we should see that on-screen. The effects of things must always be shown before their cause, like in real life. We're unaware of the causes of most of the events we witness. We see the effects and only later discover the cause.

In light of these remarks, one question I would like to ask Fincher and Refn and many Hollywood filmmakers (and even a few who work outside the Hollywood system) is: Why do you show me the things you show me? Why do I have to see the self-satisfied face of Jesse Eisenberg after he delivers another zinger? Doesn't the zinger itself suffice? Why the close-up of the agony of bloodletting in *Drive*? Think of the end of Bresson's last film, *L'argent*. A massacre occurs in a country house, but Bresson mainly shows a dog running from room to room. Only in one shot do we get close to the act of murder, and even then we don't see it. The murderer's ax is hoisted and then swung, destroying a lamp, directly after it cuts the flesh of the old woman who has taken the murderer in, but we only see the lamp and the wall behind it sprayed with a little blood—an example of cinematography and editing according to the precepts Bresson pointed out in the interview above. What are David Fincher and Nicolas Winding Refn trying to say? What they seem to communicate is a satisfaction of my own anticipation, something which disappoints, doesn't help, and finally stirs anger because I go to films for something artistic, something more mysterious than what I already know is living in the stew of my brain.

I CONFESS I PREFER to poison my outlook often by bemoaning the current state of film and literature. So excuse me for breaking a different kind of wind as I describe how I found myself euphoric one August as the summer grew elderly. Many great films do exist and I took to filling my head with a few of them.

Following the 2012 release of the *Sight and Sound* polls of the greatest films, I watched *Muriel* by Alain Resnais, *Les Dames du Bois de Boulogne* by Robert Bresson, *Playtime* by Jacques Tati, *Band of Outsiders* and *Two or Three Things I Know About Her* by Jean Luc Godard, Edward Yang's *Yi Yi*, Hou Hsiao Hsien's *The Puppetmaster* and *Café Lumière*, Bela Tarr's *Satantango*, *Werckmeister Harmonies*, and *The Turin Horse*, and, most importantly, five of Carl Dreyer's famed *oeuvre* (four for the first time): *The Passion of Joan of Arc*, *Vampyr*, *Day of Wrath*, *Ordet*, and *Gertrud*. In addition, I rewatched Hitchcock's *Vertigo*, Renoir's *The Rules of the Game*, Godard's *Breathless*, *Vivre sa vie*, *Contempt*, and *Pierre le Fou*, along with *Au hasard Balthazar* by Bresson, Altman's *The Player*, and Scorsese's *Raging Bull*. Of them all, the ones that had the greatest impact on me were *Satantango*, *Yi Yi*, *Contempt*, *Two or Three Things I Know About Her*, and Dreyer's *Ordet* and *Gertrud*. They were some of the most absorbing works of art I have ever experienced.

What makes a film by Dreyer, Bresson, Bergman, Resnais, Godard, Kiarostami, or Malick an experience? Because it is art? The first paragraph of Susan Sontag's essay 'The Spiritual Style of Robert Bresson' illuminates what the experience is:

> Some art aims directly at arousing the feelings; some art appeals to the feelings through the route of the intelligence. There is art that involves, that creates empathy. There is art that detaches, that provokes reflection.

And surely there is the synthesis of the two—art that involves, creates empathy, and provokes reflection. Does it have to detach? It well may want to, but I abjure to say so because of the negative and Buddhist connotations, because "detached" can lead to "cold," a familiar recoil from thinking—the point of not just reflective art, but all art. Is thinking such a cold exercise? It is mostly solitary. There is no doubt that, on the whole, film is not considered art in this country. It is entertainment, more akin to television. Yet, there are films which can be said to entertain as they create art, of which Hitchcock and Kubrick are the best exemplars. Should this split surprise us? Film is not thought of as art in this country because, on the whole, it is not produced as art. Directors of comic book films aside, those filmmakers interested in laying hands on some Oscar gold by producing a long line of "serious" films from *Marty* to *Gandhi* to *The Social Network* would cavil at this suggestion, claiming they are storytellers with a moral duty to point out certain ills in society and to show people how to live. But I think Kubrick rightly answered this response when he wrote:

> I don't think that writers or painters or filmmakers function because they have something they particularly want to say. They have something that they feel. And they like the art form; they like words, or the smell of paint, or celluloid and photographic images and working with actors. I don't think that any genuine artist has ever been oriented by some didactic point of view, even if he thought he was.

The great films are experiences because they are interested in addressing the questions that occupy daily existence. *Who am I? What am I doing here? Who are these people surrounding me? How do I interact with them?* Sontag says that reflective art is about the form it uses. "The effect of the spectator's being aware of the form is to elongate or to retard the emotions," she writes, and the form "imposes a certain discipline on the audience—postponing easy gratification." What makes certain films and their filmmakers great is that their art accomplishes many things at once. It tells an enticing story and creates a beautiful rhythm—where another life and another way of seeing passes before our eyes with ideally no interruption, projecting images that appeal to our senses regardless of whether they are wonderful or horrible. The characters can be assholes, and there are assholes in the world, yet the world is still beautiful. However much one might quack, the aesthetic experience in terms of cinema is a quantifiable one. There is more going on in a Robert Bresson film than a David Fincher film—more mystery and stronger images made from seeing less, images made to stick inside us like poisoned arrows and to be considered differently on different viewings. Most people tend to use the word "difficult" to describe books or films that require a reader or viewer to think more than usual—or worse: "boring." They can't read or watch them for very long because they are lost. But confusing a reader or viewer is not a symptom of great art, for as the same fusspot Arnold Bennett says in his book *Literary Taste,* "your taste has to pass before the bar of the classics. That is the point, if you differ with a classic, it is you who are wrong, and not the book."

It is funny in the most ironic, idiotic way, but I have found that as much as many Hollywood films drain me of my life spirit in a world dominated by spectral special effects teams and tawdry teenage emotions, so the great films lift me from my stupor and charge my soul with a gift to hold during my continuing days on the planet.

Seeing Carl Dreyer's *Ordet* (*The Word*) from 1955 for the first time
was a stunning experience, on the order of reading Henry James' *The
Portrait of a Lady*. *Ordet* is a film of extended scenes captured in long
takes where life develops and eventually bubbles over, so in the end I felt
like I had passed through something more than a gate. I had waved good-
bye ever so briefly to what I despise most about myself—my pride—and
gone toward a deeper truth.

There is such selflessness to *Ordet*—Dreyer's only agenda was to
make a piece of art. Based on a popular Danish play by Kay Munk, the
film proceeds as a chamber piece, but how it is presented is overwhelm-
ingly cinematic. For some time Dreyer was not given many chances to
make other films due to lack of funding (it was his first film in eleven
years) and he sat on this work like a mother hen on a prize egg. Cinematographer Henning Bendtsen recalled that everything was planned,
every camera shot and movement, but at the beginning of each shooting
day Dreyer would scrap his plans and proceed anew, though the film had
already been vastly refined. He knew the lives of the characters as if they
were his children—once even taking his lead actress to buy stockings at
a clothing store, though the stockings are never seen. The same obses-
siveness and constant working one hears about in Bergman, Kubrick,
and Tarkovsky is evident in Dreyer, who called actors in the middle of the
night with ideas. Where did all that preparation lead? It took five days
for him to edit *Ordet*.

An echo of *King Lear* is evident in the story of *Ordet* as the old widower father, Morten, has three sons—they all live together in the Bor-
gen farmhouse. Mikkel, the eldest, is married to Inger; they have two
daughters and Inger is pregnant again. Anders, the youngest, and the
most "weak" according to Morten, wants to marry Anne, the daughter of
Peter the tailor, a zealous Christian who forbids Anne from the relationship because Anders' family is not as fervent as his own. Finally there is
Johannes, who studied divinity but has had several breakdowns and now
believes himself to be Jesus Christ, sometimes walking far into the sand
dunes near the farm to stand high and admonish the people of the world,
even though no-one is there to hear him.

Each of the characters has a clearly defined role. Morten, with a Santa
Claus beard and belly, but a dark mourner's wardrobe and often scowling
eyes (except when interacting with his daughter-in-law Inger, the fount
of compassion in the film), has uneasy relations with all his sons, and it
is no wonder he asks Inger to deliver him a grandson. Mikkel doesn't believe in God, but he is in love with his wife, who helps to keep his family
together, tirelessly taking care of them. When Inger dies he is distraught,

but he holds his contempt inside so it blows out in nasty remarks until the moment when the coffin of his wife is to be sealed after the viewing. Then he unleashes and weeps, and Morten says, "Thank God, tears at last." Perhaps no other film has examined what death means and what it does to the people closest to it in such a deliberate, encompassing manner—Bergman's *Cries and Whispers* also comes to mind. All the main characters have their faults, from the hallucinating Johannes to the glib doctor who works on Inger when she falls ill, but the faults are inherent—the characters appear to the audience as complete people, and we feel for them because Dreyer's precision allows the film's form to exquisitely complement its theme. This is evident in the long takes, the floating camera (care of the dolly), the painterly compositions reminiscent of Baroque Art (see how two old men are grouped with a woman who gives her testimony during a religious meeting at Peter the tailor's house—a classical triangle, with bodies bent and contorted as in Caravaggio or Velázquez), and the dialogue. As Mikkel overflows at the end before the coffin lid is fixed in place, his father says: "Come, Mikkel, her soul is with God. You can see it is not here," to which Mikkel replies: "But her body, I loved her body, too"—a plaintive, naked cry as pointed as Shakespeare's words for the stage and intoned by the actor in a way that makes any other performance unimaginable. Dreyer's mastery is also seen in the controlled movements of the actors, in those spaces between their lines, such as the way Johannes walks, the mortified face of Morten as his family falls apart, and Inger's delayed response at the end before her hands begin to flutter.

I sat pulverized as I watched the second half of *Ordet*. The art of the film had inked me to such an extent that I lost my place in time. A real death, a real loss had been introduced to my life. An infection. I felt almost as if I had to carry the burden of the Borgens as well; Dreyer's film art had urged me to love them unconditionally. Since they were written into a play and later subsumed into a film, their lives were trying to get somewhere in a hurry—they only had two hours to show off. Isn't it amazing that we expect so much of characters in films when in real life we often wait years for the person we love to change? Morality plays aren't what they used to be—they endeavor to model but what they might accomplish instead is give false hope. Is the moral of *The Social Network* not to want to become too rich? Maybe what's missing is passion. If characters aren't at incredible crossroads, and if they don't change, most members of the audience will not be emotionally involved in their stories—this is of such a great concern to studios and megastars that script rewrites are ordered constantly. Yet film is the grand collaborative art. Passion is conferred upon it from many sources, and directed by a visionary. Good films, as the critic Kent Jones puts it,

> are made by people who don't so much transcend their moment as by-pass its clichés, its institutionalized inhibitions and prohibitions. . . . [T]hey fight their way through the movie, past their own certainties, preconceptions, and tricks, until they arrive in territory that is uncharted, for them and for their audience as well. . . . [An] artist must always be fighting against something.

And, as the novelist James Salter once said, "The secret of art is simple. Throw away everything that is good enough." This is the key distinction I see between the Dreyers and the Finchers and Refns of the world.

Dreyer could hardly find financing for his films, yet their stories are some of the most compelling, disturbing, and emotionally vibrant entries in cinema. A saint burned at the stake in *The Passion of Joan of Arc*. A vampire hunted and stabbed in her coffin in *Vampyr*. In *Day of Wrath*, an old woman accused of witchcraft is also burned at the stake, while a younger woman whose mother was rumored to be a witch falls in love with her husband's son from a previous marriage and eventually kills her husband with her inherited powers. There is a resurrection in *Ordet*. In *Gertrud*, a woman makes to divorce her husband when she falls for a younger man, while at the same time an old lover is visiting. She is rejected by the younger man and leaves the other two of them, though they both want her, choosing to live the rest of her life as a hermit. Both real and supernatural, these are the most tantalizing subjects one could seek out in drama, and yet, as with Welles, Bresson, and Cassavetes, producers felt they could not take a chance on Dreyer.

How many times is the word "love" uttered in *Day of Wrath*, *Ordet*, and *Gertrud*? Many, more than many—it is voiced so often one can't look away, because when love is the overt subject of art (we should assume it is always the inherent subject) we know the artist is not afraid, and certainly not afraid to fail, because he or she is interested in what everyone has to be interested in, even if the public isn't—that lonely, majestic syllable. Cassavetes, who often funded his own films, attests to this pull, saying:

> To have a philosophy is to know how to love and to know where to put it because you can't put it everywhere . . . you'd have to be a minister. . . . But people don't live that way, they live with anger, and hostility, and problems, lack of money . . . tremendous disappoint-

ments in their life, so what they need is the philosophy . . . a way to say where and how can I love . . . so that I can live with some degree of peace. . . . I guess every picture we've ever done has been to try and find some kind of philosophy for the characters in the film, and so that's why I have a need for the characters to really analyze love, discuss it, kill it, destroy it, hurt each other, and do all that stuff. . . . [T]he rest of the stuff doesn't interest me. . . . [T]hat's all I'm interested in . . . love.

Great art rhapsodically bears witness to love, celebrating its mysteries, while most studio-financed films push it into its familiar, hackneyed, juvenile corner so it can't contaminate the viewers they want to impress and impel to buy a return ticket. Admirers of Dreyer and Bergman would much rather continue to entertain the questions of those directors' films in their minds as they move through the world. The works of Fincher, Refn, and others don't foster thought aside from the minimal amount required to follow the stories they tell; they don't impel consideration and reflection, like how art encourages spectators to examine their own choices in life, how they've treated people, and what they want in the future. After I witnessed the resurrection of Inger in *Ordet*, that mystery and miracle stayed with me the way a weekend visit with an old friend might re-awaken a spirit grown rough and isolate. I had been taken. Emotionally and physically anguished, I was anxious to change my life and do a little good with whatever time I had left.

Great art is its own miracle because it informs as a parable with no personal political push except its own terms of beauty. The rich get richer, the concerns of popular culture more moronic and otiose, but, if for only a little while, true art, great art, can offset the gross weight of the muck on our souls and open a space in our lives for our behavior to mend; then there will be light. The gradual appearance of such a harmony, so reluctant to show its face in a sue-happy, reactionary culture, will flicker in the wind like a spring flower, but it will scatter its seeds.

Paul Thomas Anderson:
An Autocritique

I think that those that are emerging are so incredibly talented. These
young . . . directors . . . know the job well. But it's not so often that
they really have anything to say.

— Ingmar Bergman, 2002

FORM IS SUCH a spidery matter, I rarely had the desire to bend into
it until my mid-thirties. Form may be many things but it is finally how a
work of art was made and, to a degree, what it is. What does the receiver
of art respond to? Form, which is made of the same units of existence as
us and everything else—time and space. Time is usually a knotty experience, and perhaps most bullish in music, as Walter Pater says:

> All art constantly aspires towards the condition of music. For while in
> all other kinds of art it is possible to distinguish the matter from the
> form, and the understanding can always make this distinction, yet it
> is the constant effort of art to obliterate it. That the mere matter of
> a poem, for instance, its subject, namely, its given incidents or situa-
> tion—that the mere matter of a picture, the actual circumstances of
> an event, the actual topography of a landscape—should be nothing
> without the form, the spirit, of the handling, that this form, this mode
> of handling, should become an end in itself, should penetrate every
> part of the matter: this is what all art constantly strives after, and
> achieves in different degrees.

Pater died six years before the appearance of the earliest motion picture, but something full of cuts like Carl Dreyer's *La Passion de Jeanne d'Arc* may have given him as much as pleasure as the ninety-six-minute continuous shot that is Alexander Sokurov's *Russian Ark*. Because it contains music, film might not be too far from its exalted condition. Music has its notes and, as André Bazin said, "Cinema is a language. It speaks through *mise-en-scène* and montage, and the worlds it displays are greatly stabilized and destabilized by the space in the frame."

Ever since I saw *Star Wars*, I have been responding to space in art, even up to getting my dose of Georges Seurat via John Hughes and *Ferris Bueller's Day Off* at the stinky soft age of twelve. That scene in the Art Institute of Chicago may be a romantic sort of hectoring that certain art is overpowering, but it is a dutiful record of one's encounter with artistic space. Ferris' friend, Cameron, sees a little girl at the center of Seurat's *Un dimanche après-midi à l'Île de la Grande Jatte*, which may or may not be the true focal point of the painting, depending on which scholar or spectator you speak to. As an eager consumer of pop art, I saw the film three times when it débuted, but I also became a little curious about paintings. They were beautiful, but disturbing. Who can guess how many more people visited the Art Institute of Chicago to see that painting after the film came out? Because the director John Hughes had Cameron keep looking at a painting, and because he kept showing the painting on film, the audience was able to see why the Seurat is amazing.

The Caravaggio and Vermeer paintings I gloried over in college were riveting because of their handling of space, as well as light, line, and a number of other effects. Space, applied to art, is a truly awesome word. According to film critic Manny Farber, the three most important types of movie space are: "(1) the field of the screen, (2) the psychological space of the actor, and (3) the area of experience and geography that the film covers." Space is so important that it is everywhere, and spaces continually overlap in that area known as the screen—and whether in painting, photography, or film, the image that stands before us is the collective pattern of chosen spaces. How do Alfred Hitchcock and Stanley Kubrick constantly defy the strictures of narrative cinema? Through space. In *Rear Window* and *Psycho*, the objects Hitchcock settles on—Thorwald's apartment, the dog, the flower bed, the ring, the pack of money, the shower, and the Bates house—are all isolated by a certain regard of the camera, the blocking of the actors in relation to the objects, and the over- or underexposed grain of the film stock used to photograph them. In Kubrick's films what makes one overawed and fearful are the distances—the range of what he shows the audience, often in a wide-angle dream equilibrium: the vast, soundless space of *2001*; the slow backward zooms in *Barry Lyndon* that begin on people, who are mostly unaware of the true import of their surroundings, and end at a point that freezes their coming despair in grand portraiture; the hotel's golden aura and maze-like corridors exploited by the fluidity of the Steadicam in *The Shining*; and finally, in *Eyes Wide Shut*, those moments where the Steadicam again swings and sometimes stabilizes to let all the characters but the main one leap out of their metaphorical toy boxes with a brio accentuated by the fairytale-ish, Christmassy, and, at times, medicinally blue lighting scheme.

The bounty of responses to Paul Thomas Anderson and his films speak to his comparable artistry. After David Lynch and Terrence Malick, he is the star of the American narrative cinema and is certainly leagues more commercial than those two old souls, now name brands. Because he is a contemporary, I confess a competition. It is one-sided, but not drooling. What I have produced in past years may pale to what *The Master* is. Many pages and many words that don't cohere into one principled mountain can risk the dyspepsia that graces the internet, our mutual multi-glutinous mouthpiece. Our mediums are different, our means are different, one doesn't know the other exists—it sounds like many crush relationships, but it is the basis for more than thwarted love or genuine repulsion.

Critics carry the stain of envy into the thoughts they print, especially those emboldened enough to critique without having ever made the art that can exasperate them. The plexiglass irony complicating the situation is that Anderson works in the vein I presupposed would fill my life full when I was twenty. He didn't go to film school; for a few years, I did. I left with only two years completed, holding numerous Bergman-enamored screenplays that would never see production. He put in time as a production assistant, while I moved across the country to his coast to find tai chi, tofu, and people who didn't believe in underwear. Later, I farmed my way across Europe, while Anderson simply realized what Kubrick and John Cassavetes counseled—if one wanted to make a film, one had to go out, get money any way one could, and make a film. *Hard Eight*, his first, came out in 1996. Two years later, I sat in a meadow at eight thousand feet in Arizona and told myself, by pressing the words into a notebook, that I would be a writer, not a film director. The Rilkean moments of beginning to see were starting to accumulate. I began to construct fictional characters who would not be seen speaking, but whose monologues and dialogues would have to cut the internal ear of the audience.

Anderson kept pushing himself in different ways, and, after *Magno-*

lia, came a great shift in his worldview and probably his life situation, though I will only call the change aging. It's not when sadness entered—babies were born—but when his age squeezed out the adolescent endeared of pre-*Cape Fear* Scorsese, an overreliance on the Steadicam, and such Lite-Brite touches as having Georges Bizet's famous aria in *Carmen* become the final pivot of a scene between a cop and his love interest in *Magnolia*. In 2005, he served as the insurance director for *A Prairie Home Companion* because of Robert Altman's health and age and began to birth his own style: quiet, measured, and magnifying. It is with his last four features (*There Will Be Blood, The Master, Inherent Vice,* and *Phantom Thread*) that Anderson has answered Ingmar Bergman's call for a young filmmaker to have something to say, announcing this with the initial shot of the first, as he fades in to an intricately aligned long shot of three cracked mountains, accompanied by the swelling strings on the soundtrack. Images and sound more and more speak for dialogue in these films, the sound manipulation spurs mystery, and Anderson's editing produces images often offset and unexpected, if not unique in their rhythms—most triumphantly in *The Master*, in the cutaways when Joaquin Phoenix's Freddie Quell first remembers Iris and then when he tries to visit her at the end. Both scenes begin on slight roving movement (an Anderson signature) showing Quell walking toward her parents' house—from left to right in the former scene, with an old blue car in the foreground, and from right to left in the latter, with the same car a little closer to the camera (and in slow motion), so that for a moment the audience sees Quell through its windows. In these scenes the alterations of distance, speed, and longitudinal movement bring us into the moody demeanor of Quell when he pursues one of the few people he has genuinely bashful feelings for. But mostly it is the muggings and movements of Phoenix, Philip Seymour Hoffman, and Daniel Day-Lewis, often in close-up, that tailor the line, paint, swirl, and swish of Anderson's *mise-en-scène*.

When roosting in the same multiplexes that routinely feature jarring and assaulting, but not necessarily artistic images, these faces stand out. Some of Anderson's images do assault, but with a difference. Their schema has been weighed retroactively by a consciousness that has consumed Carl Dreyer, Max Ophüls, and Jacques Tati, in addition to everyone else to be expected. Anderson's worldview in the last decade—being well aware of film history, and probably his place in it—has changed. He sees things more by the light of his own heat. The *amour* between him and his main characters has become more abstract than the doting on Philip Baker Hall in *Hard Eight*, Mark Wahlberg and company in *Boogie*

Nights, and the gaggle of stars in *Magnolia*. The skin of the face is all the more naked and mature in the close-up shots of Day-Lewis, Phoenix, and Hoffman because theirs are the faces of death—their limitless malfeasance embargoes happiness and pulls the world always toward the pulchritude of darkness. Anderson has made a screen for these misfits, and the glaze of indifference in the eyes of Day-Lewis (then fear and parsimoniousness in *Phantom Thread*) or the curl to Phoenix's bitter lip makes their force shine brightly while the art flirts with the uncanny.

In Kubrick we remember the wideness and symmetrical design of space (to which the framing of the bowling alley in *There Will Be Blood* is a nod) and how, as a result, Kubrick's characters are often trapped by the spaces they inhabit. The exceptions are the moments of greatest emotional outburst—Barry Lyndon at his son's deathbed, Bill Hartford breaking down and crying to his wife in *Eyes Wide Shut*. With Anderson we remember what the faces are doing and how they react to the latest bulletin that there is pain in their lives, as in the greatest scenes when the actors take command of the frame and any cinematic space beyond them is secondary.

If Freddie Quell is a savage, and Day-Lewis' Daniel Plainview stands only a few steps from such an ethos, but is more successful because his moments of brutality are well-chosen, then Hoffman's Lancaster Dodd is the amalgamation of the two, perhaps requiring the most difficult performance. Like Plainview, he knows he is a conman, but Dodd is also a family man, a man of letters, both compassionate and bullying—a scaly soul but a powerful politician, the evil in a suit who hypnotizes others to roughhouse his enemies for him. The fat on his face guards him more from the humanity he is destined to tame. He is a provocateur and he knows that to court women is to ensure public success and private pleasure. This knowledge forms the basis of an erotics that he uses to adumbrate his screeds, making his New Age manuals twinkle for both sexes.

Because Dodd contains these multitudes, he is Anderson's most complex character. Hoffman uses his heft and certain grace notes, triggering the memory of how bumbling and offhand he could be in other films (his mugging, back-slapping, and singing) to a positive effect—the audience mostly trusts him. Except for a few flashes of fury ("Pigfuck") he is kept at a remove from any emotion that isn't rooted in rational thinking, until his sign-off song in the second-to-last sequence of the film. That tune serves to simultaneously distance Freddie and the audience so that everything we previously thought of Dodd and his integrity has to be sounded against this parabolic 'Slow Boat to China' in the final confrontation. Has Dodd realized he has fallen in love with a man who can't give back? What does he need Freddie for, now that he has unbridled success?

It is a sequence of close-ups, mirroring their first duel on the boat, in which Dodd audits Freddie. These scenes are the nexus of the film, and though the interiors change from the boat's small, drab space to an opulent English manor, the constituent parts of the *tête-à-têtes* are minimized to visages controlled by men playing pretend. In the end, one is left wondering why Dodd even bothered. Maybe he just wanted a friend, given how all his friendships are subject to his authoritarianism, his place on high. It does make a somewhat strange sense that two men incapable of true friendship should see something in each other, though the tenuous "I knew you in a past life" is more a red herring. They see themselves in each other because, at least briefly, they see an opportunity to live better. It's their only chance for intimacy before they waste away in opposite directions. What Farber referred to as the "psychological space of the actor" has taken hold of film. In a cinematic love story the faces transmit the feeling. Quell and Dodd, and the actors Phoenix and Hoffman, fall for the same faces the audience does.

My envy evaporates by wrestling with films that keep biting back. As Samuel Beckett and the Buddha might have said, the best way to forget about something is to keep thinking about it. To truly see what I see can't happen so often, but when Anderson makes spaces, I can.

Toni Erdmann and the
Anti-Hollywood Ending

SEEING *TONI ERDMANN* and stopgap guessing at its ending, wondering, *Will it end now?* (after Ines, an oil industry consultant, hugs her
prank-loving father while he is wearing a full-body woolly costume), or
Will it end now? (after he lays down in the park and puts a hand to his
heart: No, don't die! Bad ending!), or *Will it end now?* (when he gets
help to remove the costume's four-foot head piece: the all-important
unmasking!)—made me frenzied to know how I would accept the ending, whenever it came, of an earnest and undidactic work of art. But
when the film did end, and I was pretty sure it had to be the end, I was
glad it finished where it did: with Ines solitary, silent, possibly humbled,
possibly sad—it is unknown. It's my favorite kind of ending: open, evanescent, hardly anodyne.

This type of ending, an outgrowth of the mid-century European art
film—a feature of Roberto Rossellini's *Stromboli*, Ingmar Bergman's
Wild Strawberries, François Truffaut's *The 400 Blows*—has become the
pièce de résistance of many modern films, whether in the New Romanian Cinema, American "independent" cinema, or in the work of the
Dardenne Brothers, who have a patent on their own type of finale—call
it the "Dardenne Zone," in which a character is caught, paralyzed by
his or her previous actions, silently looking on. In sum, the main character goes through his or her journey on screen and a final reflection
occurs. They are alone, or if there is another character present, they
still dominate the final frames. Then there is a quick cut to black, as
abrupt as shutting our eyes. Words are, finally, meaningless. "This is a
no-filmed-theater zone," these endings say, with the obligatory nod to

Robert Bresson. There is no musical accompaniment, only background sounds—a stark departure from Hollywood's long crane shots, the most common sign-off of yesteryear, using a blaring orchestra to wipe out real sound. This anti-epiphany moment has developed into cinema's way of anthropomorphizing the final line of Rilke's 'Archaic Torso of Apollo': "You must change your life." That line makes the reader's conclusion, and, by extension, the audience's exit, as open-ended as possible, thrusting life's questions back onto them. In that instantaneous end, we are kicked back out into the world and assured that, yes, it is cruel. There will be no long romantic crane shots to mislead us.

In making such a potent work, how does director Maren Ade get from beginning to end? Kent Jones wrote of John Cassavetes that he "ma[d]e people themselves into his *mise-en-scène*," and Ade stands squarely in Cassavetes' tradition. Shot with a not-too-shaky handheld camera, *Toni Erdmann* builds on her 2009 wonder *Everyone Else* in terms of tone and psychology. There are no establishing shots, no sun, moon, or landscape inserts. The father, Winfried Conradi, dominates the first hour or so, as he leaves Germany to visit Ines in Bucharest, where her firm has placed her. Then he supposedly leaves Bucharest, and the next forty minutes belong to Ines, though Winfried keeps making appearances as his alter ego Toni Erdmann, arrayed in a shaggy wig and false teeth. As Toni, he prods his daughter—trying to lighten her up—at her home and work. The focus returns to Winfried, then to both of them on their long day together, beginning with a visit to the oil fields from which Ines' firm is planning to outsource labor, eliminating hundreds of jobs.

The core of the film is a string of incidents on that day, set in motion by Winfried handcuffing himself to Ines as a joke. It proceeds to involve a run-in with a poor family living near the oil fields; a visit to a Romanian diplomat and her family, during which Winfried compels Ines to sing a full-throated rendition of 'The Greatest Love of All'; and, finally, a naked party at Ines' apartment. The spontaneity of these latter two scenes is reminiscent of Cassavetes' *A Woman Under the Influence*, especially the "Longhetti spaghetti" scene, in which a gaggle of construction men deliver competing renditions of arias to impress their boss' wife. With all of these events spanning the real time of a few hours, Ade creates a playful spontaneity rarely seen in today's cinema, which can take itself too seriously, not knowing that comedy is inherent to drama.

Toni Erdmann is slow going at first, deceptively so, since the first act of the film carefully seeds what will later flower. Ines' character, for example, is gradually revealed to us. She is morose and plastic, but foremost a workaholic, who even on her short trips to Germany can't get off

her phone and pretends she is on a business call in order to avoid her
father. Her two-dimensional character is shed, however, when halfway
through the film she emasculates her co-worker during their tryst, making him masturbate on a dessert for her to devour. In her work and office
romance, she asserts her power, demonstrating an addiction to squalid
corporate life. But the vacuity of Bucharest's gaudy hotels—where stale,
hobnobbing meetings occur—and Ines' sterile apartment scream for an
antidote. When her father gets her to sing, her glacial spirit partially
melts.

It continues to thaw when, in preparing for a party for her cowork-
ers at her new residence, Ines decides against tall heels just before the
first guest arrives. The change in heels makes her change her dress, too.
But when she has trouble squirming out of her too-tight dress, she just
leaves it off and suddenly announces to the guests who arrive, one at a
time, that it is a naked party and they have to be nude to be there. The
contempt she has for her life breaks into fast motion—maybe the veneer
she dressed it with was always thin. It is in the contrast between the
suits (dominating the sexes for the whole movie—even the father wears
one) and the nudity at the end that Ade's art bubbles over into something vital, with bodies as only flesh battle-axing the waxen artifice usually overlaying a film's soul. Have we forgotten that nudity can be cause
for giddiness? Ade joins Alexander Payne—whose *Sideways* features an
incomparable shot of a naked man's swinging penis as he runs up to
Paul Giamatti's car—in her ability to laugh at the human body, mainly
men's. This humor doesn't dissipate the film's socio-political bite. With
the exception of Ines' father, the film's characters are the instruments
of corporate oligarchy, undercutting the human spirit and bloating the
ever-widening income disparity. They are almost all appetite and as close
to soulless as the species gets, though this is dramatized succinctly in
about ten minutes. Like any spectacular piece of art, *Toni Erdmann*
has many levels, which brings us to one of the most prominent negative
critiques of the film.

Richard Brody in *The New Yorker* appears to woefully project notions onto the film that square with a slapdash made-for-TV movie. He
claims that the relationship between Ines and Winfried is "unconsid-
ered" and that their "psychological reality" can't be brought out because
Ade "doesn't employ the panoply of devices, tracking shots or cranes or,
for that matter, any effects—visual or sonic—that break the sense of
reality captured on the fly." But why would we want to break the sense
of reality Ade creates? It is just this sense of reality, as in Cassavetes or
the Dardenne Brothers, that behooves us to identify with the work. Any

effects would diminish what is certainly Ade's triumph: namely, bringing us close enough to two people without ramping up the expressionist machinery of camera movement. Bloviating talk of a director's "vision" is usually reserved for the stylists of cinema, whose work is full of those aforementioned "devices." But Ade's achievement is to generate a soulfulness that most Mumblecore films, similarly shot and often celebrated by Brody, fail to achieve.

So why does *Toni Erdmann* get the ending it does? Ade takes us through a number of steps before arriving there. Ines and Winfried are back in Berlin for Winfried's mother's funeral. During the reception at the dead woman's house, the pair separates from the crowd and goes outside. First, the father talks somberly about life's ephemeral moments—how to remember them and how to understand them as momentous in the present. Then Ines puts on her father's fake teeth, which he has used throughout the film, along with a hat from her dead grandmother's wardrobe, and mugs for him. Is she becoming more like him? He goes to get his camera to preserve one of those moments he just spoke about, though it's already futile, because as soon as he leaves, the moment is over. Shouldn't this man, for whom "Be Here Now" is a wholesale mantra and ethic, know better? Yet, his daughter doesn't live near him—who could fault him for wanting a memento?

In this off-kilter morality tale, the ending, as constructed, is more airy than the Dardenne Zone, in which the character's choices are limited. Soon after Winfried leaves, Ines walks out of the patio into a slice of nature behind the house. She makes a few faces and looks around at the vegetation, then she wipes her face, takes out the teeth, removes the hat, and does what is probably the hardest thing for an actor to do: solitarily betray her consciousness to the audience with face and body. We have learned, in the final scenes, that Ines has moved to Singapore and to another consulting company, but in her last appearance onscreen she seems to wordlessly say, "My father will die, and someday I will die. How will the rest of my life go? What stance will I take?" Ines has made changes in her career—perhaps even changes in her relationship with her father. But those are not the changes Rilke had in mind.

Nearer My Hong Sang-soo to Me

ISN'T THE MIRACLE of art how we see the panoply of our own lives via a magical panopticon? Every time we look, we see something that's really all about us. In concert with this, I vaingloriously clutch Walter Pater's concept of how art gives "nothing but the highest quality to your moments as they pass, and simply for those moments' sake." But each of these moments, for me, is a multiplicity of moments, the past surfacing after bottom-feeding for minutes, months, or years. It might not be easy to see one's life in film—not in the narrative itself, but in the regard of the camera, the editing, how people say things and what their silences are like. It's really only happened for me with Eric Rohmer and, now, Hong Sang-soo. But it shouldn't be so surprising, since they are both romantics who capture the improvisatory moments in life, the coveted and the delusional love-at-first-sight moments (the romantic's base metal), episodes I erected plaques to in my own days, until those fancies taught me not to trust them so easily.

When *Hotel by the River* was released in February 2019, that made twenty-three films in twenty-four years (plus three shorts), and fourteen of those in the last nine, by Hong Sang-soo—a Fassbinderean rate. Over the course of a few weeks in that February and March, I watched fourteen out of those films. At the end of the cold days with a young child, my wife and I needed something light and not too long and most of Hong's films in the last decade are around ninety minutes, with two of the last four only seventy. I'm not proud that Hong's films are modern in the most unctuous consumer way—binge-watchable—nevertheless, they were made quickly and I took them in fast. Yet, this binging, as in most disorders, was not a craving to see what happens story-wise. I utilized a more topological approach, aiming to search out the essences,

lusters, and behavioral tendencies making us human—and never to en-
trap or capture the magic, but to feel its reverberations. The experience
played out more like seeing a show of Vermeers or Cézannes all in the
course of five rooms—in that zone they play off one another and one
can see the preparatory drawings for the large oils, like how Hong's *In
Another Country* (2012) is a rehearsal for *Right Now, Wrong Then* (2015),
while *Our Sunhi* (2013) and *Yourself and Yours* (2016) go into the making of *The Day After* (2017), a much more fleet of foot enterprise, and
how the themes of *Grass* (2018) get refined for *Hotel by the River*. These
weeks were like a nice extended party that we kept inviting others to,
since few outside of the cinephilia coterie I'm loosely connected with
had even heard the director's name. What is so exciting about Hong
is how "in process" everything is—he's ratcheted up his art in the last
eight years so that one day we might be talking about the fecund middle
period of Hong after the apprentice years, which were already refresh-
ing. But there is no doubt we are in the midst of something rare, like
Godard in the sixties, Altman in the early seventies, or Kiarostami in the
nineties. But what is actually or "really" (a word used multiple times in
every Hong film—*geulae* [그래]—which can be taken as affirmation or
cynicism) the stardust in his form?

His methods have been refined to the point where they are the outgrowth of his narratives, the form and content spiraling together, cadu-
ceus-like. Each film now costs around $100,000 and even if they do feel
bare bones (reminding us that you don't need a lot of Hollywood frills to
make it wear well), they astound. First, there are only around seven or
eight people on set: Hong and two assistants, the cinematographer and
his assistant, and the sound recorder, with possibly one or two students
(Hong teaches filmmaking) helping out. He sometimes edits as he shoots
and writes the dialogue for the day's scenes the morning of. There are
hardly any crowd scenes, and when there are, passersby are caught looking at the camera. Whenever people are in restaurants or bars (where
many scenes take place), they mostly are the only ones, and of late, there
are hardly any servers; music is minimal, often with one classical piece
played again and again (Vivaldi in *Right Now, Wrong Then* and Schubert
in *On the Beach At Night Alone* [2017]). Additionally, his main actress
in the last six films (model turned actress turned muse Kim Min-Hee) is
also his lover. He doesn't pay his actors much, they understand that he
"doesn't make a film to make money." Having listed all this though, as
in Rohmer, the setting of each film is of prime importance, a determining factor in the soul of the cinema. Some, as in *Claire's Camera* (the
French Rivera), *On the Beach at Night Alone* (the beach and Hamburg),

Hotel's scenic stretch of the Han River, and *Right Now, Wrong Then*'s Hwaseong Palace, a fortress built in the 18th century, are picturesque and exotic, though they are not stressed to David Lean proportions. And there is indoor Hong too: *The Day After* (mostly shot at a publishing house and a nearby restaurant) and *Grass* (at a cafe and a restaurant and the street connecting them). Hong's indoor settings are as carefully arranged as those of Ozu and Rohmer. In the publishing house, for example, the lounge area (where many long conversations take place) has two sofas facing each other with a coffee table in between. It is presented rectangularly straight on, the two sofas bookending the frame. In the background, pictures of Bach and Brahms peer out atop a ye olde sound system, with a stack of CDs and a small vase of yellow flowers on the receiver—marking another strike against Mumblecore (America's hack rejoinder to Rohmer, Hong, and their ilk) in its relatively unadventurous use of location and set design.

Hong embraces the world as it is, with no period pieces. Phones are omnipresent and texts are relayed to the audience in the sender's voice as the receiver silently reads them. Since technology encourages people to be more and more dismissive of people (they don't even need a political position to do so: Don't like that profile? Here's another!), it's a special mirror to get the perspective of someone who grew up (born in 1960) with face to face, paper and print, and bars without TVs, but who has now seen the effects of arming oneself with a phone to carry one through the longueurs of life, as in *Hotel by the River* where the phone causes people not to meet, not to see.

In the after-burn of so many Hong films, my past has been revivified—and understandably, since the compote of many of them is the eternal recurrence of scenes, with slight variations, giving the viewer less to work with so his or her memory can play more with the images. Many of his films make me feel as if I'm reliving my twenties, when pretty much every person I knew, especially myself, was like the lovelorn characters ready to immolate themselves over the least infraction to his or her ego, or even one's sense of love's majesty, bellowing in pain while love wove its own tapestry apart from them. The characters don't understand life and they ask friends and colleagues, who often don't have the answers, to help them—a most common occurrence in those green years. Similarly, characters are often traveling and meeting new people—something tamped down when more in the world of responsibilities, as the characters get older and more life-locked in *The Day After* and *Hotel by the River*.

Hong is unabashed about his own life being the direct source of his stories, unlike Woody Allen, who tries to maintain otherwise. In almost every film, at least one of the characters is a filmmaker or artist, but we never see them at work—they could just as well be word processors or meter maids—and this is mainly because the films take place over the course of a few days (the directors are always in between projects), or over the same two days twice, as in *Right Then, Wrong Now*, which, if held at gunpoint, I would have to name as my favorite. It's an artwork striving to grind out a heterodoxy where the aimlessness of life is overthrown for the bounty of living in the flaneur style. It shows those endless winter nights where you keep walking with someone because you are falling in love and no one wants to let go. The aggressor, usually the man, is unsure of when to improve on the whammy of kismet that brought them together and to bore in, tip of tongue to meet tip of other tongue—something that sometimes never happens, but not for chastity-sake, rather to achieve the numinous and go beyond our verities.

In the metaphysical turning of the camera on himself, Hong is also pushing his therapy to hit a great nerve that is central to him in all ways. He autopsies the male artist or successful man who is often always on the make, ready to fall in love, but finally unable to commit, one half of the great crisis between men and women—though he also examines the spurned woman's point of view, most closely in *On the Beach Alone at Night*. This bailiwick is a fixture in all these films, from the sobering *The Day He Arrives* (2011), where a film director returns to a woman he repudiated to cry and complain how he now needs her (in order to get sex), promptly leaving the next morning with the injunction that they should probably never see each other again, to the cessation of libido in the old poet in *Hotel by the River*, where the death drive takes over the passions, but not the need to incessantly call women "beautiful." Like Rohmer, Hong wants to eviscerate the male ego, taking to task the low-key megalomaniac who doesn't know his feelings from a Publisher's Clearing House scam.

For all the ballyhoo over Kim Min-hee, and the *cause célèbre* of her union with Hong, the male leads dominate in the best films—Jung Jae-young in *Right Now, Wrong Then*, Kwon Hae-hyo in *The Day After*, and to a lesser extent, because more ensemble, Ki Joo-bong in *Hotel by the River*. Flagrantly sloppy, yet keen about their own self-importance, these men are high-functioning, but their Achilles' heels are thinking how by falling in love they can escape the misprision of their souls. Each of these male characters is often so sure he is right, when something gets in his way, he acts out—like the *Right Now, Wrong Then* director stripping in front of two friends of the woman he wants, while she sleeps in another room—or he continually retreats, as in *Hotel by the River*. Such are the games men play, though the character in *The Day After*, while initially refusing to answer his wife's question about his mistress, almost cries when his new employee tells him her divorced father died alone, continuing a see-saw of audience identification with a man who, in the end, does the "right" thing.

In the last few years, Hong has shot a film in the summer months and then one in the winter—weather determining setting and story, again similar to Rohmer, who said his films were "meteorological." Indeed, during the opening credits for *Hotel by the River*, a voice states the exact dates of filming. *Grass* was shot the summer before that. It is a dolorous affair, there is much talk of death, suicide, and the joke of love ("Loving each other? What bullshit," and "Love, my ass," two different characters say). A cast of random characters keeps meeting and flirting, but mostly arguing, in the same cafe and a nearby restaurant. This time Kim plays a kind of auditor, of the eavesdropping variety, and with her Mac open on her cafe table, she takes in the quandaries of these odd male/female couplings, while once venturing to that restaurant to meet her brother's girlfriend, where she hears a haunting conversation between a man and a woman about someone in common who died—the camera, stationed behind the man, stays mainly on the woman as it probes forward and backward and examines nearby shadows, without showing the man's face until the final seconds of the seven-minute shot. Characters toss off rebarbative comments, but many land astray because it is unknown who these people are and sometimes the material or the actors in the miniatures are limited—the narrative topsoil is always being blown around and then settling, with some people whisked away and some reappearing, softened after their initial spikiness. Some sequences, along with the restaurant scene, are striking, like one where a young woman, waiting for her man, walks up and down the restaurant's stairs dozens of time, increasing her speed and changing her mood from chagrin to euphoria. Hong highlights the way the younger generation can seemingly, accidentally switch their mindset, at least for a little while. Near the end, some of the people are gathered together and they try to get Kim, sitting close with her computer, to join them, but she won't or can't. There's a sinister, maligned metafictional sense underlying the whole enterprise. Hong seems to be examining the process of creativity, auto-critiquing (via Kim) his series of short one-act plays as they proceed, but the melodrama of human frailty is his sweet spot, to which he returned some months later.

Parents are playing a wider role in these later films. In *The Day After*, the philandering publisher has a daughter (though we never see her) and it is the simple, yet calculated, act (also unseen) of his wife bringing the girl in an English-style blue coat ("mak[ing] her pretty") to him at his mistress's house very late one night that energizes him to say (in confessing later): "The moment I saw my daughter I decided, right then, to live for my daughter. To forget everything else. . . . To give up on my own life." In *Hotel by the River* the layers accumulate. Some films stick in you, an arrow successfully puncturing the inner ring, and given that this was the first Hong taken in by the means the medium was made for, the temple simply called a "movie theatre," it had a grander effect than his other great films: *Right Now, Wrong Then* and *The Day After*, with *Oki's Movie* (2010), *The Day He Arrives*, and *Hill of Freedom* (2014) close behind—all viewed at home. In *Hotel by the River*, an old poet, briefly residing at a hotel in winter, has his two sons visit him and reveals he has had premonitions of death during his two weeks there. This leads to the father trying to placate the two bickering sons (à la *Death of a Salesman*) as the situation finally reverberates to the unseen "Mom" (they are divorced) who he left years ago, and who still today sees no amount of goodness in him ("[She] calls you a piece of shit, every day," his older son relays). In a parallel story, two sisters, who both have their own "man" problems, are in the same hotel—they have two interactions with the old poet, but, in a ghostly way, none with the sons. The disturbed poet feels more kinship with them than his blood, whether it be the bilious reason of their overwhelming fetchingness (he continually parrots to them how beautiful they are—Hong has his types, as Rohmer) or his need of a non-judgmental presence in his last days.

The day after watching *Hotel by the River*, I took a nap and woke up, its sense-impressions still burning, my craw twisted—and so, easily ascribed to its melancholia and its death-centered theme, tears were in my eyes. Many films look at the process of death, like the celebrated *Cold War* that is a little too perfectly calibrated than Paweł Pawlikowski's more mysterious *Ida* was, but *Hotel by the River* is unique in that it encapsulates what it's like to die alone in these dark days of technologized time constantly speeding up and overtaking us. Phones are rampant in his films, but our parents, whom we constantly seek out, either in flesh or memory, to approve or infuriate us, aren't always too interested in answering theirs. We lie to appease them, because we think it's better if they don't know something (one of the poet's sons still hasn't told his father he's divorced). The old poet offers just enough wisdom and un-apologetic pathos ("You can't keep living with someone out of regret," he explains about his leaving their mother) to debauch the possibility of his hotel time being a mere sentimental journey—he also relates a quasi-parable about the two minds of a person (one of heaven and one of the street) that is tied to his younger son's name, just about the best moment all three share. Early on, he is unable to hug his younger, more emotionally fragile son after the young man tells him he has missed him and bores in for closeness (arm pat only), and soon has an idea that giving them presents (stuffed animals) will help dispatch them, as he regrets ever reaching out. The repeated call, "Dad! Dad!" (happening twice in the film—once for comic effect), acts as the cynosure, the golden fleece handed down to the audience to make us understand that: Yes, this is what the death of our parents was like, and this is what it will be like—an amalgamation so much more terrifying than anything in contemporary horror, something out of the Bergman and Dreyer (*Ordet* is listed on Hong's top ten favorite films) playbooks—black-and-white film forever the best format when tackling the nth subject.

What so excites Hong's base—that is, cinephiles, who know that the most exciting things happening in the art (not counting special effects, if that excites you) are taking place in almost every country but our own— is his impetus to simply gather a camera, his small crew, and actors who will work for little and make a film. Martin Scorsese once said of John Cassavetes, "He taught us that you can pick up a camera and shoot a movie . . . when you start shooting, it's like a drug and you keep going . . ." This, though, is not as simple as it sounds. It's incredible that artistic filmmaking can really have little to do with the story or the form employed, but all to do with the biography of the person in charge—the "what the artist has to say" bromide. Hong obliterates his personality for something higher and lasting; in a T. S. Eliot style: "[Art] is not a turning loose of emotion, but an escape from emotion. It is not an expression of personality, but an escape from personality. . . . What happens [to the poet] is a continual surrender of himself as he is at the moment to something more valuable. The progress of an artist is a continual self-sacrifice, a continual extinction of personality." The digitized frames (or the few still using ones with an emulsion side) carry the very personal thoughts, fears, and feelings translated into where to put the camera, what the actors should say, what the audience should see, and what it should be directed to, hopefully, imagine—all this comes from the right profile. As the years go by and Hong's filmography swells, his biography (the affair with his main actress notwithstanding) lessens. The work stands for the person—the goal for most artists.

Take This Waltz, Then Move On?

IN 2011, a film came and went with little fanfare, except a spattering of positive reviews, making around $4 million worldwide on a budget of about $10 million: *Take This Waltz*. More people know it as a Leonard Cohen song, from which its title comes. More people know Leonard Cohen than the film's director Sarah Polley, but as of right now, more people might know the star, Michelle Williams, than Leonard Cohen, due to her presence in other movies and a popular TV show. These jejune concerns amplify less than we know and more than we'll admit. Name recognition: it goes into the common denominators that decision-makers look for when they decide to fund a film, a book, a play. How will it sell? How will it fit? What can it capitalize on? How can we make something that will not make people think too much or depress them? We also use this type of moxie to uncover the dramas of our own lives. We silently search for the reason why someone is more fashionable or more entertaining than someone else, or ourselves, or why we might be ashamed of our lives, before we dissolve those pills with food, entertainment, or something else pro-ego. How can we keep our self-talk well-shaded inside without seeming to break stride while wearing the face we share with everyone we don't trust enough to confide in?

Today, incredibly, there is what we like and then ourselves, in that order. Thanks to profiles, to niche groups, to meet-ups, and to every bit of specialization, what we like says more to a person about who we are than what we look like, what we do, where we work, how we were educated, even how much money we have. The year 1984 might have marked *The Revenge of the Nerds*, but these days have brought us the dominance of nerds, nerdom, and nerd culture—that is, people who nerd out on specific things: games, beer, certain types of food, and the granddaddy of them all: television shows. What entertains is a criterion that creates a temporary salve between people at parties or work and the family members who hardly see one another until Thanksgiving. And by all rights, the most watched entertainments in some way inform how we conduct our lives. There is no mistaking that many of our intimate romantic relationships suffer, as nearly half of all marriages end in divorce or separation, and people spend hundreds or thousands of dollars a year on therapy of many varieties, plus dating sites, pornography, and prostitution, in order to anesthetize the holes their failed relationships leave behind.

Some works break away from the consumerist baubles. They aren't event, artifact, or artifice—they are art. *Take This Waltz* qualifies, and, together with Polley's 2012 documentary *Stories We Tell*, a companion piece about uncovering the identity of her true father and acknowledging the resilience of her mother, it is among the best films produced in the soured decade. The best are the best because they ask the most from us, because they press at our fears like few films do. In the case of *Take This Waltz*, this means dramatizing our greatest fear other than death— that we won't always love the person we think we may love forever, that time will dictate it was not meant to be, and, to make it all worse, he or she will go right into the arms of someone else. Plus, more challengingly, this is portrayed from the perspective of the one pulling away and causing the pain. Often other films and television shows try to picture this but usually fail because they don't go far enough and because their makers aren't mature enough to see into the layers of the situation; the drama is too cookie-cutter and hollow. I've talked to people about *Take This Waltz* and it has pulled them up short and shaken them out of their be-kind-in-public mode. Their disposition shifts, they become ill at ease, their voices deepen—the exact same reaction all three times I've met someone who's seen it. A friend, a roommate, a stranger at the Park Slope Food Coop—all of them women, who tetchily said, in one way or another, *Yes, I saw that—oh, God.*

The film shows a relationship coming apart, but in a heightened manner of expression. Set in summer, it takes place in Toronto's Little Portugal neighborhood and Nova Scotia, often in sunbaked frames, with reds and other primary colors also dominant. The opening unfocused shots of Margot (Michelle Williams) haunt the whole, as she soon falls away from her husband Lou (Seth Rogen) towards a thinner, more conventionally handsome man, Daniel, whom she meets in Nova Scotia at the outset and travels with on a plane back to Toronto, only to find he lives just down the street. Initially, Margot resists her obvious interest, but she and Daniel keep crossing paths, and she comes back home to security and to a husband who is mostly home, as he cooks chicken for a living while working on a cookbook. Each time she returns she has to hug him from behind as he stands at the stove. She can't breathe with her husband, she can barely talk to him. They share cutesy baby talk, which might be a stable condition for many childless couples, but she soon castigates him for employing it when they are getting ready to have sex on the kitchen floor, felling her mood as she has had Daniel on her mind and may have pictured him while getting turned on to Lou. When they sit down to eat dinner, Margot and Lou watch TV and don't talk. Margot wants intimacy and attention, not so much sex—they have their routines and they aren't that adventurous, just taking off shirts before a morning fuck. This leads to the kicker, and what may be open to interpretation—but as with any great work of art, all interpretations only enhance the memory of it: Margot would not have left her husband for better sex; but, because he did not provide the kind of intimacy she desired (cuddles, conversation, intrigue into the great questions of life, not just the childish routine they share of trying to one-up each other with insults like, "I love you so much, I'm going to put your spleen through a meat grinder"), she had no choice but to be with someone who would help her grow, who would say "yes" to life in a way that resonates with her. And although the film does have its skin moments and sexually explicit talk ("I played with you, before I entered you, before I spread your legs and fucked you hard"), it has, à la *Eyes Wide Shut*, a much deeper purpose—to unearth the perplexities of what keeps us together and what doesn't—all apart from sexuality. At the end of Woody Allen's *Husbands and Wives*, the couple who broke up at the beginning gets back together, with the man acutely saying: "We've learned to tolerate our problems more. . . . I've learned, anyway, that love is not about passion and romance necessarily. It's also about companionship and it's like a buffer against loneliness, I think. That stuff is important. Somebody to grow old with. What kills most people is unreal expectations."

Sarah Polley's most pronounced statement in regard to this uncouthness arrives in the scenes at the beginning and the end of the film. Margot is cooking at a stove (echoes of her husband) in her new apartment. She sits down in front of it and stares about, while she wonders, thinks, regrets?—we don't know—just as Daniel wanders in, unfocused, and stares out the kitchen window, though at the end she eventually goes and hugs him—from behind. How can we understand love, loss, need, and other feelings? An actress silently displaying a mix of feelings is one way to convey the spectacle, though it might only be a catch-22 leading to the great cliché: *Life is hard*. On the whole, we don't want films like this because relationships are shown in too harsh a light. Our psychology likes to dictate what success there will be, but films like *Take This Waltz* remind us how vulnerable we are and how, through no fault of our own, everything will come crashing down if that is what is to be.

Looked at on its worst days, humanity can seem jaded, presumptive, fearful, nervous, and mostly incapable of discourse or acts of humility; we receive or discard other people on unconscionable whims. A fair-use slogan of a certain coterie of people still in existence in this country is: "We create our own reality." It may also be safe to say that our technology, especially our multifarious messaging options, creates another all-mind being, absenting the body, which contains the heart. The spacing on a subway car once put me in a perfect position to see (unseen) what a man typed on his phone. I saw fragments and a few complete sentences that made it apparent he was breaking up with a person by text. On it went, with the two of them debating as he supplied more words and more reasons for his decision. My eyes closed askewly, and I wondered what it would take for me to do something like this, to mutedly emote what a torn heart must, but in public—tapping it into a machine that would send the message, while sitting still in a place of such plasticity and remoteness from light and friends that many people hold tight their faces for the thirty to sixty minutes it takes to get from the front door to work. Not to mention what it would take for me to associate with a person who would accept this type of interaction for extremely important matters like this one.

Today, when confronted with something painful, the instinct is to push it away, to reject; not to take responsibility, nor to get engaged, but instead not to allow feeling—a fine recipe for sublimation. The blame game begins, a most admired contest we have been refining for hundreds of years so that it has become our most patented reflex. Blame has become synonymous with understanding: we conceive of most of our life acts in concert with how much blame we can, should, or will endure. This happens in nearly every facet of our culture—even, incredibly, in sports, where a player, manager, or upper-management person often takes responsibility for a failure even before a hack reporter asks, "Who is to blame for this poor outing, this loss?"

Take This Waltz resists blame. The screenplay isn't interested in this cold counterpoint, but in actually feeling the pain of longing and separating. This is often conveyed through the superlative qualities of the main actor. Michelle Williams is certainly the best American actress of her generation, as she continually fills out more complex psychologies.

In *Take This Waltz* she conveys fear, surprise, awkwardness, tedium, control, regret, and fatigue with a naked spontaneity. I have seen her no-bullshit gaze in a few interviews and would like to assume she draws on the spirit of herself in order to inform her performances. I don't know how she does what she does, if she employs a method. I don't want to know, either. Her performance crystallizes as the thing itself. There is a human being on the screen and, like Daniel Day-Lewis, like Philip Seymour Hoffman, like all the greats, she gives so much of herself that it is hard not to feel she is sharing a special intimacy with the audience.

Williams takes on the most difficult roles, those that require more "presence" acting than delivering words, especially in *Take This Waltz* and Derek Cianfrance's *Blue Valentine*—a most interesting corollary. In that film, released the year before, Williams' character is also stuck in a type of loveless relationship. There is a daughter involved, though her boyfriend (Ryan Gosling) is not the biological father, even if he has raised the child as his own. The film oscillates in time between Williams' and Gosling's courtship and their gloomy future, but it is somewhere in-between (something we don't see) that the decisive moments in the relationship have occurred, because in the future she hates him from the get-go and this seems to be most engendered by his not having a career aside from painting houses, even in his forties. In Cianfrance's film, the deck is stacked *pro forma* on the side of the female character, and it isn't too interested in getting into her responsibilities for the relationship not working. Her romantic interest in a doctor she works for seems a little hackneyed and undercooked, and I can't help thinking Cianfrance succumbed in some way to pandering to the cliché that all men are jerks, with the perhaps intended result being that Williams' character comes off as slightly cruel and judgmental.

No-one can wear pain like Michelle Williams; it oozes forth in the like manner that Wordsworth defined the sublime in poetry: a spontaneous overflow of powerful feelings. Her whole body becomes a tourniquet, trying to clog the loss of spirit that marks her great characterizations. In *Take This Waltz*, she goes further. With all the chicken she's eaten with her husband, her face is a little lumpy. She's a little awkward in gait and communication, like a reluctant nerd-in-training under her husband's full-on nerdom. She's tentative about the world because she can't relate in her relationship, though we never see her before she meets Daniel. But I have a strong feeling that her problems with Lou were always there. Williams modulates her American voice differently compared to her other performances (though the film is set in Canada, she doesn't speak with a Canadian vowel shift). She was born in Montana, but here she speaks quicker than usual, probably more like someone living in the East (or Toronto) would talk. And as she embodies her wound, she also portrays how life-giving it is. She plays the raptures of the new and the pain of the old simultaneously, giving her husband many chances, albeit without the ultimatum the audience knows is in her head: that she will leave unless he becomes more than he has been—always an impossibility.

The way Polley structures the story is unexpected. *Take This Waltz* is one of the very few break-up films in which the new lover dominates early and then pretty much disappears, while the abandoned partner takes on larger significance with the break-up. In fact, we really don't know the Seth Rogen character at all until a series of Bergmanesque close-ups of anger and sadness reveal how he deals with the reality of his wife's departure, as he speaks the storied line, "I thought you were going to be there when I died." Another boon of the film's form is a flash-forward after Margot leaves Lou. A continuing circling shot in Margot and Daniel's new apartment shows a year passing in a variety of poses and situations, many carnal, including *ménages à trois* with members of both sexes, and many displaying a cuddling absent in Margot's marriage—she and Daniel even cuddle when they watch TV.

Then, one year later, Margot comes back to her house, spurred on by a subplot involving the relapse into heavy drinking of her alcoholic sister-in-law (Sarah Silverman). We find out Margot has been very out of touch—have she and Lou even divorced yet? The police are about to take away the Silverman character, but they let her talk to Margot briefly, and she says: "I'm the embarrassment? Me? Do you know we're doing the same fucking thing here? I think you're a bigger idiot than I am. Life has a gap in it, it just does. You don't go crazy trying to fill it . . ." This outburst introduces the aspect of regret to Margot's considerations, which is fortified in the penultimate conversation between Margot and Lou as she eventually shrinks from him, regretful.

The words between Margot and Lou on the porch of the house they used to live in are worth giving a font to. After some initial niceties and jokes about the chicken cookbook, which has finally been published, they frown in silence. Then, after he says he's not seeing anyone:

> MARGOT: Do you ever . . . think?
> LOU: No, I don't, I don't think so.
> MARGOT: You said you're not seeing anyone.
> LOU: Some things you do in life, they stick.
> MARGOT: I'm so sorry.

LOU: There's no reason to be sorry. How can you be sorry for doing what you had to do?

MARGOT: But I think that—

LOU: We didn't have this conversation then, I really have no interest in having it now.

MARGOT: Of course, I'm sorry, I got it.

What happens here? The line "Do you ever . . . think?" is never finished. It is probable Margot means getting back together, since just minutes earlier her sister-in-law ridiculed her decision. But why would Margot say such a thing, after a year of apparent happiness, though there is a nod to the possibility that her relationship with Daniel is becoming rote? Maybe what she means is, "Do you ever think . . . of me?" and it gets compounded because of all her self-doubt. My feeling is that many couples who break up rarely have it all out because it takes time and reflection to be able to say what we feel. Margot is weakened here. She feels she made the wrong decision.

According to the final scene by the stove, her new love is a blur, literally, as again we see what looks to be the opening scene, but it is slightly different, with Daniel walking into the kitchen out of focus and remaining so, even as Margot hugs him. Then she goes for a solitary ride on the tilt-a-whirl at the circus—what she and Daniel did on one of their Platonic dates. Her face is sad, then happy, and then baseline as the car whirs about.

How do our contemporary views on relationships read this? What exactly are our views? Do we have any? There is no guidebook in general use. In all our high schooling, the study of literature is what guides us the most about ethics and being ethical in relationships. *Romeo and Juliet, The Scarlet Letter, The Great Gatsby.* Isn't it incredible that this is still our culture's commonality aside from television shows? Manners and morals from the Roaring Twenties, let alone the Puritan Northeast and Elizabethan England, still shape what we know of love and pluck. Has love changed? In 1970, Lionel Trilling said that the vision of order, peace, honor, and beauty in those works had no place in the fiction of his time, but high schools don't teach many contemporary works; they teach *To Kill a Mockingbird.* James Joyce gave a name to these ideals—to enter "the fair courts of life," which, Trilling says, "was the very ground of the moral life as the novelists (and Shakespeare) once represented it—the moral career began with the desire to enter the fair courts of life; how one conducted oneself in that enterprise was what morality was about."

Love rarely has the answers, but it supports them. Maybe the film's ending can best be parsed as a quiet rebuke to the childish and cop-ish phrase, "move on," "moving on," "to move on," "to move past" (whatever iteration), which our society employs antiseptically as a cure-all to death, tragedy, and loss of love. This is apart from the impetuousness behind Moveon.org, a political action website. The idiom is said to come from nineteenth-century England, from police lingo: "Move on" meaning, "Get going, nothing to see here," even though, of course, there is something to see—the aftermath of an accident or other incident. Wiktionary gives the idiom two meanings: to leave somewhere for another place and to start dealing with something else. Again and again after tragedies far greater than break-ups, we hear the injunction by officials. On December 24, 2012, only ten days after the Sandy Hook Shootings, *Time* magazine ran an article with the subheading: *The last of the burials are over, but memorials to the 20 children and 7 adults killed in the Dec. 14 rampage are still growing as Newtown, Conn. ponders how to move past a senseless tragedy.*

"Move on" is basically a caveman grunt. I would certainly not be the first person to say that as we lose our language, we lose our capacity to feel, which by extension is the capacity for the purest of emotions—compassion. Fittingly, in *Searching for Richard*, Al Pacino's documentary on Shakespeare, a man of the street (where they say there are smarts) says it best: "When we speak with no feeling we get nothing out of our society. . . . That's why it's easy for us to get a gun and shoot each other; we don't feel for each other . . ." But "move on" is also much more complex than its two syllables seem to suggest, as even our most pedestrian bites of language can become imbued with a greater urgency in an attempt to make the little we say count. The two words have come to be a cudgel with various engravings and escutcheons on the handle, holding various resonances and connotative meanings like: "Grow up," or "Don't investigate the issue further," or "There is no room for discussion," or "This is a no-reflection zone," or, worst of all, "If you need to talk, go see a therapist." Yet, the way many people better themselves (therapy) is so removed from everyday life (done in private, out of view—necessarily so) that anything resembling it has no room on the national stage. This idiom is trotted out in many break-ups, as often one (or sometimes, inexplicably, both people) will refuse to say any more after a certain point, whether out of fear, grief, revenge, sanctimony, or an impulse to follow the lead of our paltry politicians, officials, and other negligible people who have greased and wound their way to a title. Telling someone to *move on* isn't only an embarrassment to our supposedly democratic souls, it's a flip of the finger to human civilization and its capacity to feel and demonstrate the empathy that the Greeks and Shakespeare, among others, helped to create. A repression, it coercively counsels: Don't learn. Don't emote.

Love's not love that's not vulnerable—that's the line of a fine-toothed poem I pondered at an age when I tried to define the emotion, the same age as all the principals in *Take This Waltz*. Perhaps I am not the best epigone of cultural critique when tallying the effects of the phrase "move on," since some years ago it stung me. I'd become suspended in a ping-pong relationship that would break up and then quickly adhere like a snowbank in a blizzard. I'd thought I wanted out, but I had nothing to catch as I fell away from it, lacking a place to stay, with desperation fueling my days. "Were we to continue," I asked her on our last day, "could we stand a chance?" "I think you should move on," my former love replied, knowing then, as I didn't, that she'd found a new man. In any case, the directive haunted. Directive—I thought of that Robert Frost poem we'd read each other in our salad days with its egalitarian ending after many iron lines: "Here are your waters and your watering place. / Drink and be whole again beyond confusion." From that poeticism to *move on*. The end of intimacy is the end of language. What should I have done with my meagre two syllables? *Move on.* How was such an injunction to be taken? Mind you, she was not a cop; she was a third-year surgery resident, but her words sure felt like a cop's bark, even though, granted, the fearful preamble—"I think you should"—has no store in police vocabulary. Surely, she told me to move on because she had already begun to; also the idiom was a slurring Swedish for: *We're not going to get back together, though we have so often—even after I was convinced it would never work out and I took you into my body and said, "I love you."* Yes, well—no, not even after that.

Again, "think" is the operative word. Did she care what I thought or was it, like, more a unilateral thing? The strong scene with the close-ups of Lou demonstrates that when we break up we truly begin to pay attention to language and individual words, and hence how we treat one another, because finally, our language colors our memories, even if they are wordless moments. We talk to ourselves about our pasts in absolute privacy. Our language is the only arbiter capable of making peace between us, our spirits, and our minds. It points the way like lights on an airstrip, however bitter or sour the remembrances.

It must be said that no break-up of a relationship taking a significant amount of time or intensity is the end of anything. It stays with one for a while, sometimes years and sometimes all remaining years. So "move on," one of those exigent phrases with a gilded, meretricious lining, must be the most wrong-headed, piss-poor, especially ugly thing to say, because it won't be heeded, not even by the person delivering it. What "move on" truly means is: *I have no way of being able to have a discourse for whatever reason—fear, anger, loss—and so I won't be engaging.* And there the door closes. As in the above dialogue from *Take This Waltz*, there is no possibility to speak what we feel, and shockingly, to even not speak what we ought to say. Margot and Lou gain no closure, even a year later, and the last thing Lou says is a stab at the one-upmanship of their old love threats. Who can know why it's so hard to communicate? Our language sickness' new strains strengthened sometime in the last twenty to twenty-five years, beginning with the rise of cable television (and all its channels), and with communication further eroded by the internet and phones—there is more of everything while there's less reciprocal interaction, less sharing, less intimacy. So it must come back to how we talk to each other. We either talk in clichés or not at all, as the age-old reluctance to say, "I love you," soldiers on.

Relationships are a nettling and funny business. The young get hamstrung over them because they want to be grown up—they are worried about their place in the world, even if they don't always know what the world is. The old treat relationships with a casual wave of a hand—if they've survived long enough with someone, they've become inured to what makes their lastingness last, and those who are alone, who've been through the cycle or cycles, often enjoy, on some level, their solitude, with their house kept in order by no-one but themselves. The French filmmaker of the confrontational and acerbic, Maurice Pialat, titled one of his films *Nous ne vieillirons pas ensemble* (*We Won't Grow Old Together*). It is the most difficult fantasy because of the *we* involved. In 1932, W. B. Yeats wrote the poem 'After Long Silence':

> Speech after long silence; it is right,
> All other lovers being estranged or dead,
> Unfriendly lamplight hid under its shade,
> The curtains drawn upon unfriendly night,
> That we descant and yet again descant
> Upon the supreme theme of Art and Song:
> Bodily decrepitude is wisdom; young
> We loved each other and were ignorant.

It's short, it's sharp, and it shocks because it takes a few readings to unfurl. "Descant" means "a melody or counterpoint sung above the plainsong of the tenor," or "discourse or comment on a theme." The poem appears to say: *We aren't wise until we are old, and we are so ignorant when young*. So what does that "love," which is no more, mean? It can't be pointed to on a resumé, only alluded to in the after-hours of new love, when we trust enough to confess, enough to know we may have a better handle. Rightly, this is the poem that would encapsulate the meeting of Margot and Lou (or each of us with whomever we choose) years after the fact. This is what they will have to say, happily or not. They will have the conversation they couldn't (and wouldn't) have had in their early thirties. Margot, on the Tilt-A-Whirl, might have had an inkling that "bodily decrepitude" is wisdom, but how would she know unless she went through the years to get there? There is a long silence for her in the cooking scene stretching into the circus scene. There are no words spoken. She isn't moving on. Her search begins and in the beginning there are a number of false starts—the mixed emotions overcoming Margot on the ride. A further definition of descant is "a variation on what is customary."

288

Mr. Turner, Boyhood, and Criticism

LET US BEGIN with difficulties. Mike Leigh's *Mr. Turner*, a film as rich as an afternoon in the Louvre, presents an austere and bilious portrait of the great English artist, as well as a ridiculous one of a young John Ruskin, a critic who explicated Turner in many words over the course of different works—a critic who drew and painted, lecturing on both practices with a great avidity. In Leigh, the drama is the classic case of critic as obnoxious foil to the artist's majesty and magic, with Ruskin's exaggerated, lisping accent—pushing every "r" out as a "w"—being the cherry on top. Leigh has said of Ruskin that "he was a kind of prick." Well, maybe.

But I must bring in one of Leigh's most passionate fans—the poet-critic Guy Davenport, whose essays are jewels, and who claimed to be "not writing for scholars or critics, but for people who like to read, to look at pictures, and to know things." Of the English filmmaker, Davenport once said that "[w]hen Mike Leigh gets to heaven, Chekhov will want to shake his hand." Dead these sixteen years, wouldn't it have tickled Davenport, a draughtsman himself who wrote frequently on painting, to see a Leigh film on a legendary artist? But what would Davenport have made of the Ruskin interlude showing the critic in a convex mirror? In an essay on Ruskin, Davenport wrote of his literary voice: "[i]t is, even at its most querulous and preacherly, not writing but speaking. It is, in a beautiful sense, thinking aloud, at its most congenial, conversational, richly anecdotal, and always observant. . . . He could make a passage from the Bible sound like words you have never heard before." And to the matter of the two Victorians meeting, Davenport added: "Ruskin and Turner never dined together, though an invitation was once sent. Turner knew that his manners weren't up to those of the refined Ruskins, and

said so, explaining graphically that, being toothless, he sucked his meat."
Leigh's film takes these truths and plays with them—Ruskin does speak
gloriously and pompously, the two only have drinks, and while Timothy
Spall's Turner is not toothless, he does make many a bovine sound in his
peregrinations and artistic struggles. Davenport, grousingly hermetic,
might have simply laughed off the lisp and reiterated that in 2021, nearly
no-one reads Ruskin.

Because I love art, particularly books, films, plays, and paintings, and
have sometimes fit a critic's assignment into my calendar, I'll try to place
Leigh's film—it is not only about an artist, but also about his time, his
loving and troubling relationship with his father, and how his successes
and failures as an artist weighed on others.

Critics have a job incompatible with their raw materials. They are
to respond promptly and pithily to a work of art—the very life of which
changes by different viewings, listenings, and readings, and at different
times in one's life. It is like being a bullrider—one being is not made to
situate itself onto the other. And yet our culture still respects some views
and honors the guidance offered. In conjunction, it is no exaggeration to
say we live in an era that disposes of language, including the etiolation
of the sentence, punctuation, spelling, and grammar by the rush to judgment, and by the ego not caring what its form of thought is like, only that
its owner's name is lit up. Our species is changing—words, because they
are not respected, boil over more easily into lies and exaggeration, dis-
regarding the best humanistic advice possible, courtesy of Shakespeare:
"Speak what we feel, not what we ought to say." Where once words were
imbricated and limned to grasp at wisdom, we now have the sweet sat-
isfactions of irony, the insulting tweet, and the ham-handed "article" on
why this or that does or doesn't meet one's satisfaction.

"What is criticism?" has been asked countless times throughout history, but there is still no adequate answer. In a series of essays treating the place of the artist, the critic, and the scholar in his book *Every
Force Evolves a Form*, Davenport twice quotes this sentence from philosopher George Santayana: "To understand how the artist felt, however,
is not criticism; criticism is an investigation of what the work is good
for." These words may express the best equation for the critic's dilemma,
though "good for" smacks of the paterfamilias making a pronouncement
from 1905—the year Santayana's dictum was published.

Within the crumbling worlds of literary arts and popular film studies,
many reviews hover near the syncopated knee-jerk pitch of press release,
for, as David Winters says, "triviality is among the allures of the form."
One advantage of the internet is that there are a bevy of places and

people not delivering half-baked thought—and many doing that for free. Still, our twenty-five-year-old "tool" has changed the ways and means of celebrating and decimating. Our culture and our politics flood the song of ourselves through the tool's giant spigot of information, bloating our bitchiness and bullshit. The zeitgeist again leans toward witch-hunts, often of the virtual variety. At every minute of every day, one person blames another, someone searches for a fault to brand on someone or something else—we (and I mean the USA) are becoming unable to accept fate, to accept that there are many forces beyond our control. In an age where everything is thought preventable, it doesn't shock that a lot of our art is cruel of heart, pandering, and dispassionate about the joy of living, with attacks on the joyousness of Terrence Malick's *Tree of Life* being particularly telling.

How else can critics respond to art? Those from the more august periodicals lead the way—though their edicts are not always subtly deployed, they are given weight due to their employers. In a 2014 issue of *The New Yorker*, James Wood wrote of the writer James Kelman that his work is "narrow . . . and can indeed be monotonous (often usefully, sometimes merely)." In the same issue, Anthony Lane said this of a film: "*Love is Strange*, however, is not about gay marriage. It is about a marriage that happens to be gay. If the film grows slightly boring, even that can be construed as an advance." These hackneyed judgments are standard fare. The analysis is godlike, involving grand pronouncements that "this" is what "that" is, what it *means*. "I wouldn't bother," or, "I would." Statements are laid down in askew opposition to the spirt of Santayana's or Virginia Woolf's, who said of critics that we ought to "ask them to be generous of encouragement, but sparing of those wreaths and coronets which are so apt to get awry, and fade, and make the wearers, in six months time, look a little ridiculous."

Into this atmosphere, I have thrown my own asinine punches, saying of Lars von Trier's *Melancholia* that its director "com[es] off like a floundering, churlish auteur who needs to again make art that communicates, and pays homage to, his own psychosis." But when fitting on the crown of a critic, it is difficult not to come across as a prig, unless, like Kent Jones and Geoffrey O'Brien (the two film critics who move me most), one mostly reviews works one extols. The dilemma and incompatibility of criticism most hit me when trying to fit my adulation for *Mr. Turner* against my cool reception to Richard Linklater's *Boyhood*, which turned out to be the work many critics and award givers backed as the best, most ambitious, most revolutionary film of 2014. Linklater may be one of our most compassionate and aware artists, but he hadn't made an absorbing film, at least not to my taste. In the months following the release of *Boyhood*, as the accolades and the honors piled up, peers passed on to me some of the exclusionary tidings offered by the film's champions. Two friends traded barbs over it, with the lover of the film eventually saying: "If you didn't like *Boyhood*, I don't know if I can be your friend"—a *cri de cœur* not far from the gas behind *12 Years a Slave* the previous year, when Chris Rock confided, via tweet, "If you don't see 12 years a slave. Then you don't deserve eyes." I'm not sure art should be utilized as a bargaining chip in relationships, like the men or women who won't step into one unless a child will be produced.

How could I or anyone contend with such bullying, pig-headed vehemence? An "us versus them" mentality. If I said what I felt about *Boyhood*—that nearly every other one of Linklater's films was more affecting, less cloying, and didn't take itself so seriously, from *Slacker's* come-what-may as ontological Americana, to the *Before* films' Rohmeresque precision masquerading as whimsy—what difference would it make? I must mind the words of Santayana and Davenport. What is *Boyhood* good for? I honestly think it's good for encouraging us to pat ourselves on the back and say, "Yes, life can be hard, but you can get through it," as some version of this advice is foisted onto the protagonist in scene after scene, especially in the last hour. When I see Linklater's not-too-distant Texas neighbor Terrence Malick examining many of the same issues in his coming-of-age film and arriving at quite a different end that parades as an end, but is really an opening for our doors of perception—similar to the work of Dreyer, Ozu, Bresson, Bergman, Kubrick, and Apichatpong Weerasethakul—I glory that he is communicating a very completed dichotomy through symbols, through the play of light and shadow, and performances that register as both mythical and naturalistic. Everyone bellows how life is unfair, but does everyone know life is unfair and beautiful, often at the same time? This art forces me to confront the specter of not only myself on the earth and then my leaving it, but that of the presence and eventual extinction of the entire human race. Malick's vision had me dreaming with "eyes wide open," as Italian director Franco Zeffirelli wrote to Kubrick of his experience of *2001*.

After Ruskin's interlude in *Mr. Turner*, the years pass more quickly and Turner's maid, whom he used to turn to for occasional sexual fulfillment, stoops more and develops larger lesions on her skin. Turner soon dies a protracted death, leaving behind another woman, a comfortably retired widow who he spent many of his last years with. Partnerless, but still happy to have known Turner, she carries in her mind's eye a picture of him painting a sunset. Meanwhile, the maid returns to his studio crying and circling his workspace, lost and feckless.

This plot summary stands in for images one needs to see for oneself. Perhaps I should agree that the early hours of criticism are recall and description of the thing itself. In the days after first seeing a unique film, I can only reimagine it and I'm not in a hurry to "understand." In the case of *Mr. Turner*, I didn't want to make sense of it beyond its straight-forward depiction of two class types, two psychological types, two types of grief, two women. We all die, so live all you can—if art is good at anything, it's reminding us of this. And if criticism has more of a fancy about it, it will dredge the morass of depictions to cry "Eureka!" at the most powerful examples.

Acknowledgments

Many of these works appeared before in the following journals, all in a much different form. The author wishes to thank all of the editors, especially Boris Drayluk, Daniel Kasman, and Andrew Gallix. Special thanks to Steve Moore, Garielle Lutz, and Ed Burns. This book (me) is indebted to Daniel Davis Wood and Jim Gauer.

3AM Magazine: 'Living Words,' 'A Year With Wallace Stevens,' 'A Rabbit as King of the Ghosts,' 'Stylized Despair,' 'The Sound is the Story'
Mubi: 'On Or About,' 'Bergman's Spell,' 'Mr. Fincher and Monsieur Dreyer,' 'Pain Pays the Income of Each Precious Thing,' 'Mr. Turner, Boyhood, and Criticism,' 'Take This Waltz, Then Move On?' 'Nearer My Hong Sang-Soo to Me'
Full Stop: 'An Adultery'
Los Angeles Review of Books: 'Remembering William H. Gass,' 'Return to Enigma,' 'Paul Thomas Anderson: An Autocritique,' 'Toni Erdmann and the Anti-Hollywood Ending,' 'William Gaddis' Compositional Self'
The Kenyon Review: 'On Influence,' 'The Self That Did So Much'
The Millions: 'Doses of Medicine,' 'William Gaddis and American Justice'
The Rumpus: 'Going Steady With Gertrude,' 'All Naked, All the Time'
The Nervous Breakdown: 'How to Love, What to Read'
The Fanzine: 'Envy, The Unsuccessful Writer's Friend'
Music & Literature: 'The Patrick White Experience,' 'Holy Hill'
Lapsus Lima: 'Oh! For Antonioni'
The Smart Set: 'On Eating Combos,' 'Highlight'
Senses of Cinema: 'Rossellini's Bergman'
A small portion of 'Paris Doesn't Belong to Us' appeared in the anthology We'll Never Have Paris (Repeater Books, 2019), edited by Andrew Gallix.